For more than a hundred centuries the Emperor has sat immobile on the Golden Throne of Earth. He is the Master of Mankind by the will of the gods and master of a million worlds by the might of his inexhaustible armies. He is a rotting carcass writhing invisibly with power from the Dark Age of Technology. He is the Carrion Lord of the Imperium, for whom a thousand souls die every day, for whom blood is drunk and flesh eaten. Human blood and human flesh – the stuff of which the Imperium is made. To be a man in such times is to be one amongst untold billions. It is to live in the cruellest and most bloody regime imaginable. This is the tale of those times.

It is a universe you can live today – if you dare – for this is a dark and terrible era where you will find little comfort or hope. If you want to take part in the adventure, then prepare yourself now. Forget the power of technology, science and common humanity. Forget the promise of progress and understanding, for there is no peace amongst the stars, only an eternity of carnage and slaughter and the laughter of thirsting gods.

But the universe is a big place and, whatever happens, you will not be missed...

I see a rising deluge of violence drowning Humanity's worlds. Like the sea crashing upon the cliffs, it grinds and crushes with every surge. Entropy. Cruelty. Lunacy and hatred. These are the weapons of the Enemy. The tides of Chaos have toppled civilisations, bringing them from supremacy to the brink of annihilation. Blindly does Mankind make that same journey, now standing on the *edge of the abyss.*

I see the trickling sands of time, blown thin in the winds of war. The celestial clock chimes loud, its deathly knell the doom of all. The hour of Ending is nigh. I see the creatures of the Warp, jealous and hungry, tearing at the fabric of reality with talon and tempest. They seek to rule over us, to wrest reality itself from our mortal grip. With each passing night, they bring the galaxy closer to eternal damnation.

I see war unbound raging across the cosmos, a black fire that consumes a million worlds. Every imaginable conflict is made manifest, and the valorous bleed and die anew each day. But beneath this battle of darkness and light there is a truth that sears the mind. The Enemy, nemesis of all, comes not from without. Our most cursed foes are the shadows of our souls made real, and they would see the galaxy burn

CONTENTS

THE EMPEROR PROTECTS.

PRODUCED BY GAMES WORKSHOP IN NOTTINGHAM

© Copyright Games Workshop Limited 2017. GW, Games Workshop, Space Marine, 40K, Dark Imperium, Warhammer, Warhammer 40,000, the 'Aquila' Double-headed Eagle logo, and all associated logos, illustrations, images, names, creatures, races, vehicles, locations, weapons, characters, and the distinctive likenesses thereof, are either ® or TM, and/or © Games Workshop Limited, variably registered around the world. All Rights Reserved.

No part of this publication may be reproduced, stored in a retrieval system, or transmitted in any form or by any means, electronic, mechanical, photocopying, recording or otherwise, without the prior permission of the publishers.

This is a work of fiction. All the characters and events portrayed in this book are fictional, and any resemblance to real people or incidents is purely coincidental. British Cataloguing-in-Publication Data. A catalogue record for this book is available from the British Library. Pictures used for illustrative purposes only.

Certain Citadel products may be dangerous if used incorrectly and Games Workshop does not recommend them for use by children under the age of 16 without adult supervision. Whatever your age, be careful when using glues, bladed equipment and sprays and make sure that you read and follow the instructions on the packaging.

Games Workshop Ltd, Willow Rd, Lenton, Nottingham, NG7 2WS
Printed by 1010 in China
games-workshop.com

THE WARHAMMER 40,000 HOBBY

Welcome to the grim darkness of the far future! Warhammer 40,000 is a tabletop game in which you command an army of mighty warriors, but it's also a wide-ranging hobby that includes collecting, building and painting Citadel Miniatures. This book is the launching pad for all this – and much more!

The Warhammer 40,000 hobby is a unique window into a world of excitement and adventure set in the Dark Imperium, where the empire of Mankind is beset from all sides. Daemon-worshipping heretics and myriad alien horrors surge from the darkness between the stars, intent upon bringing ruin and discord to the Emperor's realm. Against them stand the resolute armies of the Imperium, from the superhuman Space Marines and the pious Sisters of Battle to the innumerable ranks of the Astra Militarum and the towering war engines of the Knight households. A million worlds burn with the fires of war even as they echo to the monstrous laughter of the Dark Gods.

This apocalyptic setting provides endless opportunities for collecting, building, painting and gaming. Perhaps you're inspired to collect vast armies and fight out the epic battles described in the background. Maybe you find yourself drawn to the idea of painting beautiful display figures and building scenic snapshots of strange alien worlds within which to display them. Maybe it's all about building the most amazing war machines you can conceive of, or finding a good excuse to spend an afternoon with like-minded friends, painting or gaming together. In truth there is

no right or wrong way to go about engaging with the Warhammer 40,000 hobby – it's best to just find what you most enjoy and go for it. From gaming tournaments and campaign events to world-class painting competitions, from dining-table warfare to exciting battles at local clubs, there's a world of fun to be had with Warhammer 40,000, so strap on your armour, load your bolter and get ready for war!

Nothing brings a game of Warhammer 40,000 to life like a battlefield full of assembled and painted terrain. Here, the Ultramarines defend their home world of Macragge against the nefarious Death Guard.

COLLECTING CITADEL MINIATURES

From ground-shaking war engines to scuttling xenos swarms, heavily armed combat aircraft to brave infantrymen and the courageous heroes who lead them, the ever-growing range of Warhammer 40,000 Citadel Miniatures is incredibly vast and varied.

Grand armies surge into battle across war-torn worlds from one end of the galaxy to the other. Regiments of infantry dig in behind corpse-shored barricades. Space Marine Drop Pods streak down from orbit through burning skies to disgorge armoured warriors into the heart of the foe. Artillery pieces roar as they fling megatonne explosives into the enemy ranks, while hurtling xenos skimmers and rumbling, spike-studded tanks duel through the blazing ruins of once-glorious cities. Everywhere, storied heroes and black-hearted villains lock blades, screaming praise to their uncaring gods as they battle to the death.

A big part of the Warhammer 40,000 hobby is collecting the warriors and war machines that fight these spectacular battles, building and painting them to create an exciting and diverse collection of which you can be rightly proud. There are many ways to go about this, and all of them are equally valid. For many hobbyists, the end goal is to collect an army with which to play games of Warhammer 40,000. Such collections usually comprise a variety of heroes, warriors, armoured fighting vehicles and rampaging monsters. Others prefer to collect and paint only the mightiest heroes, or to

assemble their collections based around a theme, such as massed battle tanks, aerial armadas, or elite teams of specialist killers. Still other hobbyists might collect their models based upon the exciting stories presented in Games Workshop's novels and gaming supplements. Whatever inspires you, whether collecting for display, tabletop wargaming or both, this is an exceptionally rewarding hobby. Watching your collection grow from a handful of models to a fully realised army brings a real sense of pride and achievement, not to mention the tangible reward of having a fantastic array of dynamic Citadel Miniatures to admire.

Most collections begin with a few miniatures, whether it be a squad of warriors, a character model, or the contents of a Start Collecting! box. This Genestealer Cult army has grown to encompass a huge variety of different unit types.

In Warhammer 40,000, an army can contain massed ranks of soldiers, armoured war machines and monstrous creatures. This Blood Angels army is both mobile and resilient, with transports and fast-moving infantry backed up by tanks, heavy troops and mechanised walkers.

BUILDING AND PAINTING

Constructing and painting your Citadel Miniatures is a tactile and satisfying experience. Whether following instructions and painting guides, or creating custom conversions and inventing your own bespoke colour schemes, this part of the hobby is where you really get to personalise your collection!

Most Citadel Miniatures do not come as a single, pre-built piece. Rather, they are intended to be assembled using modelling tools and glue, and then painted in the colours and schemes that you choose. To this end, Games Workshop produces a range of specialist tools and a huge selection of Citadel Paints – with the accompanying Citadel Paint System – that allow you to easily and enjoyably build and paint the miniatures that make up your personal collection.

Many people derive a great deal of enjoyment from this, revelling in the creative process and taking pride in making the best-looking miniatures they possibly can.

A well-painted army really brings a game of Warhammer 40,000 to life on the tabletop, to the extent that you can almost hear the tank engines roar and the bolters boom. With the inclusion of a few pieces from the huge range of Citadel terrain, built and painted to complement your army, you'll have the makings of an epic tabletop narrative that will live on as a war story amongst your gaming group for years to come!

Initially, the notion of putting models together and painting them yourself might seem a daunting prospect. Yet with just a few easy-to-learn techniques from the Citadel Paint System – such as basecoating, washing

and drybrushing – and a bit of practice, you will amaze yourself with the results you can achieve. Information on the Citadel Paint System is readily available from Games Workshop staff members, Internet tutorial videos and various Citadel publications.

Whether you are carefully crafting a single, beautiful model for a painting competition, or assembling and batch-painting whole companies and squadrons of infantry, tanks and aircraft ready for massed battle, the only limit to what you can achieve is your imagination. And your skills will grow with every new project you complete, until you become a master artisan!

The Citadel Paint System works layer by layer, and takes you through building up from basecoats and washes to highlights and special effects to create jaw-droppingly impressive models. It's a straightforward system, with highly rewarding results.

Citadel Miniatures are provided unassembled and unpainted. Using Citadel Fine Detail Cutters, and following the assembly instructions provided with each kit, collectors clip their models' components out of their plastic frames and assemble them piece by piece using plastic glue. Building armies of miniatures is a satisfying experience that many collectors enjoy tremendously – and with a head swap here and a piece of re-posing there, there's also great scope for converting miniatures to become unique additions to your army.

Once your miniatures are built, the last step in bringing them to life is to paint them in the colours you choose. Games Workshop provides a wealth of painting guides, walk-throughs and instructional videos to help with this process, not to mention reams of material showing possible colour schemes to guide and inspire your creative efforts. Head to games-workshop.com to see the entire range of paints, painting-related products, books and a variety of step-by-step videos covering the schemes for a huge range of Citadel Miniatures.

WARHAMMER 40,000 GAMING

Mighty armies advance across tabletop battlefields to bring ruin to their foes. Desperate last stands and heroic duels play out amidst blasted cityscapes and carnivorous alien jungles. Every game tells its own dramatic tale, immersing you ever deeper in the war-torn galaxy of the far future.

The Warhammer 40,000 universe is vast and home to many different factions, all vying for dominance. The sprawling Imperium of Man sets itself against Chaos-tainted traitors and heretics, while vile xenos seek to invade at every opportunity. The battlefields they fight over are grand and fantastical in scale, encompassing everything from grim fortress monasteries and gothic hive cities the size of continents to arid, crystalline deserts, volcanic death worlds, ancient alien techno-crypts, and whatever else your imagination can conjure up. Just as varied as the spectacular landscapes of Warhammer 40,000 are the battles themselves. From elite commando raids and assassination missions to immense battles between millions of warriors, every sort of warfare imaginable fills the Imperium of Man from end to end.

Deadly dogfights through city spires, crashing tank battles over fiery plains, thunderous firefights between demigod war engines, and desperate battles to banish Daemons back to the hells from which they crawled; all of this and more can occur during a game of Warhammer 40,000. It really is a universe of limitless possibilities.

For many hobbyists, playing tabletop wargames is as much the desired end product of gathering and painting an army as the collecting process itself. The kind of game people look for varies immensely, however, from friendly mutual storytelling to highly competitive tournament play. Luckily, whether you are seeking to forge a thrilling narrative, play in a blistering head-to-head deathmatch, or even weave game after game into an ongoing campaign of conquest, the Warhammer 40,000 hobby offers ample opportunity to engage with any or all of these ways to play.

Many people like to start small, learning the rules by pitting a handful of squads against one another. As your collection grows, however, so too do your options. Soon enough you will find yourself plunging headlong into the grim darkness of Warhammer 40,000, and fighting battles you will remember for years to come.

Here, Steve and Natalie are using their Death Guard and Ultramarines in battle. A game this size can last a couple of hours – and later in this book you'll find many different missions to play and enjoy.

OPEN PLAY

Totally unrestricted, open play is the quickest and easiest method of playing Warhammer 40,000. All you need are some models, a copy of the rules, a few dice and a tape measure – and of course an opponent to battle against! Fun and friendly, open play allows you to use whatever models you choose, and often involves two players hurling their entire collections into the field to see what happens. Needless to say, the results are always spectacular, and provide plenty of memorable war stories for post-game discussion.

NARRATIVE PLAY

Although fighting an impromptu battle with any of your miniatures to hand is quick and fun, many people like to forge carefully thought-out narratives for their games and miniatures, developing strong themes for their armies that involve unifying colour schemes and background. Narrative play involves players using their games and battlefields to tell exciting stories, and often sees them creating an overarching narrative to bind several games into a campaign. It's a fantastic way to take your hobby to the next level.

MATCHED PLAY

Many players enjoy the more competitive element of the Warhammer 40,000 hobby, playing games to see who can come out on top. Matched play facilitates this by bringing an extra level of balance to players' armies, placing restrictions upon the units they can take and allowing them an even number of points with which to pick their forces. This type of play is most commonly seen at gaming tournaments and events, and means that no matter who you play, or with what armies, you can be assured of a close-run and nail-biting battle to the death!

DARK MILLENNIUM

'We are beset on all sides by vile
predatory aliens and sedition
gnaws at us from within; in this
dark hour the best we can do is
look to our wargear and pray
to our gods.'

- Skolak a'Trellar IV,
Imperial Commander

THE IMPERIUM OF MAN

After more than forty thousand years of war and strife among the stars, Humanity stands on the brink of extinction. Beset on all sides by hostile aliens and threatened from within by traitors, Humanity's only chance for survival rests with the continuation of the cruel and bloody regime known as the Imperium. Yet few amongst Mankind's untold population realise the full truth of their situation or the horrible fate that looms beyond the stars. If there is any future at all, it is a grim one…

The Imperium stretches across the galaxy. At its heart is Holy Terra, the cradle of Humanity and the starting point of an empire that contains countless trillions of souls. Despite its great size, the Imperium is spread thinly across this immense expanse; its worlds are dotted through the void and often divided by hundreds, if not thousands, of light years. It is therefore wrong to think of the Imperium in terms of a single, united territory; it is rather a sprawling and often hopelessly disconnected domain. Yet by the weight of its own immensity, the Imperium continues to expand, its momentum carrying it forwards even while vast segments deep within its boundaries are cut off, isolated, or remain to this day wholly unexplored.

Uncounted billions are born in squalour, labour in pain each day of their adult lives, then die in the streets, unsung and unmourned. They are blessed to do so, for in this way, they serve the Emperor. There is no greater calling.

LOST AGES OF HISTORY

Some four hundred centuries have passed since man first stepped into the cold of space. Forty thousand years. An age so long that almost its entire history lies shrouded in legend. Who knows how Mankind came to be scattered across so many disparate worlds? Who remembers the wars that split their home world of Terra asunder and dragged Humanity down to the level of brute beasts? Who would recognise the names of Terra's ancient ruins, of nations destroyed and peoples long since crumbled to dust? To these questions there can be no answers. The questions themselves died upon the lips of men tens of thousands of years past. From those times come only whispers of horror and death, of the ancient days of the Age of Technology, of the Realm of Night, of the Empire of Blood, and of the terrible long centuries of the Age of Strife.

But those eras are in the distant past; now is the time of the Emperor, the Age of the Imperium, though they are dark days indeed. It is an age already ten thousand years old and it, too, is shrouded in myth and steeped in ignorance. It is a time of superstition, an era in which great and unfathomable technologies have been enslaved by the forces of mysticism and madness. Most of all, it is an epoch of war, a grinding, unceasing war where mere survival is justly hailed as victory. Defeat can only lead to the irrevocable end of Humanity. Of the wars the Emperor waged to build his empire, of the countless agonies of his battles amongst the stars, there are no complete records, only apocryphal tales and half-remembered legends. And there is only one who might remember it all.

THE EMPEROR

When the Emperor led Mankind to spread once more across the galaxy, over a hundred centuries ago, it marked the end of a long era of history, an age of dark regression, bitter factionalism, and great isolation caused by rampant warp storms and countless alien invasions. Not even the ancient records kept by the Historitors of the Adeptus Administratum tell the full tale of how the Emperor came to unite and rule Humanity, or how the newly birthed Imperium came to be from whatever barbarism existed before it. Legends speak of the creation of the Space Marines, the launching of the Great Crusade and the brief time of illumination it brought before the terrible wars of the Horus Heresy plunged all into darkness once again. The truth lies buried under millennia of superstition, submerged beneath centuries of myth or lost to the annals of forgotten history. Perhaps there is a secret scriptorium in some oubliette of the Imperial Palace where the truth might be found, recorded in ancient tomes and locked behind adamantine doors. If there is such a place, it is best that it remains hidden. Its truths would be denied and its readers burnt for their heretical tendencies. Those ancient days will surely remain shrouded in mystery unless the Emperor himself chooses to reveal his knowledge, although none can guess what thoughts revolve inside his carrion skull.

Once, the Emperor lived and breathed as a mortal man, but his physical life has long since ended, crushed out of him by Horus, the Arch-traitor, in the final battle for Terra. Today, many thousands of years later, the Emperor lives only by the immeasurable force of his supreme will. The stasis fields and psi-fusion reactors of the machine known as the Golden Throne preserve his broken and decayed body; his great mind endures inside a rotting carcass, kept alive by the mysteries of ancient technology. His immense psychic powers reach out from the Golden Throne, enveloping and protecting Mankind across the enemy-strewn galaxy, a beacon of light in the malevolent darkness.

If the Emperor fails, then none will be able to stop the influx of the dark powers; ravenous and all-consuming Daemons will flood into the galaxy. Every living human will become a gateway for the destruction of Mankind. Reality will be subsumed by the stuff of the warp – a realm of nightmares and cruel insanity. There will be no physical matter. No space. No time. Only Chaos.

THE IMPERIUM LIVES

The Emperor has neither spoken nor moved since his incarceration in the Golden Throne. His revered body is, for all intents, dead. His psychic mind is wholly preoccupied combating the denizens of the warp. Fighting an eternal battle against the unimaginable horrors of that realm for the preservation of Mankind, all that is left of the Emperor is a consciousness divorced from the material world, a mind incapable of ordinary communication with his empire of devoted servants. He has given all so that the Imperium he founded might continue. And so it has. While it has diverged greatly from his original plan, the Imperium endures.

No longer followed merely as Humanity's leader, the Emperor is now worshipped as a god, the holy deity in whose name the Imperium is ruled. Superstition and dogma have become the rituals of worship and they are spread as gospel, with blind obedience commended and free thought viewed with suspicion and hostility. In the Emperor's name, the High Lords of Terra guide the Imperium, their commands carried out by the uncountable offices of the Adeptus Terra. Its labyrinthine subordinate organisations extend to every human world, and no man is free from its influence or from the strictures of its rule. Even with the galaxy riven by war and warp storms, information is gathered, laws are enforced, taxes are levied. So it has been done, so it continues. The cogs of the bureaucracy turn relentlessly without thought or consideration. That the sprawling Imperium is besieged from every angle by xenos and threatened with a hideous doom by the powers of Chaos has only reinforced the empire's irrational extremism.

Hunkering behind the parapets of a million scattered worlds, Mankind looks out upon a hostile galaxy with dread. Only the Imperium's armies stand between its citizens and terrors worse than extinction. And in this hour of greatest need, a Primarch returned, striding from legends of the past. As the Imperium grows ever darker, the ignorant masses are told that only their faith in the God-Emperor can now protect them. Perversely, it is true. So long as the Emperor survives, sitting in his silent vigil, there remains yet a shred of hope.

The soul is the most valuable prize of all. Souls hold the seeds of salvation; motes of divinity that flourish in the light of the Emperor. But the weeds of heresy can take root in the unwary. Beware the heretic, for he wears the face of man.

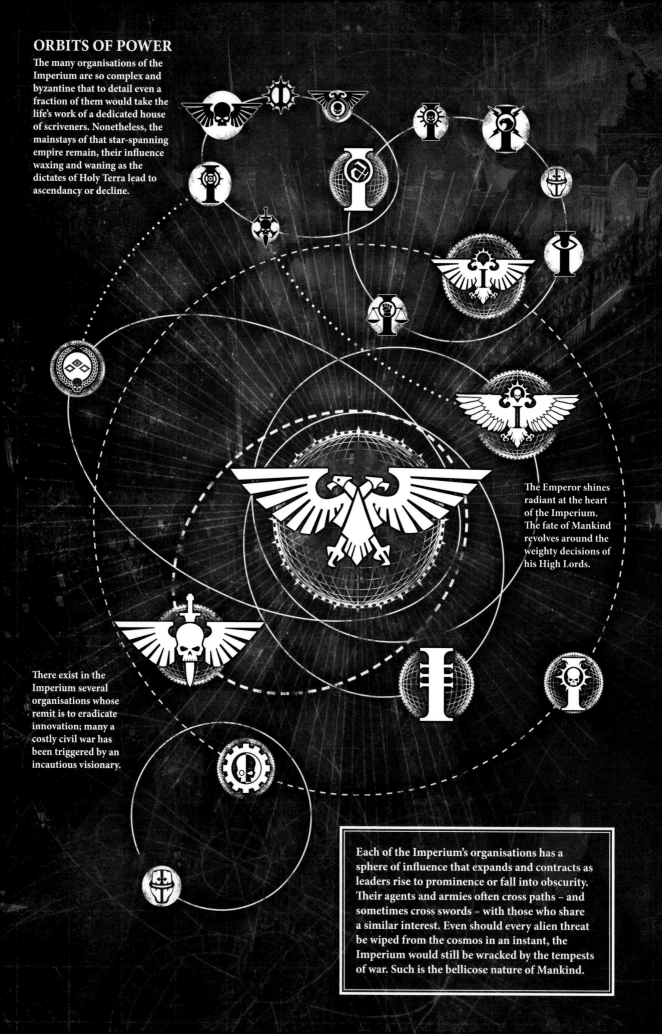

ORBITS OF POWER

The many organisations of the Imperium are so complex and byzantine that to detail even a fraction of them would take the life's work of a dedicated house of scriveners. Nonetheless, the mainstays of that star-spanning empire remain, their influence waxing and waning as the dictates of Holy Terra lead to ascendancy or decline.

The Emperor shines radiant at the heart of the Imperium. The fate of Mankind revolves around the weighty decisions of his High Lords.

There exist in the Imperium several organisations whose remit is to eradicate innovation; many a costly civil war has been triggered by an incautious visionary.

Each of the Imperium's organisations has a sphere of influence that expands and contracts as leaders rise to prominence or fall into obscurity. Their agents and armies often cross paths – and sometimes cross swords – with those who share a similar interest. Even should every alien threat be wiped from the cosmos in an instant, the Imperium would still be wracked by the tempests of war. Such is the bellicose nature of Mankind.

HIERARCHY OF THE IMPERIUM

The Imperium is colossal, the distances between its many planets immense. Even simple communication often proves impossible. Despite rampant confusion and misinterpretation, labyrinthine Imperial organisations struggle to maintain an increasingly dystopian order.

HIGH LORDS OF TERRA
They govern the destiny of Mankind.

These twelve individuals rule the Imperium in the Emperor's name. It is they who send the Imperium's fleets to war and direct its nigh-inexhaustible armies. Their task is to interpret the silent will of the Emperor, relying on his potent mind to guide their thoughts and inspire their actions. Nine seats are virtually sacrosanct, such as the Master of the Administratum, the Paternoval Envoy of the Navis Nobilite, and the Fabricator General of the Adeptus Mechanicus; other posts are filled from a range of the highest officials.

ADEPTUS TERRA
The Masters of the Earth, their will be done.

The Adeptus Terra is the central bureaucratic organisation of the Imperium and not really an agency itself. It is made up of many autonomous departments that receive the orders of the High Lords of Terra, passing them down to the different branches that then enact the commands.

ADEPTUS ADMINISTRATUM
Upon them turn the wheels of governance.

The largest organisation in the Adeptus Terra, the Adeptus Administratum is itself divided into countless different branches. It is their task to manage the Imperium, and it is they who tithe, administer, record and archive. It is enough to perform the task; understanding is neither required, nor welcome.

ADEPTUS MINISTORUM
Promulgators of the Imperial Creed.

The Adeptus Ministorum – more commonly known as the Ecclesiarchy – spreads the Imperial Cult throughout the Imperium. The Ecclesiarchy is not part of the Adeptus Terra but is a separate institution that hosts numerous subgroups of its own, the best known of which are its military wing (the Adepta Sororitas), its orthodox training orphanages (the Schola Progenium), and its missionaries who often accompany Imperial exploratory vessels (the Missionarus Galaxia).

THE INQUISITION
The eye that sleepeth not.

A highly secretive organisation, the Inquisition is bound by no authority save its own and that of the Emperor. The sole mission of the Inquisition is seeing to the protection of Humanity. Inquisitors are empowered to investigate any potential threat to Mankind and to take whatever measures they consider appropriate to destroy the danger. The end justifies any means.

NAVIS NOBILITE
Passage-makers, Bearers of the Third Eye.

The Navis Nobilite, also known as the Navigator Houses, are led by the Paternova to make up the Terra-based organisation from whence come all Navigators. One of the few sanctioned breeds of mutant, Navigators use their third eye to pilot human starships through the roiling madness of warp space.

ADEPTUS MECHANICUS
The Lords of Mars and Disciples of the Omnissiah.

The Tech-Priests of the Adeptus Mechanicus are the keepers of ancient knowledge and arcane technology. It is they who preserve the Emperor's Golden Throne and they who operate the forge worlds that feed the Imperial armouries with weapons, armour, munitions, vital spaceships and war machines. The Priesthood of Mars contains many subdivisions, including their own fleets and military wings. All follow the Cult Mechanicus – the worship of the Omnissiah – and use intricate invocations to assemble and maintain their precious machines. Unlike most major Adeptus organisations, the Adeptus Mechanicus is not headquartered on Terra, but instead upon the original and greatest of all the forge worlds, the red planet of Mars.

ADEPTUS ASTRA TELEPATHICA
Their voices pierce the darkness and cross the stars.

The role of the Adeptus Astra Telepathica is to recruit, identify and classify psykers, and then to train those found worthy. To do this, the Adeptus Astra Telepathica is divided into two main bodies: the League of Black Ships and the Scholastica Psykana; the Master of the Adeptus Astra Telepathica presides over both. The Adeptus Astra Telepathica classifies many grades of psyker, with acceptable grades being channelled to serve the Imperium in a variety of roles. Those unable to pass the battery of harsh tests they are subjected to take a final path to fulfil other, less savoury, duties.

Bring fire and bring shell, bring banner and blade – then heap all upon the pyre. With torch and gun we shall make an end to the withered husk that is human life. And in the blazing furnace of war, we shall forge anew the iron will of a yet stronger race. Let the flames of battle consume us! Let the inferno of war make ashes of our enemies!

ADEPTUS ASTRONOMICA

They fuel the guiding light of the Emperor.

The Adeptus Astronomica trains psykers to provide the raw psychic power to fuel the Astronomican, the psychic homing beacon that enables Navigators to steer through the warp. This task requires a choir of at least ten thousand psykers, and the role quickly destroys them. There are always more being trained to take their place, however.

ROGUE TRADERS

The hand that draws the map.

Licensed and equipped to explore the vast uncharted portions of the galaxy, the Rogue Traders are the Emperor's emissaries to the unknown. They hold full authority to negotiate, barter, subjugate or utterly destroy in pursuit of feeding the Imperium's rapacious appetites for information, territory, alien artefacts and raw materials.

PLANETARY GOVERNORS

They rule in His name.

Individual planets are ruled by local leaders. Like feudal lords of old, they must provide troops for the Astra Militarum, maintain order, carry out all Imperial decrees and pay all tithes levied by the Administratum, most important of which is the tithe of psykers. So long as quotas are met, a planetary governor may reign over his world in any manner he chooses.

ADEPTUS ARBITES

Keepers of the Great Book of Judgement.

The Arbitrators and Judges of the Adeptus Terra enforce law in the Imperium. They maintain order in a way that is absolute and unforgiving, A rigid adherence to the letter of the law is paramount, and they breed fanaticism.

ADEPTUS ASTARTES

They know no fear, the Angels of Death.

The Adeptus Astartes, commonly known as Space Marines, are the most powerful and dreaded of all Humanity's warriors. There are approximately one thousand Chapters, each composed of one thousand warriors. Each maintains its own identity and traditions, autonomous of the Ecclesiarchy. Although few in number, the Adeptus Astartes are highly mobile shock troops trained to deploy quickly and to do battle anywhere.

ASTRA MILITARUM

Hammer of the Emperor, the Imperial Guard.

The Astra Militarum is the largest fighting force of the Imperium. It relies on vast numbers of soldiers, armoured battle tanks and artillery to smash their foes, grinding them down through attrition and the application of devastating firepower. The provisioning of the Astra Militarum is provided by the Departmento Munitorum, the munitions and supply wing of the Adeptus Administratum.

IMPERIAL FLEET

They who ply the stars, they bear the biggest guns.

All shipping within the Imperium falls under the purview of the Imperial Fleet, with the exception of that carried out by the Adeptus Astartes and a few other Adeptus organisations. The larger part of the Fleet is the Navy, battleships that escort cargo across the galaxy and serve as the first line of defence in any invasion or insurrection. Imperial Navy fleets are composed of battleships, cruisers, escort squadrons, transports, messenger craft, orbital defences, and innumerable patrol vessels. They are vast, star-eclipsing forces that carry the Emperor's war across the stars.

OFFICIO ASSASSINORUM

The dagger in the dark, the silent answer.

The Office of Assassins is a vital, if little known, tool of the Imperium. The different temples that make up this mysterious agency are all cloaked in utmost secrecy. Each trains matchless killers who strike unseen and will go to any lengths to complete their deadly missions. Only the High Lords of Terra themselves can sanction the deployment of an Assassin.

QUESTOR IMPERIALIS

The Glorious Households, Defenders from the Old Night.

Guided by a single Noble pilot, an Imperial Knight is a giant armoured walker. Many of these proud and haughty warriors can trace their bloodlines back to Terra itself. Over the millennia, each pilot household will have sworn oaths of fealty – Imperial Knights are dedicated to the Golden Throne of Terra, and Mechanicus Knights to the Adeptus Mechanicus of Mars. Those Knights that have forsaken their household through loss, punishment, or exile will adopt new heraldry and fight on as Freeblades.

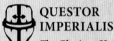

ADEPTUS CUSTODES

Bodyguards of the Emperor, Protectors of the Sanctum Imperialis.

The Adeptus Custodes, or Custodian Guard, are tasked with guarding the Imperial Palace and the body of the Emperor himself. They are ten thousand strong, each a genetically engineered superhuman that could handily best even a Space Marine in trials of combat. The Adeptus Custodes serve as the Emperor's personal guardians, answerable only to the Master of Mankind and their own leaders. On occasion they are seen off Terra, only being detached from their duties at the most dire of need.

EMPIRE LOST AMONG THE STARS

For ten thousand years, the Imperium had endured. One hundred centuries of constant war. Then a yet greater darkness descended across the galaxy. Never in all its long history had the Imperium known warp storms such as the ones that beset it following the Cicatrix Maledictum – the Great Rift. Terror washed over hundreds of thousands of planets, their last desperate calls received before all communications, even astropathic ones, fell silent. Scribes and curators in their billions sought answers. Through long-neglected records they delved, opening even the most ancient of vaults. Neither explanation nor comfort could be found, but some winnowed comparisons. The Ruinstorm had split the galaxy during the Horus Heresy, but only once had Mankind been divided as it was now: the Age of Strife. Its mere mention caused the learned to quail. Little was known of that nightmarish era, for it predated the Imperium, but the fragments that remain tell of a time when history ended, when Mankind was all but destroyed, the few survivors enslaved or reduced to barbarism. It was the end of civilisation.

For nearly ten thousand years, the Imperium had established itself as the largest single empire in the galaxy. During that time it had endured much, surviving civil wars and the loss of the Emperor's direct leadership. It had replaced the hope of enlightenment with draconian rule. By the weight of its own colossal immensity, the Imperium continued, its bureaucracy growing even throughout an Age of Apostasy when the word of the Emperor was subverted, and corrupt ideologues strove to claim power in their own names. The Imperium overcame wars beyond count. It survived schisms, betrayals, and its own religion that outlawed reason and thought. Every year planets were lost by the hundreds, sometimes by the thousands. Suns died, warp storms consumed entire systems, predatory xenos invaded, sweeping away those unable to defend themselves. Black Crusades brought further bloodshed, and always, the forces of Chaos reaped their bloody toll. So disconnected was the Imperium's communication, so unwieldy their bureaucracy, that the loss of entire star systems might never be discovered, the information lost in transit or filed beneath datastacks of minutiae.

Yet despite constant calamities, the Imperium did not just endure, it grew. Each year, hundreds of new planets were added to the fold, even while others were lost. Unstoppable in its momentum, the Imperium churned on. Explorator fleets were launched like clockwork from every forge world. Relentlessly, they sought former colonies or new planetary systems to exploit. The end result was a strange paradox. Even while crumbling at the edges, losing planetary systems by the score to

sedition, xenos invasion, or galactic phenomena, the Imperium continued. Colonies lost since the dawn of space travel were still being discovered each year.

For a time, the Great Rift threatened to end everything. Its seismic shock roiled reality. The very galaxy cracked asunder. All sentient creatures were staggered, a wave of dread washing over them. Those psychically attuned fared far worse, as the energies of the warp poured into realspace. For many, doom followed. Untold billions died, their agony a part of the cacophony that screamed inside every living mind.

Crack followed crack, running along a plane of psychic fault lines. A turbulent scar of raw, pulsing Chaos nearly severed the galaxy in two. From the Hadex Anomaly at the core of the Jericho Reach in the Eastern Fringe, to the furthest system of Segmentum Obscurus in the galactic north-west, there throbbed a horrible new presence. It was a hole that ripped open the seams of reality on a scale never imagined. The Eye of Terror – the largest and most dreaded of all warp rifts previously known – became but a small fraction of this massive new rent. The warp storms that issued forth from the gaping void swept to every corner of the galaxy. No astrocommunication could be passed from any of the million or so Imperial planets. Only those worlds that shared a solar system could remain in contact, and even that failed during the heights of the raging tempests. How many of the Imperium's planets were lost remains unknown, but for a time all of them were alone, bereft of even the guiding beacon of the Astronomican as the Emperor's Light blinked – and then vanished.

In the period that followed, psychic aftershocks washed the galaxy, and reality itself struggled to recover from the horrific trauma. Eventually, those not engulfed by the warp storms, or too close to the baleful effects of the Great Rift, discovered that Astropaths could once more transmit interstellar messages, although the risk of daemonic incursion was deadlier than ever. Crusades were launched to re-establish contact with distant star systems, to retake that which could be reconquered. The most successful of these was the Indomitus Crusade, led by none other than Roboute Guilliman. The returned Primarch had reclaimed his title of Lord Commander of the Imperium, and where he travelled, faith returned. Yet no messages and few spacecraft could cross the hellish new barrier that split the galaxy.

With the Great Rift, the always-fractured Imperium of Mankind became broken, its far-flung worlds cut off as never before. Yet it remained. The banners of the myriad armies of Mankind still flew high above planets untold.

Let every thrust of the blade, every twitch of the trigger, every step and every word be trained towards the downfall of Chaos! The galaxy is the rightful realm of Mankind, and no other. Those who would see the Emperor's works cast down will be cast by the heel into oblivion. So it is, by the might of the Adeptus Astartes, and so it shall ever be. Nightsome fiends, fear us, for we are your death!

MANKIND AND THE IMMATERIUM

The history of Mankind's greatest successes and tragedies is directly linked to warp space, also known as the immaterium, or simply the warp. In a time now long forgotten, it was the discovery of warp space that allowed the first human colonisations. By entering that alternate dimension, it was possible to achieve faster-than-light speeds over interstellar distances, allowing fleets to travel far from Terra's solar system. Mankind spread quickly, colonising the galaxy in an expansive age. It was also the warp – or more precisely, the dread powers that dwell within that realm – that caused the collapse that ended the otherwise gilded Age of Technology.

As it transpired, warp space was not an empty void to be conquered by science. Instead, it was an infinite and incomprehensible realm inhabited by many strange and malignant entities. The most powerful and dangerous of the warp's denizens were the four Great Gods of Chaos – Khorne, Tzeentch, Nurgle and Slaanesh – and their legions of Daemons. They desired only the destruction of the galaxy and longed to possess every living soul. Fortunately for Mankind, Daemons cannot easily leave the immaterium, and could only do so when they found gateways to bridge the gap between their dread domain and realspace.

Until the Great Rift, the most common gateway between the warp and realspace was the unprotected mind of a psyker. Such a being draws upon the otherworldly powers of the immaterium, whether consciously or no, yet without training or exceptional will they are vulnerable to daemonic possession. Warp storms – sudden violent outbursts of energies escaping the immaterium – also brought violent but short-lived Daemon incursions. Such tempests irregularly plagued the galaxy, waxing and waning across sectors. There had been a time, during an era known as the Age of Strife, when vast warp storms raged unchecked for centuries. It was only when that overwhelming tumult abated that the being who would become known as the Emperor rose to power on Terra. First he led the Unification Wars to unite the populations of Terra's solar system, and then he led Mankind out into the wider galaxy, to reclaim many of the lost colonies and end the greatest period of darkness Mankind had ever suffered.

With the worst of the storms receded, the Emperor ordered the construction of the Astronomican. Broadcast from Terra by a choir of psykers and focussed by the Emperor's indomitable will, this beacon shone through warp space, allowing Navigators to follow its guiding light, plotting courses through the otherwise directionless murk of endless Chaos. It was by using the Astronomican that Mankind was able to forge out from Terra once more. The Great Crusade, as it came to be known, reclaimed far-scattered and long-lost worlds, giving birth to the Imperium. For nearly ten millennia, the borders of that realm were defined by the reach of the Astronomican, the great Light of Terra.

Navigators could travel in a great radius outwards from the Astronomican, but there were many blind spots. Distant borders, like the Eastern Fringe or the Ghoul Stars, were beyond the beacon's reach. Few in the Imperium dared venture beyond such limitations save for some Rogue Traders who used conventional space travel to probe into the blackness. There were also anomalies scattered across the galaxy, near which warp travel was restricted or prevented all together. The most dangerous of these were warp rifts, such as the Eye of Terror, where a great influx of fell energies stirred fierce warp storms that dimmed or blotted out the Astronomican. Without that signal, the risk of mishap or madness, or a fate worse than either, was exponentially increased. Shorn of its guidance, even the most powerful of Navigators could neither pilot a ship nor plot a course for the immense voyages required to cross a quarter of the breadth of the Imperium. Of course, that was before the Great Rift.

A chain reaction of tears split across the galaxy, leaving behind a pulsing scar of pure Chaos. The Noctis Aeterna followed, a period when the Astronomican was swallowed, lost within the roiling masses of the storm. For some time – days, weeks, years? – only intermittent flashes could be seen, as if the Emperor himself was doing battle against the storm. For half the galaxy, the Astronomican returned, although now prone to blinks and stutters. For those in the galactic north – dubbed the Imperium Nihilus – the beam of the Astronomican was gone, leaving Navigators blind in the warp, and the Imperial worlds there lost and isolated in the dark.

NAVIGATORS

Navigators are a stable breed of human mutant whose existence predates the Imperium by many thousands of years. Founded during the Age of Technology, the Navis Nobilite, or Navigator Houses, survived through the Age of Strife to the present day, where they currently thrive as a vital part of the Imperium. Navigators have unique physiques, some of which can be quite extreme, but all are marked by a third eye. It is this that is the key to their power and value, for it is used to see the shifting currents of the warp, enabling a Navigator to steer a spacecraft through the maelstrom of the immaterium. The mutation is neither spontaneous nor natural, but rather the result of ancient genetic experimentation and engineering. Amongst humans, only Navigators can pilot spacecraft through the warp with any degree of direction. Although the guidance beacons used during the Age of Technology have long since been lost, the Astronomican provides a steering reference, allowing Navigators to pinpoint locations. Without Navigators, or their ability to see the Astronomican, all of the Imperium would be like the Imperium Nihilus, fragmented into thousands of separate stellar empires, whose spacecraft would be obliged to risk tiny, blind jumps to cover any distance of space greater than a few light years.

WORLDS OF THE IMPERIUM

Spread across the galaxy are over a million planets claimed in the name of the Imperium – a vast number, yet only a tiny proportion of the stellar systems in the galaxy. Many disconnected branches of the Adeptus Administratum are dedicated to classifying Imperial planets, their data contradictory or badly out of date.

Many worlds were settled by Humanity during the Age of Technology and then brought into the Emperor's fold during the Great Crusade. As warp storms shift, lost worlds continue to be recovered, but the exact number of worlds within the Imperium is not precisely known. Given the immense distances, poor communications, and the volatile nature of the galaxy itself, any attempt at a census would be obsolete before it was finished. To ease the difficulties of governing such a sprawling empire, the Imperium is divided into five segmentums, which in turn are broken down into numerous sectors and sub-sectors. Some Imperial worlds are clustered around relatively stable warp translation points, often branching out from key hub planets to form tightly knit alliances of trade and mutual protection, such as the Realm of Ultramar or the systems surrounding Terra. The majority of inhabited worlds, however, are separated by immense voids. Isolation and varied environments ensure a wide range of cultures and levels of technological advancement, but so long as the Imperial Tithe is paid – a charge on manpower, manufacturing and psykers levied upon every colonised planet – worlds are largely left to self-govern. Over the ages, all manner of planets have been colonised – cold, airless rocks, sweltering lush worlds and nearly everything between. During the Age of Technology, colonies were even founded upon hitherto uninhabitable orbs, such as gaseous giants where settlements were anchored above endless storms. While the secrets to taming such inhospitable environments have been lost, many worlds still cling to existence thanks to ancient machinery. The following are examples of just a few of the many thousands of different planet classifications.

CIVILISED WORLDS

η-class [HIVE WORLDS]

Hive cities are huge urban conglomerations which can stretch across continents and reach miles into the sky. Typically, their host worlds consist of many individual hives divided by areas of polluted waste or toxic seas. Hive world populations are immense, but if anarchy is properly suppressed, they can be a rich source of troops for the Imperial Guard.

μ-class [FEUDAL WORLDS]

Many rediscovered worlds are found to have regressed to a societal state described in ancient Terran lore as 'medieval'. Some of these worlds, such as those referred to as Knight worlds, maintain some technological advancements in the form of revered pieces of archeotech.

φλ-class [FERAL WORLDS]

Feral worlds contain long-isolated populations that have declined into savagery. The crudest of such societies have regressed beyond the point of using even stone tools, while others might be on the cusp of entering an iron age. Whether due to post-apocalyptic, environmental, or other factors, such planets pay the lowest tithe grade.

EXTERMINATUS

The order for Exterminatus is a death knell for a world. It calls for the complete eradication of all life on a planet. Such a command can only come from the highest ranks of the Imperium – a Space Marine Chapter Master, Lord High Admiral of the Imperial Navy, Lord Commander of the Astra Militarum, or an Inquisitor. The orders unleashing such destruction are only issued when no other solution or redemption can be seen. It has been used to combat planetwide heresy, rampant, uncontrollable mutation or disease, to prevent the opening or widening of warp rifts, or when xenos are so entrenched that the resources (population included) are beyond salvation. The methods of delivering this ultimate sanction vary, but all are equally uncompromising. The Adeptus Astartes tend towards delivering an Exterminatus device to the planet's surface, using a carefully selected kill team to ensure absolute death. By contrast, the Imperial Navy prefers sustained bombardment, using battleships to hammer the world until it collapses in on itself. The grim corvettes of the Inquisition favour cyclonic torpedoes and atmospheric incinerators.

φ-class [Forge Worlds]

Forge worlds are the domain of the Adeptus Mechanicus, planets dedicated to heavy industry and the superstitious religion of science known as the Cult Mechanicus. The first and greatest of the forge worlds is Mars, and the Fabricator General still resides there. All forge worlds are wreathed in pollution, the by-product of unceasing industry where continent-sized machines work to churn out weapons for the Imperium's endless armies.

α-class [Agri Worlds]

As many planets in the Imperium – especially those classified as hive or forge worlds – cannot produce enough food of their own, other worlds are wholly given over to the production of agricultural products. Many branches of the Adeptus Administratum ensure that such agri worlds are run to produce the maximum volume of foodstuff. It matters not how many are worked to death so long as hourly quotas are met.

Ю-class [Mining Worlds]

Planets classified as mining worlds are rich in materials coveted by manufactorums and forge worlds. Workers – whether enslaved or penal – harvest ore, rock, promethium, gas clouds or any desired minerals. Many resources are found on barren or inhospitable worlds, such as the lava oceans of Trollix, or the electro-clouds of Zeutus. The Imperium does not value its miners, only the materials they extract and refine.

ρ-class [Research Stations/Fortress Worlds]

In bureaucratic fashion, the classification of research station and fortress world overlaps. Some are planets given over to massively garrisoned continent-wide bunker complexes protected by orbital guns; others might not be worlds at all, but asteroid bases that serve as surveillance posts or defensive strongholds to safeguard shipping or watch likely xenos invasion routes.

[Chapter Planets]

A Chapter Planet serves as the headquarters of an Adeptus Astartes Chapter. This classification, which is exempt from normal Imperial Tithes, supersedes all others, as a Space Marine Chapter may claim a death or feral planet, or might not take a world at all, instead inhabiting a space station, deserted moon or asteroid. The Chapter Master rules the planet and they frequently draw recruits from the local population.

δτ-class [Death Worlds]

Death worlds are planets deemed too dangerous to support conventional human settlements. One of the best known of all death worlds is Catachan, a planet infamous for its vast jungles and myriad forms of ferocious carnivorous life – both flora and fauna. Despite their name, many death worlds support some measure of hard-fought human life, and those that survive make excellent recruits for the armies of the Imperium.

What horrors slumber amidst the stars, awaiting only the careless tread of Humankind to awaken them to wrath? What lurking terrors ply the darkened void, gazing with avaricious eyes upon the fragile lights of Imperial worlds? None can say, save perhaps the Emperor Himself, and His silence is eternal.

IN THE DEPTHS OF SPACE

The Imperium is not composed of planets and star systems alone. Defensive emplacements and man-made stations surround inhabited systems, guarding against encroaching xenos. In deep space, the Imperium maintains numerous battle stations – planet-sized ports that tether ships of the line – while at various strategic points in each segmentum are larger starforts, lynchpins of Imperial expansion since the days of the Great Crusade. Most often, these bases are stationed in close proximity to Imperial planets, although some protect trade routes or form blockades around notoriously perilous systems. There are artificial moons and doomsday bastions, as well as hazard zones made of asteroids chained together and kept in place by occasional thruster bursts. Even further into the wilderness of the void drift arrays of listening probes. Great exploratory fleets plumb the dark depths seeking to stake claims for the Imperium. Even in the most remote of places, mining stations can be found, sometimes bolted onto asteroids to strip precious metals, or as space-faring rigs designed to siphon mineral-rich nebulas. Feeding the war industry of the Imperium demands endless supplies.

The isolation of space, however, offers no safety from the hazards of war. As the Imperium's planets have been besieged, so too have their interstellar holdings. Battle stations have been boarded, no matter the calibre of their guns, and hidden watch posts have been raided. Many ships in the midst of journeys have found that space is an unforgiving environment. Malfunctions, mutiny, pirate raids, and mishap leave many ships dead and adrift. For ships that utilise warp space, the risks are multiplied a hundredfold. The vastness of space and the perils of the warp ensure few such wrecks are ever salvaged. These lifeless vessels float aimlessly, a sea of derelicts moved by eddies until they are swallowed by further warp storms. Those colossal tempests crush groups of such wrecks together, and the resultant mangle of ships, space stations, asteroids and detritus form monolithic ghost ships known in the Imperium as space hulks. Some space hulks are only a few ships compacted together, while others are massive agglomerations larger than many moons. Space hulks wander unpredictable currents, periodically dropping out of the warp and then winking away once more. During the Noctis Aeterna, also known as the Blackness, entire dead fleets were vomited into realspace, thousands of battles' worth of ship graveyards arriving at once. Amongst the derelicts were spacecraft recently destroyed and relics dating back to the Age of Technology. Others contained holds full of xenos mechanisms from lost civilisations, and many of the space hulks had become lairs for monstrous passengers.

WARP STORMS AND THE NOCTIS AETERNA

Nothing is more volatile than the warp. When those unnatural energies escape the immaterium into realspace, they roar across the galaxy, often with catastrophic effect. Throughout the centuries since Mankind's return to the stars, countless ships have been swallowed up by warp storms, never to return. Such storms were known to isolate entire sub-sectors, blocking travel and communication into and out of the region and shutting out the beam of the Astronomican. While the Age of the Imperium has seen many warp storms, none compared to those that raged during the time of the Blackness.

As the Cicatrix Maledictum cracked the galaxy, all of the Imperium was shorn of the Emperor's Light. Ships in transit were subjected to the full fury of immense storms, and entire fleets were buffeted off course, leaving crippled vessels scattered across the galaxy. They were the lucky ones. Others were torn asunder or breached by Daemons. Battleships were tugged out of moorings while defence stations were snatched into the warp to reappear on the other side of the galaxy, their crews of many millions gone. Even planets were wrenched out of their orbits and time itself was halted across swathes of space. Such storms lasted days, months, years or even centuries, depending on the location. Shock waves of warp energies flooded out from the Great Rift, appearing as multihued nebulas or writhing monstrosities. No instruments known to the Imperium could track the tempests, and ships attempting to avoid their courses found the storms following them.

Isolated, planets sent warnings and pleas for help, but no communications could pass through those storms. Astropaths attempting to send messages died horrible deaths, their last spasms attracting Daemons. Strange things moved in the inky void. The blackness itself seemed to slither. Nameless creatures hunted the starfields and the Daemon legions came, for panic and desperation drew them like predators to a blood trail. And behind them emerged the sworn enemies of the Imperium – Traitor Legions and Chaos Renegades. The worst terrors of ten thousand years strode the galaxy once more, as legendary Greater Daemons and Daemon Primarchs came forth, wreaking vengeful retribution before disappearing back into the maelstrom. Full-fledged wars tore down bastion planets whose names echoed across the Imperium. So fell Sabatine, the Chapter Planet of the White Consuls Space Marines, and Dhorthan, prime hive world of the Dhorthian System. A great feasting on the rotted corpse of the Imperium had begun.

THE ECCLESIARCHY

Necessity and fear alone cannot bind a million planets together, and from the earliest days of the Imperium, many tried to unite Mankind through faith. From a small cult full of zealous disciples, the Ecclesiarchy grew to provide the state religion for the whole Imperium. A force unto itself, the Ecclesiarchy has spread into nearly every facet of Imperial life.

As the Emperor led Humanity back to the stars, he was venerated as a leader and visionary. On the most regressive planets rediscovered during the Great Crusade, many primitive peoples considered the Emperor to be a living god – a saviour who came from the skies. After his battle with Horus and subsequent incarceration atop the Golden Throne, the Emperor was openly worshipped even on so-called civilised planets. The culmination of the civil war known as the Horus Heresy not only robbed Mankind of the Emperor's physical guidance, it brought other changes as well. In addition to the devastation of a brutal war, there was a new fear of traitors within Humanity's midst. Suddenly, the bright light that the leader of Mankind had worked so hard to rekindle was replaced with suspicion and dread. The far-flung empire felt vulnerable, and into that vacuum came a new reassurance – that of faith.

Following the Horus Heresy, many cults dedicated to worship of the Emperor appeared. These sects differed in practice, interpreting the now-silent Emperor's will in myriad ways, but all were united by their deification of the Emperor and the proliferation of the principles of human survival that he had instigated in the creation of the Imperium. Concerning mutants, psykers and aliens, anything that stood in the way of Humanity's future was to be destroyed without mercy. As the campaign known as the Scouring swept back over the human-controlled parts of the galaxy, these new sects followed closely behind. Within a few hundred years of the Emperor's sacrifice, the multitude of smaller cults had been absorbed into the largest sects, the most powerful of which was known as the Ecclesiarchy, after its elected leader, the Ecclesiarch. This aggressive body grew so dominant that, early in the 32nd Millennium, it gained the status of official religion of the Imperium and the concomitant title of Adeptus Ministorum.

THE OFFICIAL FOUNDING

The first official step of the Adeptus Ministorum was to tighten control, persecuting any remaining cults that refused to amalgamate beneath its banner. Those who

With sharpened blades and thundering guns, with disciplined warriors and cold-eyed killers, you may conquer a city, a world, perhaps an entire system. Yet with faith you may conquer the galaxy itself.

THERE IS NO COWARDICE IN FAITH.

refused were declared unbelievers and the population was stirred to violence against them. The might of the Ecclesiarchy was such that it could call for Wars of Faith – military campaigns capable of overturning planets or whole systems. Often this was done to further the Imperium's goals, ridding it of heretics, seditious unbelievers or alien subversion, but history is equally replete with examples of the Ecclesiarchy instigating bloody wars for its own gain, securing enough wealth through falsely declared crusades to build the first of the shrine worlds. Lavish cathedrals, massive statues and monolithic triumphal arches heaped praise upon the Emperor but, more importantly to many, those pivotal hub planets granted vast political sway and were often rich in mineral resources. The Ecclesiarchy's influence spread, and few dared to question its motives. By the end of the 33rd Millennium there was practically no open worship in the Imperium save for that condoned by the Adeptus Ministorum. The only exceptions were the domains of the Adeptus Astartes and the Adeptus Mechanicus, who were begrudgingly allowed to keep their unique traditions. In the long ages since, this has led to distrust, and occasionally even open war, between the differing parties.

THE HOLY MISSION

The servants of the Ecclesiarchy are fanatical in their quest to spread their religion. Given the size of the galaxy, the random nature of warp storm isolation and the widely varied levels of cultural and technological advancement within the Imperium, the Adeptus Ministorum has found many belief systems already established on planets they visited for the first time. This was not an impediment, for the Ecclesiarchy had become adept at assimilating all manner of creeds into the Cult Imperialis – the worship of the Emperor. This might mean erecting great cathedrals to impress hardened hive-dwellers, or teaching the hunting tribes on feral worlds that the sun god they worshipped was in fact the glorious light of the Emperor. The nuance of how the people bowed before the Master of Mankind was not as important as the act itself. For many centuries the Ecclesiarchy was content to play the long game. Their strategy, over time, reined in the more barbaric customs and gradually they usurped complete religious control. Any local religions that resisted were ruled heretical and actively crushed by political or military means, whichever proved the most prudent.

As the Age of the Imperium grew darker, the fervour of faith became ever louder. To the superstitious masses, the hellfire that cracked the stars and the plethora of warp-fuelled phenomenon were clear signs of the Time of Ending. In desperation, vast populations isolated and besieged by nightmare creatures called upon their Emperor to protect them. For most, the only answer was more carnage rained down from the stars.

There are those amongst Humanity who cry out for hope, for freedom and an escape from duty and toil. Decry such traitors! There can be no hope in times such as these, save that which the Emperor offers. There can be no freedom, save that which the Emperor grants. There can be no cessation of toil, save that which death bestows, and even that final gift is the Emperor's to give – as He will.

A DEADLY EVOLUTION

Since the prolific warp storms of the Age of Strife, the rate at which humans develop psychic powers has steadily increased. Psychic minds appear as bright flames in the immaterium, ripe sweetmeats for the pandemonium of planeshifters, Enslavers, and Daemons that dwell there. Recognising the substantial risk for daemonic possession and the spread of Chaos, the Emperor of Mankind attempted to control the growing epidemic. By his decree, the use of psychic powers was banned save for those sanctioned by the Imperium itself. The ruler of every Imperial planet was to set aside a levy of young psykers for transport to Terra aboard the Black Ships.

Every day of the Age of the Imperium, the vast armadas of the League of Black Ships have plied the void, racing to collect their precious cargo across the galaxy before rushing homeward to Terra, their holds crammed full of frightened psykers. Even with psychic dampeners, such journeys are fraught with danger. The threats are constant, as warp travel can unhinge unwary minds, sometimes causing psykers to release untold horrors. An untrained psyker's only chance of surviving the threats of the warp is to go unnoticed by the powers that stalk there. Without the discipline taught by the Adeptus Astra Telepathica and its Scholastia Psykana, a psyker has no chance of defending themselves against a hungry warp presence. Many psykers are innocent of any malign intentions and the implications of their abilities, although this makes them no less dangerous. Others, far fewer in number, are aware of what hunts them and actively court the dreadful attention of warp entities, tempting a terrible fate for morsels of knowledge or power. When discovered, such tainted psykers are quickly eliminated.

Many psykers die en route to Terra, but those who survive are rigorously tested to work out their best use. Upon reaching the Imperial home world, the psykers are sorted, graded and assigned to various duties. The vast majority are sent to the Astronomican to serve the great beacon – their lives are short, painful and culminate in an agonising death. A goodly number are deemed too unstable even for that duty. Most of these are lobotomised, becoming mindless servitors, but a few are spirited away to the Obsidian Keep in the heart of the Astra Telepathica palace complex where an unknown fate awaits them. A very few are deemed fit for more active service. Of these, the main part are sent to the Imperial Palace to undergo the Soul Binding ritual. More die there, but the maimed survivors are inducted into the ranks of the Astropaths. Others are sent to various departments – one in ten million may be mind-scrubbed and sent to serve the military as a

sanctioned psyker, one in a hundred million may be mind-scrubbed and sent to a Space Marine Chapter to be reborn as a Librarian, and one in a billion may be worthy of serving as an Inquisitor or other high-status official. Since the eruption of the Great Rift, the supply chain of the Black Ships has been severely interrupted. Planets cut off from their Imperial Tithe are forced to implement their own restraints upon their populations of untrained psykers.

AGES OF MANKIND

Knowledge of the long ages of human history has been wreathed in shadow, buried beneath the aeons or simply lost over the expanse of time. Some Historitors continue to seek knowledge, but their work can be compared to holding a candle against the dark abyss.

The Historitors of the Adeptus Administratum seek, gather and dutifully collect the history of each planet within the Imperium. Once, perhaps, this was done with purpose. Now, however, it is most often an indiscriminate compilation of data, a process where scribes unthinkingly copy content onto scrolls, preserving complete records in constant fear of missing a single inconsequential letter. The ability, or even desire, to translate what these facts mean in any larger sense is almost entirely absent, found only in a few individuals who are eyed suspiciously, or perhaps punished for their enthusiasm.

The largest and most complete collection of such records exists beneath the surface of Terra, where the colossal under-halls stretch out of sight – endless vistas of datascrolls tower upwards like mountains. With flickering candlelight provided by floating servo-skulls, processions of curators, scriveners, and ciphers wind through the valleys, attempting to illuminate that which was. Over the years, old truths have been lost to the adjustments and redactions made by revisionists of the Adeptus Ministorum, the Inquisition and even the High Lords of Terra themselves.

AGE OF TERRA: M1-M15

Little is known of this period save that, during this time, Mankind made its first forays from Terra into space. Mars became the first planet to be terraformed when it was settled by industrial cartels. The red planet soon became synonymous with technical expertise and scientific advancement. Colonies had to be self-sufficient, as many were isolated from Terra by long, dangerous journeys.

AGE OF TECHNOLOGY: M15-M25

This era is referred to as the 'Dark Age of Technology' so often that its original title might seem incomplete. There are few reliable records dating back to this epoch and even they seem to contradict themselves with regularity. What is known is that from roughly M18 onwards, Mankind discovered the warp and how to enter it. Slowly, through many disasters, Humanity learned to use the warp to make faster-than-light journeys out of their own star system. It was during this time that the first alien races were encountered.

Soon after, Mankind embarked upon the discovery, development and cultivation of the human Navigator gene, a controlled mutation that allowed human pilots to make longer warp jumps than previously thought possible. Navigator families, initially controlled by industrial and trade cartels, had become individual forces in their own right by M19. By M20, Humanity had proliferated and settled many of the countless star systems. It was a golden age for scientific achievement; technology provided all the answers. Thinking machines aided civilian and military production, allowing enormous labours to be accomplished at a frenetic pace. Perfection of the Standard Template Construct (STC) system permitted an explosion of colonisation that reached the furthest limits of the galaxy. This was the zenith of technological development and knowledge-sharing, for even the most far-flung colony had access to the entire inventory of human invention.

For the rest of the age, Mankind spread across the stars, becoming widely dispersed and divergent. Evidence exists of many wars, but none that threatened the stability of human space. Amongst the records are lists of xenos enemies that have long since gone extinct, along with more familiar names such as Aeldari and Orks. During this time period, interplanetary trade was established and great fleets carried goods to and from

'We endure an age of darkness, it is true, but still we shall be the lucky ones who do not live to see its end.'

- General Valtor, IV Drovian Dragoons

the ends of the galaxy. As planets became overpopulated, the recently invented construction mediums of plasteel, plascrete, ferrocrete and rockcrete were used to build colossal cities, which became the proto-hives.

As quick as the expansion of Mankind's domain had been, it was eclipsed by the speed of its collapse. The decline was so rapid and so nearly complete that little of those colonies, or the civilisations they spawned, remain. Speculation is rampant, but there are few facts. What is known is that human psykers were first mentioned towards the end of M22, making a sudden appearance on almost every human world within a relatively short span of time. By the end of M23, there was widespread anarchy, descriptions of what must be daemonic possessions and great turbulence in the warp. Some records also cite betrayal by the machines and a great war with robotic armies. Whether factual or allegorical, the histories leave no doubt on one point: the golden age had come to a spectacularly swift and brutal end.

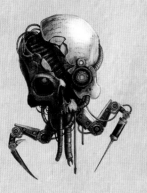

AGE OF STRIFE: M25-M30

Marked by terrible wars and massive invasions that tore Humanity apart, this age was a time of collapse. Warp storms of unprecedented ferocity isolated Mankind's colonies. The great distances prevented almost all contact between colonised planets, and those who were close enough to remain in communication often became embroiled in internal battles for control.

The separated human cultures rapidly diversified. Humanity itself began to evolve, with mutations regularly appearing on most planets and, on some worlds, altering into something new altogether: the first of the abhuman races. Civilisations that persecuted the recently developed psykers fared the best. Worlds where such abilities were encouraged seem to have been destroyed altogether. Some of the wonders of the Age of Technology were lost or destroyed in the flames of conflict while others fell into neglect. Mankind was brought to its knees, and this horrific state continued for nearly six millennia.

When it finally emerged from the long darkness, Humanity was forever altered. Science was no longer the answer, but instead something to be feared. As legends tell, late in the Age of Strife, a force slowly reconciled the old grudges held between the warring factions of Terra and Mars, and the long campaign later called the Unification Wars was ended. This new leader was known only as the Emperor, and even as he prepared to reclaim the wider galaxy, a final mighty surge of the Age of Strife's warp storms lit up the skies. This phenomenon was so large that the event was recorded by planets all across the galaxy. When the scintillating burst died down, it left the warp somewhat becalmed and the galaxy scarred by what would later be known as the Eye of Terror.

With the sudden quelling of the warp storms that had raged unabated, the Emperor and his newly formed Legions of Space Marines turned their attention to the stars, beginning the Great Crusade. Using the psychic beam of the newly created Astronomican, Navigators could plot courses through the warp to cover vast distances of realspace quickly. So did the Great Crusade advance outwards in many directions at once, driving back xenos and creatures of the warp alike. Over hundreds of battles, the Emperor reclaimed many of the earlier colonies, and was reunited with the lost Primarchs – his superhuman creations whose gene-seed had been used to make the Space Marine Legions. The Primarchs had been stolen from the Emperor, whisked away by the Dark Gods while still in their gestation pods. The Emperor's crusade brought an end to the dismal despair and loss of the Age of Strife and began a new period of human history.

'DIVEST YOURSELF OF MERCY, FOR MERCY IS A WEAKNESS. DIVEST YOURSELF OF COMPASSION, FOR COMPASSION IS A WEAKNESS. DIVEST YOURSELF OF HOPE, FOR HOPE IS A WEAKNESS. WHEN NOTHING REMAINS WITHIN BUT HATE, AND THE PURITY OF YOUR PURPOSE, THEN YOU WILL BE STRONG.'

- *Sergeant Golgaar, Iron Hands Clan Company Raukaan*

AGE OF DARKNESS

A new era had begun, but the bright new dawn for Mankind envisioned by the Emperor was not to be. The fledgling Imperium was instead torn asunder by the great betrayal of the Horus Heresy. Human pride and ambition opened the door for the treacheries of the Dark Gods. So did an age of enlightenment grow dark, as Humanity was forced to barter reason for superstition, and hope for survival.

The Great Crusade was spearheaded by the newly formed Space Marine Legions, who were armed by the recently allied factories of Mars. Supported by the new Imperial Army, the forces of the Emperor proved unstoppable. Xenos and warp creatures were driven back, and planet after planet was reclaimed in the name of Humanity. Further and further the campaigns pushed outwards from Terra. One by one, the twenty missing Primarchs were found and added back into the fold.

During the Great Crusade, the Emperor preached three great truths in his reconquest of the galaxy: genetic corruption must be sought out and eradicated; psykers were to be uncovered, kept controlled, and handed over to Imperial agents for evaluation, and destructive xenos were to be rendered powerless. With triumph on all battlefronts, the Imperium of Mankind was re-established as the largest single empire in the galaxy. Deciding it was time for the next phase of

enlightenment, the Emperor handed control of the new Space Marine Legions over to his sons, the Primarchs, while he returned to Terra. In the Emperor's stead, Horus, Primarch of the Luna Wolves (later renamed the Sons of Horus), was named first amongst equals, and given the title Warmaster.

THE GREAT BETRAYAL

In the dawn of this expansive new era of Mankind, great sacrifice was demanded. Turning his back on the teachings of the Emperor, it was the Warmaster, Horus, the Emperor's most trusted and gifted commander, who committed the ultimate betrayal. Embracing the will of the Dark Gods and infused by their ruinous powers, the traitor Horus led a rebellion that set the galaxy aflame with bitter civil war. A full third of the Imperium's military forces joined Horus, including half of the Space Marine Legions. So it was that brother fought

No being is more accursed, more hateful and despised, than the traitor. Show neither mercy nor compassion to such heretics; they deserve only your hate.

against brother, creating myths and grudges that still echo throughout the galaxy. On both sides there strode warriors out of legend, and the very planets cracked apart beneath their titanic struggles.

Seeking to slay the Emperor, the traitors carved their bloody way to Terra itself, invading the Emperor's Palace, howling their rage in an orgy of slaughter and war. Yet finally, heroically, the tables were turned and, at last, Horus was struck down – but not before he dealt the Emperor a mortal blow. The shattered body of Mankind's leader remained intact, however, held strong by his indomitable spirit until it could be interred within the recently forged machinery of the Golden Throne. There, deep within the Imperial Palace, towering banks of arcane technology sustained the Emperor's spirit so that it could continue to watch over Humanity. Although his withered form was bound, the Emperor's psychic powers were unfettered; he was still the Master of Mankind and custodian of the human race.

VICTORY'S HEAVY TOLL

The Emperor's survival is paramount to the survival of the Imperium, because only the mind of the Emperor is powerful enough to survive the never-ending process of directing the psychic beacon of the Astronomican out of the raw psychic forces supplied by the servants of the Adeptus Astronomica. The same survivability does not hold true for those members of the Adeptus Astronomica themselves, and their fate is a tragic one. The effort of generating so much mental energy soon destroys them, leeching their souls and reducing them to empty husks. Many die every day, but they are not the only psykers who make the ultimate sacrifice. The Emperor cannot eat as men eat, or drink or breathe air, as his life has long since passed the point where such things could sustain him. The only viable sustenance for the Emperor is human life force – souls – and he has an insatiable appetite.

Not just any human will suffice for the Emperor's table, for they must have psychic powers. Therefore, the Imperium is scoured by the vast flotillas of the Black Ships in a tireless search for emergent psykers. During their long journey back to Terra, some of the psykers are found to have the strength of mind to be recruited to the Adeptus Astronomica, but many more serve their Emperor in a more gruesome way. They are given wholly to the weird machinery that surrounds the Master of Mankind, and their souls are siphoned, slowly and agonisingly, to feed his mighty spirit. Many hundreds, even thousands, must die in this way every day for the Emperor, the Imperium, and all of Humanity to survive.

The Emperor's dream of an age of enlightenment, a time when Mankind was freed from superstition and ignorance, turned into something far different. His Imperium has endured, but only by virtue of an oppressive and necessarily harsh rule carried out in his name. It became an age of tyrants and of unreason, an era of stagnation and intolerance. His people regressed into religious obfuscation while the Emperor sat immobile, his thoughts unknown – the creature whose will extended over a million worlds was unable to lift a shrivelled finger.

REPERCUSSIONS

The bitter fighting of the Horus Heresy was the beginning of a new age founded in blood. After the death of Horus, the traitors splintered, but many hard wars remained. The time of the Scouring demanded countless victories before the fledgling Imperium was wrested back from the brink of destruction. In the midst of the turmoil, the hierarchy of the Imperium underwent fundamental alterations, morphing from the direct rule of the Emperor to a realm ruled by a council in his name. Suspicion fuelled many changes, as it was uncovered that far more planets than first thought had been lulled into treacheries of one form or another. The roots of these betrayals ran deep and were hard to flush into the light. Distrust and paranoia were rampant and a new era of fear and mistrust began.

Changes swept the military and government offices. The Legiones Astartes, the vast fighting formations so instrumental in Mankind's victories during the Great Crusade, were broken down into many smaller Chapters. Overseen by Roboute Guilliman, the Primarch of the Ultramarines Legion, this transition allowed for greater tactical flexibility without placing the command of an entire Space Marine Legion into the hands of one individual – never again would the awesome power of one hundred thousand Space Marines be misused.

Another change redefined the Imperial Army. Once including both the great battleships that plied the stars and the countless soldiers that landed to fight planet-side, now the two were divided into the Imperial Fleet and the Astra Militarum. Across all the agencies of the Imperium, offices and institutions were split, their previous responsibilities fractionalised. Many branches of the Adeptus Administratum were spawned at this time. It was not unusual for two separate organisations, each unaware of the other, to be tasked with the same jobs. These byzantine systems were fail-safe measures that have since spiralled out of control. Beyond such bureaucracies, standing watch over all, was the newly formed Inquisition, a secretive organisation outside the established hierarchies. Ever vigilant, their role was to question everything in their constant search for threats to Humanity. None save the Emperor himself could escape their uncompromising and watchful gaze.

AGE OF THE IMPERIUM

Following the Horus Heresy, Mankind became hidebound within the organisations and institutions of the Imperial administration. The Emperor, having reached the end of his natural life, existed only by the artificial means of the Golden Throne and continual human sacrifice. Psykers continued to emerge in ever growing numbers and were barely controlled through constant suppression and vigilance. There is only war and constant battle, and the menace from the warp looms ever larger.

THE SCOURING: M31

The entire millennium was marked by the sprawling campaign of vengeance fought against the heretic traitors still found across the galaxy. Loyalist forces, led mostly by the Ultramarines and Space Wolves, drove back the traitors who survived Horus' fall. A great number were purged, but the foes were many, and included thousands of fallen regiments, star fleets of the Imperial Army, whole Titan Legions and the Dark Mechanicum, in addition to the Traitor Legions themselves. The core of the corrupted Space Marines fell back and found refuge within the swirling chaos of the Eye of Terror. They were declared Excommunicate Traitoris, and all records and memory of the Traitor Legions were to be expunged from Imperial archives.

The Scouring, however, was far from over. It was a time of grim realisation for the Imperium, as in the war-torn aftermath the true scope of the Horus Heresy's betrayals was revealed. A great many more planets had been lured into helping the traitors than was at first known. Some had embraced their corruption, while others had been misled or beguiled. The search for the disloyal took on epic proportions. In the midst of the Scouring came the Second Founding and the formation of the Adeptus Astartes. It was but one of many such precautionary moves intended to prevent so great a betrayal happening again. Henceforth, suspicion, guilt and recrimination became rife in the Imperium of Man.

XENOS RISING: M32

With so much strength siphoned off by the countless battles of the previous millennium, the Imperium was ill-equipped to deal with the growing threat from the myriad xenos races, which became ever bolder and more predatory, closing in on all sides. Even star systems once thought impregnable were besieged. Tragedy heaped upon tragedy as Roboute Guilliman, Primarch of the Ultramarines and Lord High Commander of the Imperium, was mortally wounded by the Daemon Primarch Fulgrim.

THE FORGING: M32-34

During this golden age of the Imperium, the Adeptus Terra began to bind its most important star systems under ever tighter control. Astropath choirs were set in relay positions across the galaxy, with major hubs on the best-garrisoned worlds, such as Armageddon, Bakka and Macragge. The Imperial Cult became the official religion, and the Ecclesiarchy added more measures of control over the masses. Without the Emperor's guidance, the best direction for the Imperium was left to interpretation. To avoid prolonged dissension, strict rules were put in place. Fear ruled the highest levels of authority, while ignorance dominated the lower menials. The Imperium's reign became ever more harsh and uncompromising.

NOVA TERRA INTERREGNUM: M35-36

Also known as the Time of the Two Emperors, the Ur-council of Nova Terra denounced the High Lords of Terra and claimed rule of the entire Segmentum Pacificus. For nine centuries, the Imperium was split in twain in an age marked by civil wars for reunification, disputes over old trade terms and wavering allegiances. Chaos cults were discovered behind many, but not all, of the uprisings. So prolific was the corruption that the 21st Founding of Space Marines went horribly wrong, and the Grey Knights were called on by the Inquisition to expunge the threat.

THE AGE OF APOSTASY: M36

Following the Nova Terra Interregnum, a new age of dissent and power struggles erupted. It included both the Reign of Blood – a struggle between the ruling Ecclesiarch and the other High Lords of Terra – and the Plague of Unbelief – a galaxy-wide uprising of corrupt demagogues. Only during the Horus Heresy had more blood been shed in internal strife.

THE AGE OF REDEMPTION: M37-41

The sins of apostasy were purged in blood, including a systematic culling commanded by the High Lords of Terra. The Imperial Cult spread as never before, leading to the burning of heretics on hundreds of thousands of planets. Uncounted crusades of faith were launched, depleting both Imperial Guard regiments and Space Marine Chapters. Perhaps the most infamous example was early in the period, when the judgement of Saint Basillius found thirty Space Marine Chapters wanting in faith. The guilty were given the choice of instant death, or embarking on a crusade into the Eye of Terror. All chose the latter mission.

THE MACHARIAN CONQUESTS: M41

Many Imperial Lexographers and Historitors consider this to be the last of the Redemption Crusades, as well as the zenith of their achievement. Lord Commander Solar Macharius mustered the greatest army the galaxy had seen since the Emperor united his Primarchs beneath him in the Great Crusade. In seven years, Macharius' armies reconquered a thousand worlds on the western reaches of the galaxy, and his glory carried him into the darkest sectors, places where the Emperor's light had never been seen. Upon Macharius' death, the whole Imperium wept. Soon afterwards, the vast territories he had conquered fell into rivalry and war. The Macharian Heresy, as it came to be known, lasted for seventy years and was only ended through the combined efforts of over one hundred Space Marine Chapters.

THE WANING: M41

With Imperial armies exhausted by the Redemption Crusades, many outlying worlds fell to Ork invasions, Chaos insurgencies or other xenos menaces. To combat the spreading anarchy, the Adeptus Terra imposed ever stricter rules, doling out ever harsher punishments. Portents of doom were both incessant and relentless. The prescient foretold of great ripples in the warp, like a swell in the water disturbed by some colossal but unseen menace.

TYRANNIC WARS: M41

The Tyranids entered the galaxy and the Tyrannic Wars began. Hive Fleet Behemoth destroyed the planet of Tyran and the Thandros System before being halted at great cost in the Realm of Ultramar. Other Hive Fleets emerged, including Hive Fleet Kraken which ravaged the Aeldari craftworld of Iyanden.

THE GREAT RIFT: M41

A galaxy-spanning tear in reality known as the Cicatrix Maledictum, the Crimson Path, the Mouth of Ruin, the Warpscar, the Dathedian, Gork's Grin and a thousand other names besides, was ripped open. It brought with it a terrible darkness that enveloped the galaxy and ushered in a new epoch.

THE LONG WAR: M31-41

The great rebellion begun by the arch-heretic Horus has never ceased. Every year, decade and century since the Horus Heresy, the Long War – the term used by the Traitor Legions to reflect their desire to complete what the Warmaster began – has continued in every segmentum. The Traitor Legions, along with the cults and rebellions they foster, have rapaciously assailed the worlds of the Emperor. Thirteen times, Abaddon the Despoiler has launched Black Crusades – massive invasions where the oft-feuding Chaos powers united in force against their common foe. Yet the Long War has never been limited to open combat alone. Plagues are propagated, anarchic iconoclasts created, and covert cults intertwined into the very fabric of bureaucracy that binds the Imperium.

Fight until your blade is blunted, until the last round in your gun is spent. Fight until your armour is rent and battered, until your flesh is bloodied and your bones are splintered and smashed. Fight until your lifeblood spills from your body, and nothing but your duty is left to sustain you. The Emperor expects no less.

HOPE REKINDLED

When the Cicatrix Maledictum roared into being across the galaxy, it brought with it a terrible darkness that fell like a shroud across much of the Emperor's realm. Yet even as that unholy gloom was beginning to spread from star system to star system, a handful of courageous heroes and mighty champions fought to keep the light of hope alive. Records of that turbulent period are fragmented, riddled with allegory and thrown out of order by catastrophic temporal distortion, but it is generally accepted that the crux point of fate was Cadia.

By uniting the disparate factions of the Eye of Terror, Abaddon the Despoiler brought ruin to the world that had proven his nemesis for millennia. The Imperium's mightiest heroes opposed him – amongst them Belisarius Cawl, Saint Celestine and Inquisitor Katarinya Greyfax – but though they bled in Cadia's defence, they too were overcome and hounded to the ice-locked world of Klaisus. Upon Cadia, Abaddon brought low the mysterious geometric pylons that dotted the wind-swept outlands, and in doing so weakened the barrier between worlds, for these ancient megaliths were fashioned to keep the stuff of Chaos from the material dimension. This same act his agents repeated on every world that harboured such structures. Without these lynchpins to hold the material dimension sacrosanct, warp storms tore the galaxy along its length.

Meanwhile, the civilisation of the Aeldari underwent its greatest upheaval in millennia. From amidst the ranks of craftworlders and Drukhari alike arose the Ynnari, a new faction of grim warriors who followed their newborn deity, Ynnead, on a radical path that they believed would see Chaos defeated and the Aeldari race resurgent. Compelled by fate or circumstance, the Ynnari lent their aid to Cawl, Celestine and Greyfax in their darkest hour, and together, these champions of the light forged a path through their foes to Ultramar.

No matter how confused or divergent accounts of this time may be, all agree upon one point: upon Macragge, within the Fortress of Hera, these unlikely allies wrought a miracle. Roboute Guilliman, Primarch of the Ultramarines, was reborn. Clad in the raiment of war, the Lord of Ultramar drove the heretic hosts from his star system and harried them into frantic retreat. He then set out upon a desperate pilgrimage, his fleet surging through the warp even as the storms that would become the Great Rift roiled around them. Through fire and fury they battled, Guilliman defeating the mightiest champions of each of the four Gods of Chaos and finally winning through to Terra. There, he communed alone with his father, the Emperor of Mankind, and from that meeting the Primarch emerged with grim new purpose.

IMPERIUS DOMINATUS

Imperial Record GHR 14/556 Map used by Roboute Guilliman in the latter half of the Indomitus Crusade

SEGMENTUM OBSCURUS

HALO STARS

SCARUS SECTOR

NAOGEDDON

DIMMAMAR

STORM OF THE EMPEROR'S WRATH

COE

CALIXIS SECTOR

FINIAL SECTOR

GOTHIC SECTOR

IMPERIUM

CYPRA MUNDI

MORDIAN

VALHALLA

THE EYE OF TERROR

NACHMUND GAUNTLET

ALARIC

BAA

CHINCHARE

CADIA

BELIS CORONA

PISCINA

NECRON MEPHRIT DYNAS'

AGRIPINAA

FENRIS

MOLOV

CICATRIX MALEDICTUM

HYDRAPHUR

ARMAGEDDON

ELYSIA

SEGMENTUM SOLAR

THE ROCK

LASTRATI

PROSPERO & Planet of the Sorcerers

GOLGOTHA

VORDRAST

RYZA

SEGMENTUM PACIFICUS

TERRA & MARS

CATACHAN

THE MAELSTROM

GATHALAMOR

NECROMUNDA

BADAB

MACHARIA

ULTIMA MACHARIA

KRIEG

LUTHER McINTYRE

TALLARN

CHIROS

UHULIS SECTOR

OPHELIA

NOCTURNE

BALOR

V'RUN

SIREN'S STORM

ALEUSIS

BANE'S LANDING

HOLY TERRA
Blessed in his authority, here dwells the most beneficent Emperor.

SOLSTICE

RYNN'S WORLD

NEPHII SECTO

SEGMENTUM TEMPESTUS

REDUCTUS SECTOR

AGRAX

Imperial Primus Palace

Scholastica Psykana

Orbital Defence Systems

BAKKA

ANTAGONIS

SAN LEOR

Hall of the Astronomican

Ecclesiarchal Palace

GRYPHONNE IV

The Cathedral of the Emperor Deified

The Halls of Judgement

ILLUSTRIS

THE VEILED REGION

NEW DREKPORT

STEC PRIME

MALFACTUS

LUNAPHAGE

ISTO'ROL

GHOUL STARS

ANGELIS

COELIA

DESPERATION

ASTRO TELEPATHIC DUCT

NEXUS III
ASTRO STATION

ASYLUS

LE

ULTIMA
SEGMENTUM

SOMNIUM STARS

FORMUND

HEXOS

NIHILUS

KAR DUNIASH

CORINTHE

ATTILA

THE EASTERN FRINGE

TEMPORARY
RIFT CORRIDOR

VENGEANCE

IRILLO PRIME

THE YMGA MONOLITH

SCHINDELGHEIST

T'AU
EMPIRE

NECRON
SAUTEKH DYNASTY

HADEX ANOMALY

CHARADON
SECTOR

ICHAR IV

THE SCOURGE STARS

MACRAGGE

DUS

BLACK REACH

CRON
ILAKH
NASTY

FALSE HOPE

SALEM

The vast spread of the galaxy contains an estimated four hundred thousand million stars. The total number of planets in orbit across all these star systems is beyond measure, but approximately one million worlds are claimed beneath the dominion of the Imperium and ruled by the Emperor of Mankind.

To govern and protect the galaxy, the High Lords of Terra originally divided it into five zones of control known as the Segmentae Majoris. These are the Segmentum Solar (home of Terra), the Segmentum Obscurus, the Ultima Segmentum, the Segmentum Tempestus and the Segmentum Pacificus. The Cicatrix Maledictum, or Great Rift, necessitated the addition of a further classification: the Imperium Nihilus – the portion of the galaxy cut off from the guiding light of the Astronomican.

Each segmentum is further divided into sectors and sub-sectors. Although space is three-dimensional, the galaxy is largely planar, and so Astrocartographers refer to galactic locations using cardinal directions derived from those of Holy Terra. Thus, the Eastern Fringe was so named as it was far to the galactic east of Terra.

DARK IMPERIUM

Such was the turmoil during the creation of the Great Rift and the period following it that there could be no reliable accounts. As limited communications returned, Historitors and Chronotechs struggled to understand incoming reports. With the influx of warp energies, time passed strangely, speeding up in some sectors, slowing in others.

THE NOCTIS AETERNA

As the chain reaction of the Great Rift cracked open the galaxy, tidal waves of unnatural energies spilled outwards in sporadic fashion. Warp storms swept across everything – not even the furthest reaches of the galaxy were spared their corrupting touch. With a great surge, over a million planets of the Imperium were cut off from the Light of the Emperor as the Astronomican went out. During that time, the Imperium of Mankind ceased to be – each planet was isolated, a speck of sanity buffeted by a raging tempest. It was a warp storm beyond the ability of any technology in the Imperium to record – indeed, it was greater in size and power than anything that had ever been recorded, the most powerful of its kind since perhaps the lost era of the Age of Strife.

During the Blackness, as many came to know it, all long-ranged astrocommunications proved impossible. The warp was in far too much upheaval to permit travel, and those starships in transit at the time were destroyed in horrific fashion or subjected to the worst battering their crews had ever experienced. It is impossible to count all those who lost their lives in the turmoil. Those who survived found themselves carried far off course by the insane tides of unnatural energies.

Riding the crest of the warp storms' shock waves, or following swiftly in their wake, came the forces of Chaos. The Daemon legions were the vanguard, followed hard by the fleets of the Traitor Legions and the ragged masses of the Renegades and their associated cults.

THE DEFENCE OF TERRA

As the first warp storms broke over Holy Terra, its pollution-filled skies turned a roiling crimson. Khorne, heedless of the plans of his brothers and hungry to prove his superiority, sent forth eighty-eight cohorts of his Daemon legions to assault the Emperor's Palace. The Blood God wanted the glory of tearing down the Golden Throne for himself, and so the skies of Terra congealed into blood-clouds that deployed the red host directly before the Lion's Gate.

The gun batteries of the Imperial Palace are second to none, yet they alone could not halt this red tide. Led by Roboute Guilliman, the newly reappointed Lord Commander of the Imperium, the Primaris Space Marines, Adeptus Custodes and Sisters of Silence fought side by side. Although the rash Chaos assault was turned back and broken long before it could reach the Eternity Gate, the High Lords were shaken at the boldness of the foe. Without the beam of the Astronomican, their arcane machinery and protective devices were not enough to halt the fell powers from materialising even on Holy Terra. Khorne, upon receiving the returning forms of his slain, grew so apoplectic in his rage that his fortress trembled. So great was the heat from his outburst that the essences of the eight Bloodthirsters that led the failed attack were wholly obliterated.

THE GATE IS BROKEN

Cadia had stood so long, and so proudly. The gate through which the enemy could not pass. For the whole Age of the Imperium, that bastion planet bore the brunt of countless Chaos assaults as the daemonic forces attempted to reach Terra. Cadia, and the fortified worlds of its system, were for long centuries a redoubt that withstood every horror that issued from the Eye of Terror. In the Dark Imperium there was no assurance, however, from which direction the Chaos forces would attack; the only assurance was that they would.

'THOSE WHO ARE PURE OF HEART AND STRONG OF FAITH HAVE NOTHING TO FEAR FROM THE BLACK TEMPLARS, THIS IS TRUE. BUT WHO THEN, AMONGST THE HEAVING, SINFUL MASSES OF HUMANITY, CAN TRULY COUNT THEMSELVES AS SAFE FROM OUR WRATH?'

- Marshal Gideon,
Black Templars,
Mephistari Crusade

Although Cadia was ultimately reduced to a burning wasteland by Abaddon's endless assaults, the worlds in the wider Cadian System fought hard to destroy the spearhead the Despoiler had plunged into their midst. The Great Exodus of Cadia had seen swathes of the Imperial defence redeployed to the sister worlds of the fortress planet, and not before time. Every realm touched by the Cicatrix Maledictum was blighted by intense Daemon storms, howling tempests that carried a thousand types of death upon their fell winds. Where those baleful hurricanes blew strongest, the scions of the Dark Gods would stride from the aether and bring battle anew to the defenders of Mankind's realm. Hundreds of battles. Uncounted billions of casualties. The skies of Belis Corona were lit with fire as the conquering fleets of Abaddon's endless armadas clashed with the Imperial Navy of the Segmentum Obscurus. The forge world of Agripinaa, its legions bold enough to have raided the Eye of Terror in the past, was assailed by covetous Warpsmiths and the menageries of Daemon Engines that stormed forth at their behest. Again and again the stakes were raised as the forces of Chaos rode upon the winds of the Great Rift.

THE HOUR OF THE DAMNED

Although all communications were cut, they received the distress calls. When travel was impossible, they arrived unlooked for. When all hope was lost, they strode forth out of the Blackness, a legion of vengeance, a brotherhood of flame. The Legion of the Damned appeared on Baal, Armageddon, Antagonis and hundreds more planets besides. They spoke only with bolter and chainsword, meting out terrible punishments upon the enemies of the Imperium before themselves vanishing without a trace. Truly the hour of the damned had come…

A LIGHT IN THE DARKNESS

From blackness there came a light. A brief flash, then distant blinks. Intermittently, the rays of the Astronomican lanced outwards from Holy Terra. Deeply the beam pierced the maelstrom that smothered the galaxy, but it could not pierce the Great Rift. In the north-eastern half of the galaxy, they could see little or none of the Emperor's guiding light – the Cicatrix Maledictum simply swallowed its illumination. Now that messages could once again be sent through the warp, Terra received such a backlog of terror shrieks that half of the already-depleted Astropath core were instantly driven insane. The survivors were appalled to discover how many planets, even on the Terran side of the Great Rift, did not respond. Slightly less than half of the one thousand Space Marine Chapters remained unaccounted for, and no less than twelve Space Marine Chapter Planets were reported as destroyed during the Noctis Aeterna and the bitter campaigns that followed. Some Space Marines, like the White Consuls, escaped the destructions of their fortress worlds. Others died to a man, as did the Sky Sentinels, when their home world of Pranagar was overrun by none other than Magnus the Red, Daemon Primarch of the Thousand Sons.

Should the isolated Imperium Nihilus regain contact, the number of known losses will only grow, as the Lords of Terra learn the grim truth.

THE INDOMITUS CRUSADE

After his defence of Holy Terra, Roboute Guilliman gathered a new armada. Along with elements of the Adeptus Custodes, a small contingent of the Silent Sisterhood, and a vast war host of Primaris Space Marines from many newly founded Chapters, the Primarch set a winding course. Strike forces from over a dozen pre-existing Chapters of Space Marines, led by the Imperial Fists, joined the fleet. Thus began many new legends as Guilliman travelled to aid beleaguered planets, breaking sieges and sweeping away invaders to bring hope back to the desperate defenders. It was not long before word began to spread, as all those planets that could receive astropathic messages hailed the return of a hero out of myth. Once more, one of the demigods of the past fought for the Imperium of Mankind.

'BUTCHER YOUR ENEMY'S WARRIORS WITHOUT MERCY. CRUSH HIS ARMIES AND LEAVE NONE ALIVE. BUT DO NOT STOP THERE. BURN HIS CITIES. BOMB HIS WORLDS FROM ORBIT. SLAUGHTER EVERYTHING AND EVERYONE UNTIL HE KNEELS IN THE ASHES OF THOSE HE SOUGHT TO PROTECT. ONLY THEN WILL HE UNDERSTAND THE TRUE FURY OF THE DARK GODS.'

- *Haakor of the Black Legion*

THE STAND AT ARMAGEDDON

For much of the millennium the planet of Armageddon had been a battleground. First invaded by Chaos, it was later the site for a massive war between the Ork hordes of Ghazghkull Thraka and the forces of the Imperium. Although the infamous greenskin leader left to establish new stomping grounds, the onslaught continued. Not even the hellstorms unleashed by the Great Rift could halt the fighting, but they did change its nature. During the Noctis Aeterna, reinforcements were cut off for both sides, and those en route to the system were swept into oblivion. Those that remained on Armageddon were forced to fight off not just each other, but the oncoming waves of Daemons. At times, so desperate were the defenders that Ork and humans fought alongside each other against the greater threat. Such temporary ceasefires never lasted long.

By the time the Astronomican returned and travel through the storm-ridden immaterium was once again possible, the Imperial relief force arrived to find the landscape greatly changed. At the height of the warp storms, the forces of Tzeentch and Khorne had battled each other. The Orks and Imperial forces sought cover as titanic Greater Daemons duelled for supremacy. Fully half the planet had warped into what looked like a Daemon world – a hellish landscape merged over the top of what had once been a war-torn hive world. The Imperial forces, with elements of nine Space Marine Chapters led by the Salamanders, succeeded in halting the ritual that would have brought Angron, the Primarch of the World Eaters, back to the planet that had defied him in ages past.

DEVASTATION OF BAAL

After sacrificing the shield worlds of the Cryptus System to fend off the xenos' earliest advance, the planet of Baal itself came under intense attack by Hive Fleet Leviathan. The Tyranid fleet was of such mass, even after its considerable losses, that it blotted the stars from the skies. Lord Commander Dante bolstered the formidable defences of the Blood Angels' home world and her moons like never before. Never one to await attack, he also sent forth scores of pre-emptive strike forces to delay, mislead, and whittle down the living armada. Hundreds of splinter fleets were thus defeated. Dante's call, beseeching the Blood Angels' successors to send immediate aid to their parent Chapter, did not go unheeded. The Flesh Tearers were the first to arrive, and ultimately all the successor Chapters save the Lamenters answered. Even the Knights of Blood, who had been declared Excommunicate Traitoris by the High Lords of Terra, arrived to bolster the defences. It was still not enough.

Learning at an exponential rate, Hive Fleet Leviathan could not be thwarted by the same strategy twice. Advancing steadily, their superior numbers cleared the sector of life before the xenos made planetfall upon Baal and her twin moons. The first nineteen waves, each larger than the last, were driven off at great loss to the Blood Angels and their successor allies. Five Chapter Masters fell in that bitter fighting, three in the Battle at the Dome of Angels alone. The Tyranids began the process of draining Baal and her moons, absorbing even the rad-poisoned deserts of Baal Secundus. With their defences in ruin and the moons stripped and broken, the remaining Space Marines retreated back to the rubble of the Blood Angels' sprawling fortress monastery. There, they prepared for a last stand as the next wave swept downwards. Doom, it seemed, had at last come to the Sons of Sanguinius.

It was then that the Great Rift cracked open the galaxy, and the withered Baal System was blasted by the aetheric storms. Although no further attack waves came from the Leviathan fleet, not a single Imperial defender remained alive upon the last moon, Baal Prime. On Baal itself there were already enough Tyranids there to destroy the Imperial troops many times over. Even with no chance of victory, Commander Dante led his troops, each fighting retreat seemingly more hopeless than the last. As the final perimeter was broken, the stars reappeared. Looking skywards, the Tyranids sought contact with their hive fleet, but it was gone, replaced by a newly arrived Imperial fleet.

Like an angel of vengeance came Roboute Guilliman and his crusade. After many more battles, Baal was finally cleared of the xenos threat. A great rebuilding of both world and Chapter was undertaken, for the Blood Angels and their successors were sorely needed elsewhere. What became of Leviathan is a mystery, although a clue was found upon the now-barren moon of Baal Prime. Xenos skulls were piled impossibly high in the much-reviled, eight-pillared symbol of one of the Blood Angels' most terrible and ancient nemeses: the Bloodthirster Ka'Bandha.

TERRA RETALIATES

In an effort to seize the initiative, a strike force was mustered on Terra, supported by an entire army of Adeptus Custodes.

The Custodes for a while... the ...ed ... the Master of Mankind dead.

PLAGUE OF PLAGUES

Something terrible came out of the warp storms as they roiled through the southern reaches of Ultima Segmentum. Where the seeds of corruption had been planted by the Plague That Walks, a new and terrible contamination spread. The diseased dead rose to claim the living. Previously, the walking corpses could be destroyed, but now doing so only released hordes of Nurglings that writhed impossibly out of the withered flesh of the fallen. Hive worlds were toppled, and as the Blackness descended, there was no escape. In the horrific ruins, Cults of Corruption slithered out of hiding, summoning forth further aid from the Realm of Chaos itself.

So did systems fall, creating the Scourge Stars – a trio of sickly systems that had fallen to Nurgle. From that power base, the Death Guard and Plague legions issued, systematically reaping planet after planet. On they spread. It was none other than the Daemon Primarch Mortarion that brought the fabled Realm of Ultramar, gem of the whole segmentum, under siege. Plague bombardments rained down, so severe

that once gloried hives became pits and agri worlds became slime-ridden ruins. Chaos was encroaching on many fronts when Roboute Guilliman returned. It was his tactical acumen that first stabilised the many war fronts, and his Spear of Espandor counter-attacking campaign that successfully bought the forces of the Imperium still more time. At the Gates of Parmenio, Roboute Guilliman defeated the Greater Daemon Septicus and his Plague Guard. At Iax, once a glorious garden world, Primarch met Primarch as Guilliman confronted Mortarion, the two brothers fighting to a deadlock before the Chaos forces mysteriously withdrew under cover of a virus bomb.

NO SAFE PASSAGE

An intermittent passage through the Great Rift was discovered, yet it brought little hope to the Imperium. The Cicatrix Maledictum had at least one gap, although others were reported but not confirmed. The passage was near the Eye of Terror, which had been avoided by Navigators since the Great Crusade, for warp storms and strange anomalies had always made the region too dangerous to travel. There, when the swirling nebula lulled, was revealed the Nachmund System. Its Tyrant King, Kaligius, ruled over a Household of Fallen Knights that had not been seen since the Horus Heresy. Claiming Old Night had returned, Kaligius rejected communications from the Imperium, instead making pacts with Renegades and pirate fleets. Some starships have run the Nachmund Gauntlet successfully, but many more have been destroyed attempting the journey – the ruined hulks of innumerable craft hang suspended in space as a ship graveyard.

ONLY WAR

As the Imperium gradually realised the extent of the nightmare conditions created by the Great Rift, they tried to adapt to the horrifying new dynamic. There were no more shield worlds, no more bastion systems. Every planet – even Holy Terra – was now on the front line of the war for Humanity's survival.

Thus did a dark age grow darker.

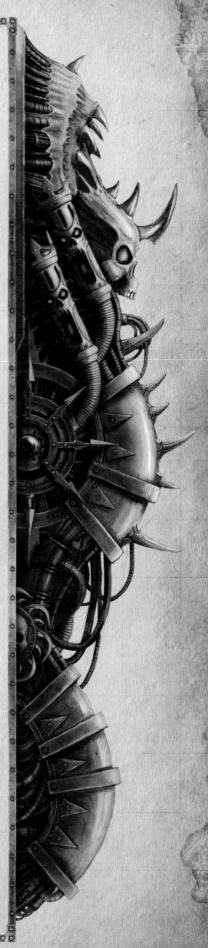

ARMIES OF THE IMPERIUM

The Imperium of Mankind was founded by force of arms and it is only through military might that the empire has been maintained. The galaxy has proven to be a hostile place. Planets, space stations, trade routes – all are beset by dangers. There is no peace amongst the stars – it is an age of unrelenting war. The battle is no longer for colonisation or for supremacy, but for survival.

War, invasion, sedition, corruption to Chaos – as the threats to the Imperium are multifarious, so too are the agencies that fight for Mankind. Some of these, such as the stalwart Astra Militarum or the legendary Adeptus Astartes, are generally known, their efforts lauded by the common man. Other military branches, such as the shadowy Officio Assassinorum or the Ordo Malleus, are wholly unknown. Their existence is only guessed at by a small percentage of those in the upper echelons, but their role is no less vital than the more visible forces.

Each branch of the Imperium's military is independent, with their own duties, rituals, chain of command, tactical acumen and gear of war. Though diverse, the forces of the Imperium often work in conjunction with each other, and the larger the battle, the more likely it will be to see multiple Imperial factions engaged in the same war. Massive conflagrations, such as the Chaos invasions known as the Black Crusades or a major war zone such as the one surrounding the planet Armageddon, will attract representatives from all of Mankind's military institutions.

There are many variables, but a typical Imperial response begins with a planetary defence force holding the line, broadcasting its situation. As the threat level warrants, the innumerable assets of the Astra Militarum are called upon. Countless soldiers and tanks seek first to stabilise a front and then, as further reinforcements arrive, drive the foe into submission. In addition to ferrying the Imperial Guard to and from war zones, the Imperial Navy supplies orbital bombardments and fleets of atmospheric aircraft to dominate the skies. The Adeptus Astartes specialise in key missions, and strike forces streak in to devastate vital enemy positions, slay powerful leaders or capture key terrain features or strategic assets. Then the Space Marine forces are quickly off again, deploying elsewhere for another rapid strike. Where their interests are involved, such as the recovery of lost STCs or the defence of a forge world, the armies of the Adeptus Mechanicus are also drawn to battle. In the most sprawling of conflicts, the Titan Legions are deployed, their world-shaking firepower reserved for the most impregnable of fortresses and the direst of enemies. Imperial Knights might join the fray, bringing squadrons of their enormous walkers at the behest of their home world, or in honour of fealty oaths to the Golden Throne or the Adeptus Mechanicus. As fanatical shock troops, the Sisters of Battle mercilessly purge any who would deny the Emperor's true way, while unseen and unheard Imperial Assassins ply their deadly craft. And as always, the influence of the Inquisition is everywhere, imposed by its dauntless agents.

To coordinate such diverse forces upon linked battlefields that might stretch across whole star systems, the Imperium will assign a supreme commander to direct the various branches. Given time, such assignments are the purview of the High Lords of Terra, but in the maelstrom of battle the selection is often made by the members of impromptu war councils.

> 'ALONE, WE STAND AS BASTIONS OF STRENGTH. BUT WHEN WE FIGHT SIDE BY SIDE, WE ARE A FORTRESS OF FAITH THAT NO FOE CAN OVERCOME.'
>
> *- Warmaster Solar Macharius*

THE EMPEROR WILL NOT JUDGE YOU BY YOUR MEDALS AND DIPLOMAS; HE WILL JUDGE YOU BY YOUR SCARS.

ADEPTUS ASTARTES

They stand apart from those they protect. Indeed, in many ways, they have given up their humanity in order to better serve it. They are a warrior brotherhood unlike any other, made for, trained for, and utterly dedicated to war. They are the Space Marines, and they know no fear.

The foremost of Humanity's defenders, the Space Marines sweep into battle, shattering their foes before leaving as abruptly as they arrived. The Adeptus Astartes are genetically engineered super-soldiers, living weapons raised up from the ranks of Humanity through arcane science. Like all legends, there is a mythology woven around the Adeptus Astartes, and the line between fact and fabrication is often blurred. This is no surprise, as the Space Marines were created at the very dawn of the Imperium by the Emperor himself. Over the long centuries, Chapters have been destroyed and replaced, but some can trace their history directly back to the fabled First Founding, when Space Marines were organised into twenty vast Legions.

The Adeptus Astartes follow the example of their Emperor and their Primarchs, from whose gene-seed they were created. With the many threats to the Imperium surrounding them – Daemons, heretics, and xenos – the Adeptus Astartes are tested as never before. Many of the bastion walls of the Imperium have crumbled, but the rapid strike forces of the Space Marines fill the breaches. Led by a Chapter Master, most Chapters are composed according to the Codex Astartes – a doctrine written by Primarch Roboute Guilliman of the Ultramarines Chapter soon after the Horus Heresy. The Codex Astartes dictates all aspects of Chapter organisation and battlefield tactics to ensure the efficiency and loyalty of the most effective military force the galaxy has ever seen. According to its regimen, a Chapter is broken into ten companies, each of which is made of ten squads of ten warriors that fulfil specific battlefield roles. Other Chapter war assets include armoured vehicles, Dreadnoughts, atmospheric strike craft, bikes, and a fleet to transport it all to wherever it is most needed.

GENE-SEED

The warriors of the Adeptus Astartes surpass human excellence, being far stronger, faster, and more resilient than ought to be possible. The secret to their superhuman nature is the bio-engineered gene-seed of the Primarchs, the potential of which was further exploited in the creation of Primaris Space Marines.

A Chapter's gene-seed is the fundamental genetic material required to grow and develop the specialised organs that, alongside intensive psycho-indoctrination and countless hours of physical and spiritual training, transform a novitiate into a Space Marine. These organs react with an aspirant's physiology to stimulate muscle growth, bone-hardening and many other augmentative changes. The creation of a Space Marine is a long and sometimes fatal process, the different stages of which must occur in a precise order. Various Chapters use a number of their own specialised rites during these stages, revered rituals from a time when the Emperor himself led the Space Marines to battle. Should a recipient survive the initial steps of this ordeal, he will receive a second heart, a multi-lung, and numerous other glands, nodes, and organs that boost his physical and mental abilities, as well as granting him superlative healing characteristics and increased resistance to poison, the hard vacuum of space, and the ability to interface with his power armour. Space Marines that complete their transformation have heightened senses, an ability to spit acid, and an enhanced frame ready for the rigours of endless war. Their new progenoid glands replicate further gene-seed, allowing their genetic superiority to be passed down to future battle-brothers. On the battlefield, this takes the form of the harvesting of the progenoid glands of fallen Space Marines by their Apothecaries. It is the grim duty of these warriors to ensure the noble lineage of their Chapter continues, and by use of narthecium and reductor, they reclaim the gene-seed from their fallen comrades.

All in all, nineteen specialised organs are found in nearly every Space Marine created since the First Founding, with an extra three appearing in their Primaris brethren. This is due to adjustments in the gene-seed implantation process, pioneered by Archmagos Dominus Belisarius Cawl on orders he received from Roboute Guilliman soon after the Second Founding. In the wake of the Great Betrayal, Guilliman foresaw a potential future in which Humanity was besieged as never before by heretics, aliens and worse. He set Cawl to augmenting the process of Space Marine creation to make even mightier warriors for the defence of Mankind, better defended against bullet, blade and mortal injury. To assist the Archmagos in this endeavour, Guilliman entrusted Cawl with many wondrous artefacts, including the Sangprimus Portum – a device containing genetic material harvested from the Primarchs that went beyond even gene-seed in its potency. Thus were created a new generation of Adeptus Astartes, the Primaris Space Marines – taller, stronger and clad in mighty Mk X power armour – though it had taken Cawl nearly ten thousand years to finish his work. The Primaris Space Marines were presented to Guilliman after his resurrection, and were deployed en masse in the Ultima Founding, bastions of hope in a galaxy torn apart by the Great Rift. The Indomitus Crusade saw them spread throughout the galaxy as part of Guilliman's strike against a new age of darkness, to lend their strength wherever it might be needed.

As such, existing Chapters across the galaxy welcomed Primaris reinforcements, and new Chapters composed entirely of Primaris Space Marines were created. So did the Emperor's Angels of Death carry forth the genetic heritage of the Primarchs with a fierce new potency and savagery, a power set to match, and perhaps conquer, the dreadful cataclysm that had befallen the galaxy.

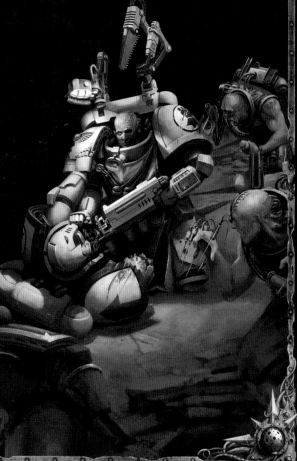

THOUGHT FOR THE DAY: THERE IS PURITY OF PURPOSE IN THE FAITH OF THE JUST.

59

PRIMARIS ARMOURY

When the locked forge vaults of Archmagos Dominus Belisarius Cawl at last were opened on Mars, a new arsenal of armour and weapons was made ready for the new forces of the towering Primaris Space Marines.

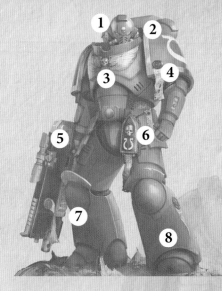

BOLT RIFLE

Shown above is a Mk II Cawl-pattern bolt rifle. Like all weapons in the bolter family, the bolt rifle fires small, self-propelled missiles known as bolts which explode with devastating effect. The bolt rifle has a longer range and slightly more penetrating power compared to the standard-issue boltgun.

ASSAULT BOLTER

Centuries of tinkering improvements by Archmagos Cawl resulted in the creation of the assault bolter – a handheld pistol version of the conventional heavy bolter. Although short-ranged, its rate of firepower and hitting strength are considerable, with the recoil contained by a mag-shield.

PLASMA INCINERATOR

Imperium-produced plasma weapons all fire searing bursts of energy, but the Mk III Belisarius-pattern plasma incinerator is the most advanced of its kind, firing a potent armour-melting blast with no risk of overload. The same cannot be said when the plasma incinerator is fired on its deadly overcharged setting, however.

1. Mk X power armour does not have a single appellation (like Mk VII 'Aquila' armour). Instead, different variants are worn depending on the Space Marines' role. Intercessor Squads, for example, wear Mk X Tacticus armour.

2. Sloped pauldrons, or shoulder pads, are used to deflect enemy fire. Space Marines are trained to use these angles to deflect shots.

3. The thickest layer of ceramite is over the chest-plate, protecting not just the power armour's cables, but also most of a Space Marine's vital internal organs.

4. Dominus-class purity seal. These wax seals and parchment are inscribed with the holy words of the Crux Imperius.

5. The Mk II Cawl-pattern bolt rifle is wielded like an extension of a Space Marine's weaponised physique.

6. Absolutis ballistic-appeasement auto-reliquary, allows for autosanctification of bolt weaponry in combat.

7. Flanged poleyns, made of melded plasiron and ceramite, provide extra protection over vulnerable joints.

8. Greaves. These incorporate gyroscopic stabilizers and can magnetise the soles of the armour's boots, allowing Space Marines to walk on metal surfaces in treacherous terrain, including zero-gravity environments – essential for boarding actions in the cold battlefield of space.

A THOUSAND CHAPTERS

As outlined in the Codex Astartes, Space Marines are organised into independent armies, called Chapters, of which there are roughly one thousand spread throughout the galaxy. Each Chapter maintains its own fleet, heraldic uniforms and distinct identity.

Imperial Fists
1st Founding

Dark Angels
1st Founding

Iron Hands
1st Founding

Blood Angels
1st Founding

Black Templars
Imperial Fists Successor

Crimson Fists
Imperial Fists Successor

Knights of the Chalice
Blood Angels Successor

Blades of Vengeance
Dark Angels Successor

Fulminators
Ultramarines Successor

Rift Stalkers
Raven Guard Successor

Salamanders
1st Founding

White Scars
1st Founding

INNOCENCE PROVES NOTHING.

ULTRAMARINES

The exemplary Chapter, the Ultramarines are perhaps the most honoured of their legendary kind.

The Ultramarines have covered themselves in glory since the fledgling days of the Imperium, when they liberated more planets during the Great Crusade than any other Legion. The triumphs continued during the Indomitus Crusade where they aided their recently returned Primarch, Roboute Guilliman, in battles across the galaxy.

MACRAGGE

The planet Macragge is the home world of the Ultramarines Chapter. The heart and capital of the Realm of Ultramar, Macragge is a great bastion of the Imperium. It has come under assault many times, but always, the Ultramarines have emerged victorious.

The bulk of the Ultramarines Chapter consists of Space Marines clad in existing marks of armour, such as this Mk VII battleplate.

Sergeant	Veteran Sergeant	Veteran	Lieutenant

Each of the ten companies of Ultramarines – except the Scout Company – is designated by a different edge colour on its battle-brothers' shoulder guards.

By order of Primarch Guilliman, the Ultramarines were the first Chapter to receive the new Mk X Space Marine armour.

Space Marine squads indicate their overall battlefield role through a clear, simple system of markings applied to their shoulder guards. Battleline squads, for example, make up the strategic core of any given force. By comparison, fire support provide heavy firepower, while veteran units are especially experienced.

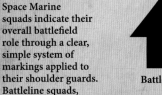

Battleline

Fire Support

Close Support

Veteran

BLOOD ANGELS

Known for their ferocity, the Blood Angels bear within them all that is good and noble, yet their gene-seed also contains a destructive flaw. So must every Blood Angel rein in his fury, holding in abeyance the blood-madness.

Created during the First Founding, the Blood Angels are one of the oldest and proudest of all Space Marine Chapters. In the Great Crusade they established their bloodthirsty zeal, favouring aggressive tactics, close combat and the use of jump packs, and they have maintained this fierce reputation ever since. The Blood Angels are equally noted for their unceasing quest for perfection in all their endeavours – from the flawless execution of a battle plan to the aesthetics of their wargear. Yet for all their honours, for all their storied accomplishments fighting at the forefront of the Imperium's many wars, the Blood Angels are deeply marred. Since the closing days of the Horus Heresy, when their angelic, winged Primarch, Sanguinius, was viciously killed at the hands of Horus himself, the Blood Angels have been haunted by a curse. That the Sons of Sanguinius fight on, despite the blood rage that seeks to overwhelm them, body and soul, only makes their selfless sacrifice all the nobler. Although held in awe and feared in equal measure by those they protect, the Blood Angels continue to smite the Imperium's foes, compiling a battle history second to none.

THE BLACK RAGE

On the eve of battle, Blood Angels are prone to apocalyptic visions that can plunge them into a spiral of madness. Death is the only release from this malady. It is almost inevitable that this fate will eventually overtake every Blood Angel. This Black Rage is a psychic imprint left by their Primarch Sanguinius' death. Left in a frenzied state, those warriors suffering from the Black Rage seek only to charge and hack their foes. Over the centuries, the Blood Angels and their successor Chapters have learned how to best wield these warriors, forming them into a Death Company from which these berserkers are hurled into battles that no sane warrior would risk. It is better that they should achieve an honourable death in combat for the cause of the Imperium than face the final stages of uncontrollable fury, turning the once noble warriors into little more than snarling beasts. In the Blood Angels, those suffering from the Black Rage don black armour daubed with red crosses, signifying the wounds of Sanguinius.

DARK ANGELS

The Dark Angels shun glory and fight only to punish transgressors against the Emperor. Behind their stern facade, however, lies a dark obsession. Haunted by their past, they remain the Unforgiven.

The Dark Angels were the first Legion created by the Emperor. Theirs is a mysterious and taciturn Chapter, their every action steeped in secretive traditions and rituals. What is known about the Dark Angels is that time and again they have stubbornly stood their ground against overwhelming odds until they eventually emerge victorious. Despite a history full of such heroics, they are viewed suspiciously by many in the Imperium, who claim that the Dark Angels follow their own clandestine agenda. Such allegations are never answered – or even acknowledged – the Dark Angels remain silent and brooding. The organisation of the Dark Angels differs from the practices laid out by the Codex Astartes, most notably in their 1st and 2nd Companies – elite formations known internally as the Deathwing and the Ravenwing.

DEATHWING

The Dark Angels 1st Company, the Deathwing, are distinct from their brothers in several ways. The formation consists entirely of veterans and Masters-in-training known as Deathwing Knights, and the entire company goes to battle in Terminator armour. Their triumphs against impossible odds are lauded across the Imperium. A single squad teleporting into the thick of fighting can turn the tide of almost any battle – the entire company deployed en masse can win an entire war. The Deathwing bear their own heraldry and don armour of bone white, not the dark green armour of their brethren. As members of the Inner Circle they are privy to some, but not all, of the Dark Angels' many secrets.

RAVENWING

The Dark Angels 2nd Company, known as the Ravenwing, are even more unusual than the Deathwing. A highly mobilised formation used for scouting and lightning-fast strikes, they use speed and surprise to catch their quarry. To this end, every single Space Marine in the company goes to battle atop an armoured assault bike or within a Land Speeder or atmospheric fighter. Organised into Attack and Support Squadrons, they work in coordination with the rest of the Chapter, chasing down foes, heading off retreats, and often working as a one-two punch with the Deathwing, using teleport homers to bring their brothers into the heart of the battle. The vehicles and power armour of the Ravenwing are both an ominous black.

SPACE WOLVES

Though some may see them as little more than savages, the Space Wolves are a proud brotherhood, every bit as loyal as they are fierce. They are amongst the most notorious of all the Adeptus Astartes, and their raucous, boastful ways can rankle the sternest of other Chapters, but none can deny the bold heroism that they display again and again.

The Space Wolves are a fiercely independent Chapter that has served the Imperium with distinction since the First Founding. Courageous to the extreme, each Space Wolf strives to perform great deeds on the battlefield worthy of song. Made feral in thought and appearance by the genetic heritage of their legendary Primarch, Leman Russ, the Space Wolves revel in their unorthodox nature. They have little patience for fawning religious rites, Codex Astartes rules, or strict adherence to the conventions of others, preferring to follow the warrior traditions from their savage home world of Fenris. In war zone after war zone, the Space Wolves have spent the entire Age of the Imperium building upon their outstanding reputation, earning one of the most

impressive tallies of victory in the Imperium. Their ability to strike quickly and savagely has made them a peerless shock-assault force, and they are also known to tirelessly pursue villainous forces, hunting them down and destroying them no matter the obstacles. Yet despite their long and excellent service, the only known successor Chapter of the Space Wolves were the ill-fated Wolf Brothers. A flaw was recognised in the genetic seed of Leman Russ – which would later manifest itself in the emergence of the Wulfen – and it is because of this aberrance and their blatant disregard for authority that the Space Wolves have gained many naysayers within the Imperium, particularly the often scoffed-at and ignored officers of the Adeptus Administratum.

WULFEN

The Wulfenkind were the 13th Great Company of the Space Wolves Legion, the most savage warriors of all. It was they who pursued the Thousand Sons Primarch, Magnus the Red, into the Eye of Terror when he fled the Massacre at Prospero. They were lost until shortly before the Noctis Aeterna, when they returned from the Eye, having grown even more bestial in appearance and savage in war.

GREY KNIGHTS

Created to fight Mankind's most dreaded foe, the Grey Knights are a Chapter unlike any other. They are devoted, reclusive, and each is powerfully psychic.

Amongst the elite brotherhood of Space Marines, there exists a Chapter destined to stand apart, for it is their sworn duty to fight Chaos in its most terrible form. The Grey Knights act as the military arm of the Ordo Malleus, the Daemonhunters who form the oldest branch of the Inquisition. Founded on an order from the Emperor himself, each Grey Knight is a potent psyker, pure of heart and just of cause. This is essential, for in their battles, they seek out and confront the most horrible of Daemons wherever the warp fiends appear. Privy to the darkest secrets of Mankind and armed with deadly Nemesis force weapons and the most advanced wargear in the Imperium, the Grey Knights are the ultimate foil to the warp-spawned minions of the Ruinous Powers. With the outpouring of Chaos from the Great Rift, the Grey Knights have been called upon as never before.

DEATHWATCH

Against the Xenos threat there can be no respite. When a Necron tomb world stirs, or the perfidious Aeldari make their move, they are stymied, for the long vigil of the Deathwatch stands over Mankind.

Just as the Adeptus Astartes are recruited exclusively from the most promising warriors of all Mankind, so are the Deathwatch formed from only the most proven of all Space Marines. Many Chapters have pledged a tithe, lending a portion of their strength to the endless war against the xenos threat. Thus, the Deathwatch is formed from an amalgamation of the best warriors drawn from many different Chapters, each bringing with them their own unique strengths. Typically working in conjunction with the Inquisition's Ordo Xenos, Deathwatch Kill Teams are deployed to counter the direst of encroaching alien threats. The Deathwatch are a brotherhood of heroes, the elite of the elite, and each unit is distinctive in their skills and armaments, yet all are clad in the black armour of the Deathwatch. To the Deathwatch, there are but two options – to contain the xenos, or to purge them.

ASTRA MILITARUM

Manpower is the Imperium's greatest resource, and it is a currency readily spent. The forces of the Astra Militarum are so numerous that not even the Departmento Munitorum knows how many soldiers are in uniform. From across the galaxy regiments form up and rise from the trenches, taking their place at the head of a battlefront that stretches across one million planets.

The Astra Militarum, also known as the Imperial Guard, is Mankind's primary and most numerous defence. With soldiers, battle tanks and artillery beyond number, they are a sledgehammer force that delivers a devastating payload against the Emperor's foes. Soldiers of the Imperial Guard are not gene-enhanced super-humans and they do not fight with the most finely crafted armaments in the galaxy. They are but men who fight with whatever weapons and armour can be cheaply mass-produced. They are, however, the largest coherent fighting force in the galaxy, able to move massed regiments and armoured vehicles to join any fray. The Astra Militarum achieve their victories through hellstorms of firepower, grinding attrition and sheer dogged determination.

When the Imperial Guard go to war, they do so organised into regiments. Each regiment is largely uniform in composition, meaning an infantry regiment will be made up primarily of foot soldiers, with little in the way of heavy artillery or armour. Likewise, an artillery regiment will be made up entirely of serried batteries of big guns and other long-ranged weaponry, and will contain little, if any, infantry. If an Imperial Guard regiment were forced into battle individually it would struggle, for each homogeneous force is vulnerable without support – infantry by themselves can be smashed by armoured foes, while tanks alone are poor at holding ground, finding themselves prone to ambushes, especially in areas of dense terrain where manoeuvrability suffers. Such is the immense size of the forces deployed by the Imperial Guard, however, that the idea of lone regiments is preposterous. Every Imperial Guard army is composed of many regiments, and a wise commander will marshal his myriad divisions to fight as a combined-arms force – drawing men, vehicles, elite squads and even abhumans from different regiments, brigading them together as suits availability and the needs of the battlefront. It is beneath the banners of the Astra Militarum that the fate of Mankind rests, for by their victories does the Imperium survive.

THE HUMBLE LASGUN

The most lethal weapon wielded by the Astra Militarum is not a massive missile, nor is it a super-heavy battle tank. More enemy kills are accounted for by the standard-issue lasgun than any class of missile or tank. It is steady, reliable, and rugged – the perfect infantry weapon. A lone lasgun might give few xenos pause, but when deployed in billions-strong formations, it has proven capable of defending a galaxy-wide empire for nearly ten thousand years.

There are numerous patterns of lasgun in use, from the Lucius-pattern No. 98 lasgun used by the Death Korp of Krieg to the Mk IV Catachan lascarbine. They are often named after the forge world or manufactorum that made the original model (as in the Mars-pattern version).

REGIMENTS OF DISTINGUISHED SERVICE

Countless human worlds provide regiments for the Astra Militarum, and some have done so since before the Horus Heresy. Most regiments serve honourably but are little known outside of their own systems. Others, however, become renowned through great deeds, and their names are praised throughout the Imperium.

Cadian Shock Trooper

Catachan Jungle Fighter

Valhallan Ice Warrior

Vostroyan Firstborn

Death Korp of Krieg

Armageddon Steel Legion

Tallarn Desert Raider

Mordian Iron Guard

ARMOURED MIGHT

The Leman Russ is the workhorse battle tank of the Imperium. A lone Leman Russ can shore up any infantry line, while a Leman Russ Squadron can spearhead an attack from a war zone's centre and an Emperor's Fist Tank Company can collapse a whole enemy front. With thick armour and many variant armaments, the Leman Russ is a deadly tool in the arsenal of any Imperial Guard commander.

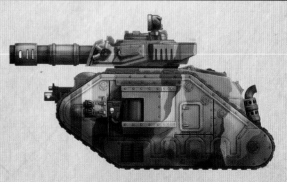

A common weapons loadout for a Leman Russ includes a turret-mounted battle cannon and hull-mounted heavy bolter. The side sponsons shown here bear heavy flamers.

AN IGNORANT MAN IS A DANGER TO HIMSELF; A LEARNED MAN IS A DANGER TO ALL.

SPECIALIST DIVISIONS

MILITARUM TEMPESTUS

An elite, specialist subdivision, the Militarum Tempestus train at the Schola Progenium. They are honed to a proficiency beyond even veteran Astra Militarum formations. Militarum Tempestus squads, or even entire armies, are used to break open fronts or capture key objectives. They are zealots to the Imperial cause and will succeed at their mission or die in the attempt.

MINISTORUM PRIESTS

Every regiment of the Imperial Guard is required to have at least one attached Ministorum Priest. It is their duty to administer holy rites as dictated by the Ecclesiarchy, and their fiery oratory can steady a wavering battle line or drive their flock into an impassioned frenzy. Whether this ability truly does channel the Emperor's powers or merely mass hysteria is irrelevant so long as it leads to victory.

OFFICIO PREFECTUS

The Officio Prefectus is the section of the Departmento Munitorum that oversees the activities of the Commissar officer corps within the Astra Militarum. The Officio Prefectus attaches one or more Commissars to regiments of the Imperial Guard. These stern authoritarians inspire, boost morale, and if necessary, take control when commanders or men demonstrate an improper lack of zeal or competency.

ENGINSEERS

The Adeptus Mechanicus are masters of technological mysticism, and it is they who look to the well-being of the Imperial Guard's engines of war. Enginseers are the most common Tech-Priests within the ranks of the Astra Militarum. These cybernetic holy men stand aloof from the Guardsmen, concerned only with tending to the machine spirits of their foster regiment's many vehicles and weaponry.

MILITARUM AUXILLA

As the nascent Imperium regained contact with the rest of Humanity, they discovered populations that had developed into subspecies. Most of these abhumans were killed, but some, such as the Ratlings and Ogryns, proved their worth as specialists in the Militarum Auxilla. Indoctrinated in the Imperial Creed, they are taught self-loathing, and watched closely by the Commissars and Priests.

ADEPTUS ASTRA TELEPATHICA

The Adeptus Astra Telepathica is responsible for the training of psykers into the service of the Imperium. Most die during testing, but those who survive might become sanctioned into duty with the Astra Militarum. Primaris Psykers or formations of Wyrdvane Psykers are valuable assets to any Imperial commander, even if they are feared by their superstitious comrades.

The rapid-firing gatling cannon allows the Leman Russ Punisher to lay down an overwhelming dose of firepower that can mow down enemy infantry or light vehicles.

Armed with a short-ranged but powerful siege cannon, the Leman Russ Demolisher is ideal for blasting foes out of even the densest of cover.

ADEPTUS MECHANICUS

The Adeptus Mechanicus, like the Adeptus Astartes, is an autonomous Imperial institution. It is led by the priesthood of the Cult Mechanicus – an organisation older even than the Imperium, first formed before the Unification of Terra – and provides technological expertise to the Imperium. In the name of the Omnissiah, as they know the Emperor, they send forth their armies. Each of their forge worlds commands its own formidable forces, including hosts of battle servitors, congregations of Electro-Priests, the fabled Legio Cybernetica, the Centurio Ordinatus, the Ordo Reductor, and the Skitarii and Titan Legions.

MARS, THE RED PLANET

The red planet is the birthplace of the Cult Mechanicus, the holiest of worlds save only Terra itself. Its surface is covered with vast, smoke-choked forge complexes and sprawling refineries, a hive of industry unmatched in the Imperium. Around the entire planet is a massive encirclement of orbital constructs known as the Ring of Iron. The many armies of Mars wear deep red as homage to their home planet.

MARS41

LUCIUS

The hollow planet of Lucius has at its core a fusion reactor so large many have likened it to a captive sun. In addition to vast Skitarii Legions, the planet is home to the Legio Astorum, a loyalist Titan Legion.

AGRIPINAA

Agripinaa has always been at the forefront of the Imperium's wars against the encroaching darkness of Chaos. They have even launched fleets into the Eye of Terror, seeking to take the fight to the traitors.

STYGIES VIII

No forge world yearns after xenos tech more than Stygies VIII. They send forth army after army of Skitarii to feed their studies, even drawing the Aeldari's ire after breaching the webway in search of the fabled Black Library.

GRAIA

Graia resides in a geometrically perfect network of space stations known as the Graian Crown. The forge world's priests claim their interest in warfare represents a desire for enlightenment, though rivals claim they go to war for war's sake.

RYZA

At great cost, Ryza defeated the invasion of Warlord Grax. Only the influx of Astra Militarum regiments from that campaign allowed the forge world to survive subsequent Daemon attacks during the Noctis Aeterna.

METALICA

Metalica's Tech-Priests have an obsessive revulsion for disorder. Since the first War for Armageddon, the priesthood has taken special interest in that war zone, sending forth many legions and collecting vast amounts of data.

LEGIO CYBERNETICA

One of the mightiest weapons in the arsenal of the Adeptus Mechanicus is the Legio Cybernetica. Though the robots of the Legio Cybernetica once numbered enough to shatter entire alien empires, a great many have been lost to the ravages of time. They were pivotal in the days of the Great Crusade, but their existence stretches back to predate the Imperium. Most battle-automata were destroyed and banned, but those deemed righteous enough were allowed to continue their duties. The secrets of their construction are all but forgotten. Because of this, it takes a Tech-Priest of surpassing rank to sanction their use, and absurd lengths are taken to retrieve those that fall in action. When their use is permitted, the Legio Cybernetica are organised into cohorts each consisting of four full-strength maniples. Legio Cybernetica Datasmith Tech-Priests accompany each formation of robotic warriors, programming their charges' every move. Accompanying those relics of Humanity's past are many of the faithful Electro-Priests. All are led by a Tech-Priest Dominus who is flanked by his hulking battle servitors. Incanting codes and complex war-blessings, they relentlessly seek to further the dominion of the Machine God, for such is their sole purpose.

CENTURIO ORDINATUS

Engines of the Omnissiah

COLLEGIA TITANICA

God-Machines of the Titan Legions

AUXILIA MYRMIDON

Savants of War

A QUESTIONING SERVANT IS MORE DANGEROUS THAN AN IGNORANT HERETIC.

LEGIONES SKITARII

Whether in the vanguard of the Quest for Knowledge or in the front lines of a forge world's defence, the Skitarii Legions are the mainstay armies of the Adeptus Mechanicus. On titanium limbs, the Skitarii stalk the galaxy's war zones, collecting data and doing as their Tech-Priest masters bid. They take pride in their holy work, glorying in the power of the Omnissiah as their Machine God drives them to ever greater feats.

Despite much of their flesh being plated over or grafted into machines, the Skitarii Legions are human. Barely. Each warrior has been dismembered and rebuilt to better serve the Omnissiah. Bionic replacements ensure not only the Skitarii's lethality, but also their utmost obedience. Neurosync implants allow the strictly ordered Skitarii cohorts to fight in perfect concert, each maniple uplinked to their masters. Far from the battlefield, a legion's overseer monitors each action, sending encoded commands. If needed, the Skitarii can be forced into suicidal engagements, or possessed entirely. The devout Skitarii see these incidents as the divine spirit of the Omnissiah entering them. Tirelessly, the cohorts stride forwards, wielding archaic weapons so dangerous that anyone in close proximity becomes rad-saturated. Accompanied by crab-legged vehicles and bipedal walkers, Skitarii cohorts operate ceaselessly until their task is complete or they are themselves destroyed.

SKITARII RADIUM WEAPONS

Radium weapons are deadly on several counts – if the shot does not kill its target outright, the bullet is so thoroughly bathed in radium that it can cause instant rad-poisoning.

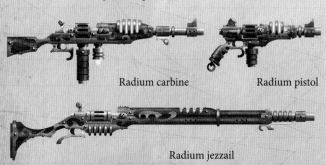

Radium carbine   Radium pistol

Radium jezzail

LEGIONES SKITARII

Warriors of the Machine God

LEGIO CYBERNETICA

The Host Robotic

ORDO REDUCTOR

Bringers of Blessed Ruin

QUESTOR IMPERIALIS

Knights are legacies of an ancient time. Rich in heritage and heraldry, each Knight is a survivor from the Age of Strife, a relic passed down to new generations. Once, when the galaxy was dark, they alone protected Mankind.

Knights are massive, single-pilot war machines crewed by a Noble. Even a lone Knight can turn the tide of battle, for each is an adamantium-armoured giant whose weapons speak in roars of thunder, its thick armour and ion shields shedding enemy fire like spring rain. Most Knights do not fight alone, but rather in Households – groupings that can often trace their heritage back beyond Imperial reckoning. There are two types of knightly household: Imperial Knights who align themselves with the Imperium, and Mechanicus Knights directly aligned to the Adeptus Mechanicus. Individuals detached from Noble houses can also fight on their own as Freeblades. It is a lucky Imperial commander who can add a Knight to his order of battle.

TYBALT, FURY OF VOLTORIS

Tybalt is the High King of Imperial House Terryn, one of the Great Houses. The House Terryn crest is proudly displayed upon his tilting plate and the Fury of Voltoris is further bedecked with battle honours and kill markings. It is said that the telling of High King Tybalt's triumphs takes well over twelve days to complete, and it is a tale that is still growing.

WALKORN, UNYIELDING IRON

Walkorn belongs to House Raven, a household closely allied to the nearby forge world of Metalica. Walkorn and his Knight, Unyielding Iron, have been inducted into House Raven's revered Order of Companions, but the Knight bears no mark to distinguish its elite status, for House Raven does not use such iconography.

GERANTIUS

Known as the Forgotten or Green Knight, Gerantius is a legendary Freeblade Knight said to reside at the centre of Sacred Mountain, a blessed peak that rises from the heart of Alaric Prime's largest island. There is rumoured to be a vault of archeotech and lost lore there, over which he stands guard.

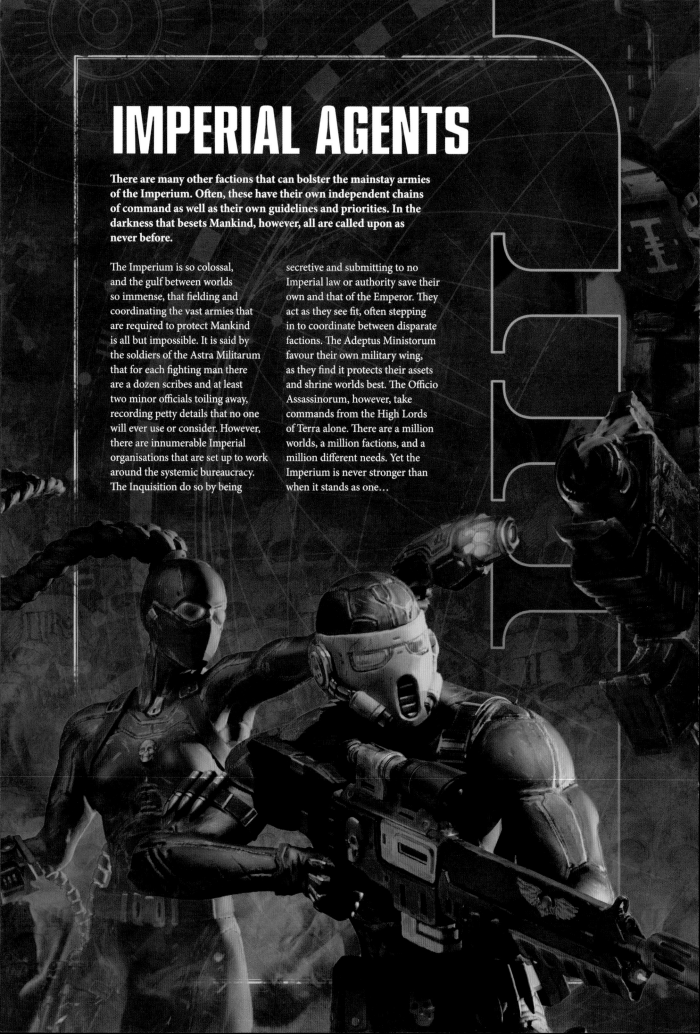

IMPERIAL AGENTS

There are many other factions that can bolster the mainstay armies of the Imperium. Often, these have their own independent chains of command as well as their own guidelines and priorities. In the darkness that besets Mankind, however, all are called upon as never before.

The Imperium is so colossal, and the gulf between worlds so immense, that fielding and coordinating the vast armies that are required to protect Mankind is all but impossible. It is said by the soldiers of the Astra Militarum that for each fighting man there are a dozen scribes and at least two minor officials toiling away, recording petty details that no one will ever use or consider. However, there are innumerable Imperial organisations that are set up to work around the systemic bureaucracy. The Inquisition do so by being secretive and submitting to no Imperial law or authority save their own and that of the Emperor. They act as they see fit, often stepping in to coordinate between disparate factions. The Adeptus Ministorum favour their own military wing, as they find it protects their assets and shrine worlds best. The Officio Assassinorum, however, take commands from the High Lords of Terra alone. There are a million worlds, a million factions, and a million different needs. Yet the Imperium is never stronger than when it stands as one…

THE INQUISITION

The Inquisition is divided into different factions known as Ordos, each specialising in combating a particular threat to Mankind. The Ordo Malleus stalk all creatures of Chaos. The Ordo Xenos are alien hunters who combat non-human elements, and the role of the Ordo Hereticus is that of witch hunting – dealing with psykers, mutants, and traitors.

OFFICIO ASSASSINORUM

The Imperium's covert agency of trained killers consists of many different Assassin temples. Each specialises in a particular murderous art or eliminating specific types of targets. The four largest temples are Vindicare, Callidus, Eversor, and Culexus, and there are many smaller ones as well. They all work in secrecy and shadow.

ADEPTUS CUSTODES

They who guard Mankind's past, present and future. The Custodian Guard are the Emperor's personal bodyguard. Before the Great Rift they rarely left the Emperor's side, standing vigil over the Golden Throne. In the dark days since, however, they have, on occassion, been seen throughout the galaxy fighting alongside the Emperor's forces.

ADEPTA SORORITAS

The promulgators of the Imperial Creed, the Adeptus Ministorum, more commonly known as the Ecclesiarchy, hosts numerous sub-factions, the best known of which are their military wing, the Adepta Sororitas, along with the orthodox training orphanages of the Schola Progenium, and its missionaries, the Missionarus Galaxia.

ADEPTUS ASTRA TELEPATHICA

Psykers of the first rank chosen off the Black Ships are given further training. Those who survive fight amongst the ranks of the Imperial Guard as Wyrdvane and Primaris Psykers. Although feared as witches by their own side, these Psykers can crumple tanks and halt an oncoming tide of greenksins with destructive blasts of mental energies.

Exemplars of all that the Space Marines stand for, the Ultramarines Chapter battle the enemies of the Emperor wherever they are found. Led into battle by their mighty Primarch, Roboute Guilliman, they are the bane of heretics and traitors alike.

IMPERIUM AT WAR

From the massed ranks of the Astra Militarum and the Adeptus Mechanicus, to the superhuman Space Marines and the towering war engines of the Knight households, the armies of the Imperium are spectacular in their martial might and uniformed grandeur.

Hellblaster

Intercessor Sergeant

Roboute Guilliman, Primarch of the Ultramarines

Stubborn masters of siege warfare, the Imperial Fists will fight to the last rather than give ground. Their rivalry with the embittered traitors of the Iron Warriors Legion is the stuff of dark legend.

Hailing from the volcanic world of Nocturne, the Salamanders are a stern and honourable Chapter of Space Marines. They excel in the use of flame as a weapon, cleansing their enemies from the battlefield amidst roaring streams of promethium death.

Stealth, speed and misdirection are the hallmarks of the Raven Guard Chapter. Striking and fading, feinting and ambushing, the sons of the Primarch Corax pick their enemies apart like so much battlefield carrion.

'As our bodies are armoured with adamant, our souls are protected with loyalty. As our bolters are charged with death for the Emperor's enemies, our thoughts are charged with wisdom. As our ranks advance, so does our devotion, for are we not the Space Marines? Are we not the chosen of the Emperor, his loyal servants unto death?'

- Chaplain Fergas Nils

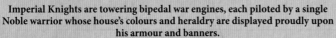

Imperial Knights are towering bipedal war engines, each piloted by a single Noble warrior whose house's colours and heraldry are displayed proudly upon his armour and banners.

Many knightly houses are aligned with the Adeptus Mechanicus, venerating the Omnissiah and dedicating the spectacular slaughter of entire enemy armies to his glory and that of the forge worlds.

Imperial-aligned Knight households, such as the ancient and honourable House Terryn, fight their battles in the Emperor's name. Hidebound by notions of duty, valour and courtly conduct, these insular warriors are nonetheless terrifying foes to face in battle.

Hailing from mighty forge worlds such as Mars or Metalica, the Adeptus Mechanicus deploy vast armies of cyborg Skitarii into battle. Here they fight alongside the Daemon-hunting brotherhoods of the Grey Knights against the minions of Khorne.

'A man may die yet still endure if his work enters the greater work. Time is carried upon a current incepted by forgotten deeds. Events of great moment are but the culmination of a single carefully placed thought. As all men must thank progenitors obscured by the past, so we must endure the present that those who come after may continue the greater work.'

- The Chime of Eons,
Garba Mojaro, Prefectus of the Adeptus Mechanicus

Amongst the greatest of the Adeptus Mechanicus priesthood is Archmagos Dominus Belisarius Cawl. The acquisitive, amoral genius responsible for the creation of the Primaris Space Marines, Cawl has worked long on his own cyborg body to transform himself into a living weapon.

Even amongst a gathering of heroes as auspicious as the Grey Knights, Grand Master Voldus shines as a beacon of piety and might. Gifted with phenomenal psychic abilities, he has banished vast hordes of Daemons back to the warp whence they came.

The ground shakes and the air turns to flame as the massed might of the Astra Militarum attacks. Rank upon rank of infantry, abhumans, mobile artillery and lumbering battle tanks roll forwards to crush the enemy without mercy.

Vostroyan Sergeant

Cadian Sergeant

Catachan Jungle Fighter

Steel Legion Trooper

Cold-eyed killers all, the Tempestus Scions are raised as psycho-indoctrinated soldiers almost from birth. They are elite specialists who strike hard and fast, and will gladly give their lives for the Imperial cause.

Master of Ordnance   Tech-Priest Enginseer   Sanctioned Psyker   Commissar

Potent witch hunters, the Sisters of Silence and Culexus Assassins sever their foes' connection to the power of the warp.

For the first time in ten thousand years, the mighty warriors of the Adeptus Custodes bestride the stars in force.

The Deathwatch draw their warriors from almost every Space Marine Chapter to exterminate the xenos threat.

OUR THOUGHTS LIGHT THE DARKNESS THAT
OTHERS MAY CROSS SPACE.
+
WE ARE ONE WITH THE EMPEROR, OUR SOULS
ARE JOINED IN HIS WILL.
+
PRAISE THE EMPEROR, WHOSE SACRIFICE IS LIFE
AS OURS IS DEATH.
+
HAIL HIS NAME, THE MASTER OF HUMANITY.

- extract from The Credo of the Astronomican

Most pious of all the Emperor's servants, the Battle Sisters of the Adepta Sororitas manifest miraculous powers through the sheer power of their faith. Greatest amongst their ranks is Celestine, the Living Saint.

FORCES OF CHAOS

From the shifting seas of the warp, fearsome entities espy Mankind. From that realm of madness, great powers conspire to bring about a doom so absolute that the entire galaxy would be consumed – swallowed into an endless oblivion of darkness and torture. If such a cataclysm were to happen, there could be no hope of recovery, only Chaos. Despite the incessant xenos invasions that beset the Imperium, it is this apocalyptic fate that looms largest over Mankind.

Few in the Imperium understand the true ramifications of what lurks in the warp, plotting Man's demise. It was the Emperor, the Master of Mankind, who first fathomed the dangers that the Ruinous Powers posed to Humanity. It was his ill-fated plan that protected the Imperium for so long from the worst predations of the Dark Gods and their daemonic scions. Secretive agents of Mankind work tirelessly to thwart daemonic incursions into realspace. Even after the Great Rift, most citizens of the Imperium remained ignorant of the true scope of the Chaos threat, for the terror that seeks to possess them is so vast it is almost impossible for the untrained mind to comprehend.

The Ruinous Powers attack the galaxy in interwoven ways, using unexpected guises. It is beyond mortal comprehension to follow such machinations. Was the slaughter on Van Horne's World related to a greater plan, or was the bloodbath merely an opportunity for the denizens of the warp to enter realspace? What was the endgame for the corruption of the planetary governor of Drakus Prime? Only now can it be seen what foul seeds were planted upon the worlds infected with the Zombie Plague. What hope has Mankind to fathom such random, bloodthirsty and immortal foes?

What can be recognised is that the forces of the Dark Gods are legion and increasingly seen outside the warp. Humanity itself has been corrupted. Many have willingly opened their hearts, allowing their own hubris, greed or envy to lead them astray. Disaffected traitors follow selfish goals, unknowingly serving a larger purpose. Outcast mutants harbour secret resentments, unwittingly

nurturing a festering malignancy. The actions of such groups spread over time and space, yet work towards the same goal – the breakdown of barriers between realspace and the warp, and the downfall of Man.

The most powerful of the Chaos forces are the Daemons. The servants of the Chaos Gods, Daemons are all that is vile made manifest. They are not fashioned of flesh and blood but of malevolent intent – supernatural beings who dine on the terror and ambition of man. Although the different factions are often rivals, Daemons are united in their quest to transform the mortal plane into a playground for their hateful needs. The Daemon legions are innumerable, but they are not alone. The Lost and the Damned are mortals corrupted into the service of the Dark Gods. Of these, the mightiest are the Chaos Space Marines, traitors who have bargained away their souls, discarding oaths of allegiance for material power, sensual freedom and the chance to attain immortality. They are joined by cultists beyond count. On every human world there are those who lust for power. Such minds are easy prey for the Ruinous Powers, and Chaos cults coil their way into all levels of the Imperium. Who can say which of their fellow citizens are pure and which are tainted?

'WE FIGHT THE LONG WAR, NOT THROUGH VAIN NOTIONS OF DUTY OR HONOUR, BUT THROUGH A FAR PURER PURPOSE: HATRED.'

- Ferrous Ironclaw, Warsmith of the Iron Warriors

IT IS THE BITTER TEARS THAT THE GODS WEEP THAT BIND US TO THEIR HEARTS.

93

THE CHAOS GODS

From beyond the boundaries of reality, the Chaos Gods look upon the galaxy with covetous eyes. It is their nature, their all-consuming purpose, to destroy. Relentless and unstoppable, all of their incomprehensible energies are directed to collapsing reason and perverting order.

Far from the light of sun or star lies the infernal, ever-changing Realm of Chaos. There, the four Dark Gods rule supreme – the mutable landscapes serving as battlegrounds for their daemonic legions. Their rivalry is eternal, each god seeking dominance over his brothers. As one power gains mastery through warfare, manipulation, corruption or sorcery, the others combine against him. New pacts flourish until another conqueror emerges, only to be thrown down in his turn. Yet there is one thing that can compel these opposing powers to put aside their differences for a time and work together. For, above all else, the Chaos Gods lust to push through the boundary that separates them from the mortal plane, to unleash their wanton destruction upon the physical galaxy. Nothing short of total annihilation will ever sate these fiends, the dragging of all reality into the Realm of Chaos.

KHORNE
The Blood God

Khorne is the god of war and murder, the patron of ferocity. He broods upon a throne of brass atop an endless mountain of skulls. Carnage is his only desire.

TZEENTCH
The Changer of Ways

The eternal schemer, Tzeentch is the god of magic and change, master of the timestream. He is the Great Conspirator and the Architect of Fate.

There is no peace amongst the stars, only an eternity of carnage and slaughter and the laughter of thirsting gods.

NURGLE
The Great Lord of Decay

Nurgle is the lord of entropy and fecundity, the joyous bringer of plague and physical corruption. His is the cycle of purification, rebirth and morbidity.

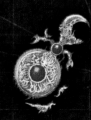

SLAANESH
The Dark Prince

The youngest of the Chaos Gods, Slaanesh alone is divinely beautiful. He epitomises boundless excess – the Dark Prince is all things decadent and debased.

DAEMONS OF CHAOS

There are no foes more terrible. From out of the warp they come, bringing ruin and unimaginable horror. They are the armies of the Dark Gods, the Daemon legions, and they will only cease their relentless assault upon the mortal worlds when reality itself has been torn apart.

In the warp, there exist countless Daemons of myriad abhorrent shapes, each the spawn of the nightmares and vices of mortal creatures. Daemons are but aspects of the Chaos Gods made sentient. The appearance and behaviour of a Daemon always betrays the character and ambition of its creator. So, Bloodletters, the rank and file of Khorne's legions, are ferocious creatures, eager to reap and slay, as befits minions of the God of Battle.

There are numerous ways in which Daemons can invade reality. Human psykers present the most common means of entry, for their minds shine like beacons within the warp. Ships entering the immaterium are also vulnerable, for if any of their safeguards fail, a horrifying fate awaits all on board. Permanent gateways to the warp exist throughout the galaxy, torn open by psychic activity or dark rituals. The Cicatrix Maledictum is the greatest of these, and it continues to degrade the veil separating the Realm of Chaos from the galaxy. Near such places, the powers of Chaos run rampant. Warp storms, great stellar trauma or vast psychic emanations can also draw forth the daemonic legions. When the Daemon armies emerge, they do so with great purpose –

bringing war and corruption. If enough unnatural energy spills out, the most monstrous denizens of the warp can cross over – the powerful Greater Daemons. At their command, daemonic hordes slaughter entire populations. To drive Daemons back into the Realm of Chaos requires depleting the warp energies sustaining them. Physically slaying them will do, but only for a while. The destruction of a Daemon's physical form will banish it from realspace, but the malefic presence will gradually reform again in the warp, nursing its grudge. Given a chance, it will return, its hatred further stoked with a horrible vengeance in mind.

DAEMON WORLDS

Planets near major rents in reality can become imbued with arcane energies. Those most corrupted of worlds – where creatures from the warp walk freely – are classified as Daemon worlds by the Imperium. Few encounter such hellish places and survive. Often, Daemon worlds are gifted to powerful Greater Daemons, Daemon Princes, or the Traitor Primarchs as rewards. Since the days following the Horus Heresy, they have served as refuges for the Heretic Astartes, sanctuaries of dread from which terror raids and Black Crusades are launched. Daemon worlds are located near major rents in reality, clustered near the baleful energies that pour forth from such ruptures as the Great Rift, the Eye of Terror or the Maelstrom. It is a rare individual who can travel into such perilous phenomena and emerge unaltered.

HERETIC ASTARTES

The Heretic Astartes, also known as Chaos Space Marines, are fearsome foes. They have a Space Marine's abilities, along with his gear of war, but since turning to the darker powers many also now bear powerful mutations or gifts from their patron Chaos Gods, making them mightier still.

Not all creatures of Chaos are its direct offspring. Once proud warriors armoured with faith, the Chaos Space Marines are now bitter and corrupt champions. They are hateful reavers who war to serve their own fell needs and, in so doing, also serve their new masters. Between their long histories of service, STC-designed wargear and the Codex Astartes, there are more similarities than differences between Space Marine Chapters. This is not the case with the Heretic Astartes. A dark mirror to their Imperial counterparts, Chaos Space Marines share the same genetically enhanced abilities, but beyond that, the ranks of the traitors are more greatly varied. The superhuman frame of a Space Marine can survive more mutations than any other mortal could bear. Heretic Astartes become marked by mutations, such as tentacles or bestial visages. Over time, the corruptions grow. Yet time moves strangely within regions that are awash with the unnatural energies of the warp. Those from the ranks of the Traitor Legions are the same warriors that joined the rebellion under Horus all those long years ago. After the Warmaster's fall they fled into the Eye of Terror. To this day they still continue that war…

BLACK LEGION

The history of the Black Legion resounds with the din of both glorious victories and the most bitter of defeats. The Black Legion will never cease until they succeed where Horus failed.

The sixteenth of the First Founding Adeptus Astartes Legions, they were once called the Luna Wolves, before the Emperor renamed them the Sons of Horus to honour the accomplishments of their Primarch. It was with that title that the Legion rebelled, fighting as Horus' bodyguard during the Horus Heresy. After Horus' defeat, they recovered his body from the loyalists and fled into the Eye of Terror. There, they feuded with other Traitor Legions, eventually losing the Warmaster's body, and were nearly destroyed. Only the matchless leadership of Abaddon, who had been Horus' second in command, kept the remnants of the old Legion together. It was this new Warmaster's edict to repaint their armour black in eternal memory of the shame of their losses. Abaddon directed the newly named Black Legion and reclaimed their vaunted reputation once again. Since that time, the Black Legion have been a scourge on the Imperium, appearing at the forefront of Black Crusades where they unite the usually anarchic Chaos factions. There are no Heretic Astartes more infamous and none are more focussed on toppling the Imperium of Man and ripping the Corpse-Emperor off his Golden Throne.

THE LOYAL SLAVE LEARNS TO LOVE THE LASH.

DEATH GUARD

The Death Guard were one of the original Legions, but with lies and half-truths Horus swayed their Primarch, Mortarion, to his rebellion. The Death Guard would pay a nightmarish price for that betrayal, falling under the sway of Nurgle, the Lord of Corruption, to become the first of all the Plague Marines.

Few sights are more loathsome than the corrupted forms of the plague-infested Death Guard. Their oozing power armour has rotted away in places, exposing festering wounds and pestilence-filled innards – yet their bloated bodies do not feel the agony of their mutations. If anything, these afflictions only make them stronger, their necrotic bodies so numb to pain that only total destruction can stop them. Relentlessly they march forward.

Abominations against nature, the Death Guard advance within clouds of flies, their weapons spitting death, their miasma spreading unnatural disease. Truly, Nurgle has blessed the Death Guard – their flesh bulging with corruption – and they wish to share these gifts of virulence across the galaxy.

For a long period after his ascension to daemonhood, the Traitor Primarch Mortarion allowed his Death Guard to fractionalise. He was content to rule from his throne upon the Plague Planet – a Daemon world inside the Eye of Terror – only rarely issuing forth. In the wake of the Noctis Aeterna, however, Mortarion has taken a more direct role in leading the Death Guard. The time for the planting of corruptions had ended, and the time for reaping has begun.

THOUSAND SONS

Remorseless. Cursed. Tragedy and fate conspired to drive the most psychically gifted of the Space Marine Legions into the clutches of Chaos. Thus they became an enemy of the Imperium like no other.

The path of damnation for the Thousand Sons was longer than most. One of the original Legiones Astartes, the Thousand Sons had many psykers within their ranks – hardly surprising as their Primarch, Magnus the Red, was a psychic giant. During the Great Crusade, the Thousand Sons continued to study arcane lore despite the Emperor's warnings. They remained loyal, using their occult powers to warn the Emperor of Horus' impending betrayal. The Emperor declared the Thousand Sons' arcane arts to be heresy, however, and unleashed the Space Wolves upon them. Forced into a war they did not want, the Thousand Sons turned to Tzeentch in order to save themselves. Escaping certain destruction by fleeing into the Eye of Terror, the Legion continued their magical studies, although they were soon wracked by mutations. Disturbed by their decline, a cabal, led by the sorcerer Ahriman, risked the wrath of their Primarch, now risen to daemonhood, to cast a spell known as the Rubric. The spell placed his kin beyond mutation, but reduced their mortal forms to dust sealed inside suits of armour – no more than magical automatons. The cabal was banished by the enraged Primarch, forced to scatter and fight for different Traitor Legions. After an age-long exile, however, the Legion has reconciled and reformed.

PROSPERO

Prospero was a world of mutants and psykers, refugees that chose it as a good place to hide. In the end, it was not even that. As their home world was devastated by the Space Wolves, Magnus used his powers to whisk the last city and his Legion from the fiery ruin. He settled in the Eye of Terror upon the Planet of Sorcerers, as Tzeentch promised, but Magnus vowed one day to return. Prospero remained a blasted ruin, declared Purgatus by the Inquisition. After long ages, however, Magnus used a mighty spell to wrench the Planet of Sorcerers out of the Eye of Terror, bringing it to rest next to the husk of Prospero. The Space Wolves feel it was this unnatural act that precipitated the arrival of the Great Rift.

RENEGADES

The traitors of the Horus Heresy were not alone for long, and many have followed their path. The taint of Chaos can infect even the strongest mind, and just as Space Marines are above men in strength and skill, so do they fall further – becoming mockeries of their former glory.

Although it is rare for Adeptus Astartes to turn from the light of the Emperor, over the span of thousands of years countless Space Marines have done so. Sometimes they fall from grace individually, or in squads or companies, and on very rare occasions, in entire Chapters. Freed from the dogma of service to their Chapter and the Imperium, these individuals fully indulge their superhuman bodies and prodigious fighting skills. Modified to be the ultimate warriors, these defectors most often gather wealth or power, becoming tyrannical leaders of pirate fleets, despot warrior kings on frontier planets, or the leaders of mercenary warbands or cults, out to claim their own fortunes.

As doomed as any traitor from the Heresy, these Renegades eventually turn to the Chaos Gods, sometimes willingly, seeking more power, sometimes at desperate need. Although none have gained the infamy of the Traitor Legions, some have carved their names in blood across the Imperium. Names like the Red Corsairs, the Purge, the Invocators and the Crimson Slaughter are enough to cause any planetary defence force to quake. Some Renegades dwell in the Eye of Terror, but many more are scattered across the galaxy. Some live in hidden moon bases and drifting space hulks that flit in and out of the warp. Some have conquered whole worlds to claim as their own, or established furtive bases on

Imperial worlds, hiding beneath their enemies' noses. From these sites, the Renegades launch their raids – taking what they want for their own needs or continuing a war of hate against the Imperial whelps and their cursed Emperor. Across hundreds of worlds, the banners of these Renegades are held aloft.

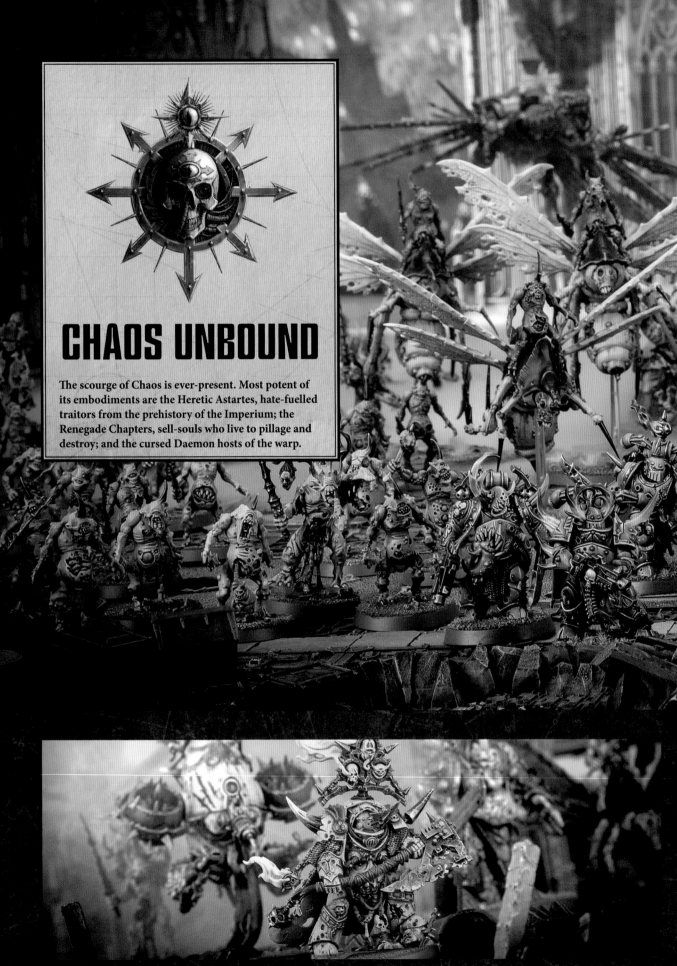

CHAOS UNBOUND

The scourge of Chaos is ever-present. Most potent of its embodiments are the Heretic Astartes, hate-fuelled traitors from the prehistory of the Imperium; the Renegade Chapters, sell-souls who live to pillage and destroy; and the cursed Daemon hosts of the warp.

Lords of Contagion stamp their filthy footprints across the domains of the Imperium, leading corrupted monstrosities in their wake.

Amongst a stinking miasma of infectious gases, the legions of Nurgle advance with slow but unstoppable momentum. The air fills with the drone of bloated flies and chanting Plaguebearers, their vile chorus punctuated by the crash and roar of gunfire.

Plague Marines bring to their victims the foetid gifts of Grandfather Nurgle – amongst them disease, despair, and boundless entropy.

'Be warned! Many are the guises of the mutant. They may appear to you as a normal person but beneath this benign countenance may lie a wretched and twisted beast. An abomination, a witch or worse. Mark the beast and expel it, it has no place with us!'

- Inquisitor Czevak

The favoured armies of the Chaos God Tzeentch are masters of sorcery. Only the brave or the insane dare to bar their path, for the enemies of the Changehosts are horrifically transmuted, twisted in body and soul as they meet truly spectacular deaths.

With the berserk warriors of Khorne in his wake, the butcher of men known as Khârn the Betrayer has slaughtered his way across the galaxy for ten millennia. Only he knows how many hundreds of thousands of skulls his axe has claimed in the name of the Blood God.

Khorne cares not from whence the blood flows, only that it flows. The devotees of the Blood God hurl themselves into the crucible of war with wilful abandon, soaking the battlefield with the gory remains of their enemies – or spilling gouts of their own lifeblood should fate demand it.

A Wrath of Khorne Bloodthirster leaps into the sky in its haste to seek worthy prey. A terrifying incarnation of the Blood God's rage, the very presence of such a monstrosity can sear the mind beyond recovery.

Though the warbands and warrior servants of Chaos are daunting in their variety, they will put aside all rivalries in pursuit of a common cause – usually the pitiless execution of those their eldritch masters deem unfit to live.

The Iron Warriors are bitter, twisted siege-breakers and warsmiths who revel in the thunder of unbound destruction.

Hopelessly addicted to the mind-numbing clamour and spectacle of war, the Emperor's Children seek excess in the name of Slaanesh.

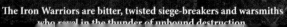

Fear the cruel and vindictive Night Lords, for they are masters of psychological warfare as well as brute force.

The Word Bearers are fervent worshippers of the Dark Gods, their unholy zeal driving them to commit ever-greater acts of slaughter.

THE XENOS THREAT

Mankind is not the only race to walk among the stars. Since they first travelled beyond the Sol System in the early days of the Age of Technology, Humanity has encountered alien races, most of which have proven hostile.

The galaxy is full of creatures, the majority of which are capable of great acts of destruction. While some xenos exist only on a single planet, other civilisations might occupy a whole star system, and there are a few that are widely spread across the galaxy. It has never been in Humanity's nature to share worlds with aliens, and bloodshed has ever formed the foundation of empires. Sometimes, humans and aliens are forced to fight over inhabitable planets or vital resources; at others, humans must do battle with the most dangerous types of xenos, whose only aim is to eradicate Humanity wherever their paths cross. Down the ages, there have been innumerable wars against the xenos, planet-wide battles of annihilation and long campaigns of genocide that have stretched over vast distances and eras.

Many Imperial planets were usurped from xenos races long ago, some during the initial colonisations of the Age of Technology, and now the aliens' very existence on such worlds has been forgotten. This explains why great monuments of inhuman design are occasionally unearthed, strange technologies found buried beneath levels of stone and metal, crushed down beneath long ages of human construction. How many xenos species have been eradicated is not known. The Lacrymoles are gone, the last of their kind wiped out, relentlessly ground away before the end of the Great Crusade. The same can be said of the Vrakk, the Uluméathic League, the Losh, the worm-like Drugh, and others beyond count.

Although many xenos races may have been forgotten, the alien peril to the Imperium is incessant. Even worlds and systems that the Imperium has cleared of xenos find that such purges are not an ultimate triumph, merely a respite. It is never long before those same planets are again under threat, whether by the returning foe or some new alien species. Sojourns into unexplored sectors often find thriving colonies, and even nearby planets once deemed lifeless become infected. Other xenos drift into human territory, perhaps expanding their own empires, or seeking to escape an impending threat.

Some alien races are ancient beyond Mankind's reckoning, while others are nascent powers – newcomers that have just learned how to leave their home planets. No few xenos species care nothing for civilisation or empire, being sheer monsters that wish only to prey on the unwary. Countless such abominations have been encountered and tales of the ferocity of creatures like the Donorian Clawed Fiend, the crystalline Dracolith, the dread Ambull or the Catachan Devil have spread across the galaxy. All must be fought tooth and nail, for the Imperium learned long ago that only the strong survive and that no mercy can be found amongst the stars.

Led by the fervour of the Adeptus Ministorum, most of Mankind believes in the extermination of all xenos, even those deemed peaceful. Against such foes, vigilance and intolerance can be Humanity's only safeguards. Still, the effort to fight xenos drains the Imperium, diverting much-needed military strength from the battles against the never-ending corruptions of Chaos.

'THEY CAME FROM THE DARK PLACES BETWEEN THE STARS, FROM THE ABYSS INTO WHICH EVEN THE EMPEROR'S ANGELS FEAR TO GAZE. MONSTROUS IN FORM, ENDLESS IN NUMBER, THE SWARM DESCENDED TO DEVOUR ALL.'

- Anon

ZEAL IS ITS OWN EXCUSE.

THE ALIEN DREAM IS TO DANCE ON THE GRAVE OF MANKIND.

THE AELDARI

The Aeldari are a space-faring race that ruled the galaxy long before Mankind's ancestors crawled from the Terran seas. It was the pride of their own supremacy that led to their downfall, yet still the elite armies of the Aeldari fight on against the upstart races that would reign in their stead.

The galaxy-spanning Aeldari, known to some simplay as Eldar, are an ancient and enigmatic xenos race. One moment they act as an ally to Mankind, the next they launch inexplicable strikes against them. Partly, this confusion arises because the Aeldari are splintered into factions radically different from the each other. The term Aeldari is also ancient, used before the Fall to describe craftworlders, Harlequins, Exodites, Drukhari and Corsairs when they were all one, and their race ruled the galaxy. They nearly went extinct, becoming remnants of a shattered civilisation. Although only a shadow of their former glory, the Aeldari splinter groups are each still formidable in their own right.

All the factions share a confidence in the superiority of their wisdom, technology and martial prowess, so that, as a whole, the Aeldari look down on the barbaric usurpers that have overrun the galaxy. While Aeldari armies and fleets are not numerous, they make up for this lack of quantity with quality, displaying consummate skill, wielding advanced wargear, and methodically planning well-choreographed assaults. Interlocking manoeuvres allow even small Aeldari armies to strike quickly, whittling down more-numerous foes with a series of rapid, interwoven attacks which leave their enemies vulnerable to a swift killing blow.

THE FALL OF THE AELDARI

The Aeldari themselves never speak of the Fall, as they call it, to other races, so it is difficult to get an accurate picture of exactly what happened. Rumours tell of planets swallowed by the warp, and how the darkest Daemons from within the minds of the Aeldari overcame them for their arrogant sins. Some say that the captive souls of long-dead Aeldari are still tormented to this day by their sadistic conquerors. Others say the Aeldari received their just punishment and it is only a matter of time before the rest succumb to whatever dreadful fate destroyed their reign. What is indisputable is that the area of the galaxy which was once the central region of the ancient Aeldari empire became dominated by the Eye of Terror, and that the Aeldari are haunted by their past.

THE MANY FACES OF THE AELDARI

The Aeldari are a complex and fractured people, more so than even the Mung xenolexicors can comprehend. That said, there are distinct and divergent cultures that have spun outwards from the great cataclysm of the Aeldari. The most far-sighted sought refuge before the Fall, becoming those we call Exodites. As the birth of the Dark Prince came ever closer, the ark-like craftworlds took to the void; many survived the apotheosis that laid the Aeldari low. Others roam the stars as Corsairs, wanderers and Outcasts, or make their lair in dark Commorragh. Amongst them are the savage slavers known as Drukhari, the enigmatic Harlequins of the Black Library, and the Ynnari, who seek to reclaim the glory of ages past.

- Obelius Mung the Fourth, Echoes of Paravax

LEGEND

1. Aeldari
2. Exodites
3. ++REDACTED++
4. Craftworlders
5. Corsairs
6. Outcasts
7. Drukhari
8. Harlequins
9. Ynnari

CRAFTWORLDS

Craftworlds are colossal yet graceful vessels of living wraithbone and various psychoactive materials. These world-ships were originally created as space-faring arks by those ancient Aeldari who foresaw the horrifying fate of their empire and sought to flee far enough to escape the hunger of She Who Thirsts.

Each of the surviving craftworlds represents but a small fragment of Aeldari civilisation. Their inhabitants are the guardians of their people's culture, history, traditions, and their dead, and strive to preserve an echo of their past greatness. The craftworlds are self-sufficient, able to grow organically, and capable of repairing damage. The largest and most important of the craftworlds identified by the Imperium are Alaitoc, Iyanden, Saim-Hann and Ulthwé. There are smaller craftworlds too, including the mysterious Black Library, the doomed craftworld of Mero, the legendary lost craftworld of Chto, and the former craftworld of Biel-Tan, which became a fleet-based faction during the awakening of Ynnead.

Undoubtedly there are others, for the craftworlders are isolationists even among their own kind. Aboard their world-ships these Aeldari live their lives as they have done for millennia, following ascetic Paths to hold off the decadence that doomed their forefathers. When the shadow of war falls upon them, all citizens will take up arms, forming warhosts mighty enough to conquer worlds. Craftworlds do not, indeed cannot, use warp travel in the same manner as the Imperium. Instead the Aeldari use the webway, a labyrinth dimension that exists between the warp and realspace. The webway leads to many sites across the galaxy, although few of its portals are large enough to accommodate craftworlds.

CRAFTWORLD AELDARI

The most numerous of the Aeldari are those who live on craftworlds. Since the Fall, these craftworlders have been forced to fight for survival, contending with a galaxy that is no longer theirs. They are a proud race, determined to see the flame of their kind blaze brightly once more rather than flicker and die out.

The craftworlds are home to vast populations of Aeldari, although the majority of them are no longer living. Legends tell that at the moment of the Fall, the Aeldari gods were slain, devoured by Slaanesh. The war god, Khaine, was torn apart and scattered across the galaxy, the fragmented shards of his spirit coming to rest deep within the hearts of the craftworlds. Only Cegorach, the Laughing God, escaped. Without the protection of their ancestral gods, the souls of all Aeldari have since been vulnerable to the predations of Slaanesh when they die. To stay this terrible fate, the craftworld Aeldari wear objects known as waystones. These gems of psycho-receptive crystal capture the wearer's essence upon death,

thereby becoming spirit stones. Precious beyond measure, these glowing gems are gathered from fallen Aeldari and returned to their bearer's craftworld. There, the soul within is transferred into the wraithbone skeleton of the ship itself. Thus, the Aeldari live on even after death as ghostly echoes trapped in the shadowy limbo of the infinity circuit. At need, Autarchs – the war leaders of the Aeldari – can call upon ghostly legions of wraith-constructs, each one powered by a reinterred spirit stone. It is not the way Aeldari wish to respect their ancestors, but the call of war comes too often for them to do otherwise. Despite their isolationist tendencies, the craftworld Aeldari frequently find themselves forced

to battle simply for their survival. Yet they are prepared. In times of need, all civilians on a craftworld – male and female – don armour to fight as Guardians. Dotted across every craftworld are warrior shrines dedicated to the myriad Aspects of Khaine, in which the Aeldari's most elite fighters train endlessly to hone their skills to a level of perfection beyond human ability. Within the Dome of Crystal Seers, Farseers – powerful Aeldari psykers – commune with the dead, searching both the future and the past for the best fate-path to follow. Most sinister of all is the chamber at each craftworld's heart, where a towering statue of iron sits upon a giant throne: the Avatar of Khaine, awaiting war's call.

HAPPINESS IS A DELUSION OF THE WEAK.

SAIM-HANN – *The Wild Host*

Bold. Impetuous. Proud. The warriors of the Saim-Hann craftworld have a fierce reputation. So it has always been. One of the first to abandon the Aeldari home worlds as the Fall approached, other craftworlds see those of Saim-Hann as barbarous and rash, but their bravery is legendary. Like Khaine's bloody spear, the Wild Rider clans of Saim-Hann strike from above, the greater part of their warriors mounted upon jetbikes or taking to the skies in grav-tanks. In streaks of crimson the Wild Host attacks with blurring swiftness, true masters of hit-and-run tactics.

IYANDEN – *The Ghost Warriors*

Iyanden was once among the most populous of the craftworlds until it was targeted by a tendril of the Tyranid Hive Fleet Kraken. Only the return of the exiled Prince Yriel and his Corsair fleet saved the craftworld from being completely annihilated. The craftworld cannot recover its losses and many Iyanden Seers believe extinction looms. Their rapid decline has led the Iyanden Aeldari to a reliance upon wraithbone constructs to form the backbone of their armies, as well as an unusual number of Spiritseers – warrior mystics skilled at communicating with the dead.

ULTHWÉ – *The Damned*

Craftworld Ulthwé sails close to the Eye of Terror, an inescapable reminder of the Fall and the doom that eagerly lusts after them. It is this memory that drives the Aeldari of Ulthwé in their war against Chaos, a fight not just for an ideal, but for their continued existence – and perhaps even that of the galaxy. Home to many powerful psykers, Ulthwé relies upon its Seer Councils more than any other craftworld. Using runes to see the strands of fate as they form the future, Farseers have led the Black Guardians of Ulthwé to many seemingly impossible victories.

BIEL-TAN – *The Swordwind*

The Fracture of Biel-Tan was a traumatic event that shook the galaxy. During the split, Biel-Tan was broken into fragment vessels, leaving the husk of the craftworld, and its infinity circuit, in ruin. This released enough death energy to bring Ynnead, the Aeldari god of the dead, into being, stymieing Slaanesh's plans. The surviving members of the Biel-Tan warhost, the Swordwind, have resolved to maintain the warlike traditions of their craftworld, and they have since vanished into the webway to continue to scour ancient Aeldari worlds of alien usurpers.

ALAITOC – *The Starstriders*

The Aeldari of Alaitoc puritanically adhere to the Aeldari Paths. A side effect of this zeal has led to many becoming Outcasts. These nomadic individuals are still loyal to their kin, however, and some become space-faring Corsairs, bolstering Alaitoc's navy in times of war. Others choose the way of the Ranger, acting as the craftworld's eyes and ears in the galaxy. Some trapped upon the Path of the Outcast become Pathfinders, supernaturally adept at concealment and ambushes. Many foes have likened a fight versus these elusive wanderers to hunting phantoms.

DRUKHARI

Where the Aeldari aboard the craftworlds attempt to overcome the anguish of their past with inhuman discipline and rigid self-control, their dark kin have gone the opposite way. The Drukhari have become an indulgent race of vicious killers, whose existence depends upon the pain and suffering that they inflict.

Nestled far from prying eyes, the vile and sadistic city of Commorragh was once a grand nexus point within the labyrinthine dimensions of the webway. Before the Fall of the Aeldari, the hidden destination was renowned for its depravity, especially in the right circles of the cults of excess, for it served well those who wished for privacy. Shielded from the raw power of Chaos and the psychic backlash unleashed upon the galaxy during the Fall, those in Commorragh were not slain like so many of their kin. From their safe haven, the depravity of these Aeldari grew, until the city was a monstrous den of absolute villainy. It was this Dark City that was the

birthplace of the race that later came to be known as Drukhari, or Dark Eldar, the corrupt cousins that splintered from the Aeldari.

Hidden within the webway, the Drukhari were largely immune to the passage of time, with the exception that their souls began to wither. Their only counter to this gradual loss was to refill that void by steeping themselves in extreme sensations and outrageous evils. The agony and suffering of others replenishes them, granting them an unholy vitality and vigour. In order to exist, the Drukhari must have a constant supply of living beings on which to practise their foul crafts. To fulfil such needs,

they have become masters of the lightning raid – darting attacks that eliminate all resistance, allowing the victors ample time to gather up the spoils. While not above taking technology and material goods, it is live captives that the Drukhari seek above all. The mortal creatures taken into captivity suffer a terrible and often prolonged fate in order to satiate their loathsome captors. To launch their assaults, the Drukhari travel using the webway, moving unseen across the galaxy where no space fleet, patrol, or listening station can detect them. And no matter how many captives they take, their needs soon require more. Many are the armies that leave Commorragh every day…

KABALS

The Kabals of Commorragh are the black heart of most Drukhari armies. They are autonomous organisations somewhere between criminal cartels, pirate fraternities and noble households.

When the Kabals strike, they do so in rapid fashion. With no warning, they darken the skies, hurtling downwards upon razor-edged anti-gravity craft. Led by Archons, the hallmark of a Kabalite raid is a combination of speed and firepower, applied in precision assaults. There are some, however, who prefer to feel the splash of blood that only close combat can offer. Although often set at each other's throats, the Kabals are largely responsible for the flow of slaves into Commorragh – and so temporary alliances are common, as all Drukhari rely upon the supply of soul-stuff that such captives provide.

HAEMONCULUS COVENS

Beneath the Dark City lurk the terrifying beings known as Haemonculi. Masters of the flesh, be it alive or dead, the Haemonculus Covens are universally feared.

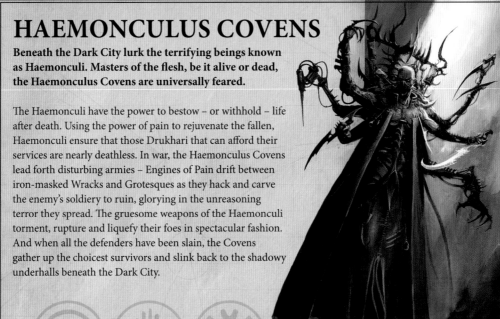

The Haemonculi have the power to bestow – or withhold – life after death. Using the power of pain to rejuvenate the fallen, Haemonculi ensure that those Drukhari that can afford their services are nearly deathless. In war, the Haemonculus Covens lead forth disturbing armies – Engines of Pain drift between iron-masked Wracks and Grotesques as they hack and carve the enemy's soldiery to ruin, glorying in the unreasoning terror they spread. The gruesome weapons of the Haemonculi torment, rupture and liquefy their foes in spectacular fashion. And when all the defenders have been slain, the Covens gather up the choicest survivors and slink back to the shadowy underhalls beneath the Dark City.

WYCH CULTS

Because of their unending need to bathe in murderous sensations, the Drukhari have evolved Wych Cults – gladiatorial sisterhoods that provide maximum carnage.

Each Wych Cult is a thousands-strong organisation of gladiators that put on nightly displays of incredible violence to edify and sustain the masses. Yet the martial acrobatics of the Wych Cults are not confined to arenas alone. These trained killers relish the thought of proving their deadly superiority to lesser races in war, often competing amongst themselves to take trophies in the most gruesome fashion possible. Led to war by a Succubus, Wyches twirl, spin, and slice a deadly path through any foe. Beastmasters drive bloodthirsty creatures into the mayhem, while some Cults add flying support in the form of Hellions and Reavers.

HARLEQUINS

One of the strangest of all the splinter groups of the Aeldari are the Harlequins. These lightning-fast warrior acrobats make no distinction between war and theatrical art.

Since the Fall, the Harlequins have waged a clandestine war against She Who Thirsts. In the name of Cegorach, the Laughing God whom they worship, the Harlequins travel the secret paths of the webway, emerging with no warning to combat Chaos. Alongside death-dealing, the Harlequins possess another, ritual duty: they journey between the realms of their divided kin – craftworlds, Exodite worlds, Corsair fleets and the Dark City of Commorragh – performing the dances and plays of the Aeldari mythic cycle. These performances are not so different from their war manoeuvres, for the colourfully costumed Harlequins flow and twist through battle like silk streamers in a hurricane. A Troupe Master choreographs the carnage, directing the Harlequins in spinning, graceful ballets of death. Supported by jetbikes and streaking gunships, the Troupes move in blinding blurs. Then, in a multicoloured flash, the Harlequins are gone, leaving only death in their wake.

Cegorach, known as the Laughing God, or the Great Harlequin, escaped the clutches of Slaanesh and fled into the webway. He dwells there still, always one step ahead of his ancient nemesis.

YNNARI

As the strength of Chaos increases across the galaxy, a new faction of Aeldari has risen. These Ynnari, also known as the Pathless or Reborn, have found a way to defeat Chaos and revenge themselves upon Slaanesh. Or so they claim.

The Ynnari are the disciples of Ynnead, the Aeldari god of the dead. They have learned the secrets of absorbing the souls of the deceased, bringing them closer to their ancestors and the ways of the Aeldari before the Fall. The Ynnari gain the knowledge of those souls they have taken, and have travelled across the galaxy attempting to recruit others of their race. On every craftworld some have turned to Ynnead's cause, but not all agree, and many see the Ynnari as fiendish or already themselves dead. Ironically, in attempting to unify the Aeldari, the Ynnari have instead polarised them, making the race more splintered than ever, despite their continued efforts to the contrary. And wherever the Reborn travel, trouble follows. Internal clashes between disputing factions have been inevitable, and the forces of Chaos are never far behind. Slaanesh especially covets the Ynnari, for each is a walking hoard of souls, a treasure of delectables for the Chaos God.

THE RUNES ARE CAST

It is the Ynnari's plan to fulfil ancient prophecies of Slaanesh's defeat by dying. However, their version of the prophecy does not involve their race's extinction. Instead, by absorbing the souls of dead Aeldari themselves, the Reborn intend to starve She Who Thirsts out of existence. It promises to be a lengthy battle, but Ynnead is eternally patient. The god's agents are not, however. Members of every Aeldari faction have joined the Ynnari, but more stand opposed. Amongst the Drukhari, the Haemonculus Covens refuse their vision, desiring the souls of the dead for themselves. The gladiatorial champion Lelith Hesperax has joined the Reborn, along with many of the Wych Cults, while the Kabalites' reactions to Ynnead's disciples are varied. Harlequins, naturally, fight on both sides.

NECRONS

After aeons of slumber, the Necrons have begun to waken. Rising from their stasis tombs, the Necrons have returned to complete their terrible purpose.

Long ago the Necrontyr forsook mortal flesh for bodies of near-impervious metal. When their dreams of galactic conquest soured, they sealed themselves inside hidden tomb worlds, awaiting a new age. So long did the Necrons slumber that the galaxy all but forgot their existence. Even in the minds of the Aeldari, who once strove against the Necrons for mastery of the stars, did their memory grow dim. The cold-hearted Necron Overlords and their implacable legions awakened to find their once great empire in decay and primitive life forms squatting in their ancient domains. They were not impressed. No longer creatures of flesh and blood, Necrons are androids that can survive crippling damage. Once rent, the metal from which they are formed flows back together, and severed limbs scrabble to reattach themselves. Should irreparable damage occur, the Necron 'phases out', its body and consciousness teleported back to the nearest tomb-complex to remain in storage until a new shell can be forged. The technologies by which this is accomplished are a mystery, and many contingencies, including self-destruct mechanisms, prevent that knowledge from falling into the covetous hands of lesser races. While their technology is beyond the grasp of human understanding, the Necrons' purpose seems brutally clear: they seek to cleanse the galaxy of upstart primitives and re-establish themselves as rulers.

NECRONS AT WAR

From vast crypt-fortresses, the burnished legions emerge into the dying light of a war-torn galaxy. The Necrons are an implacable foe, a steel sea that ripples with the crackling energy discharge of their gauss weaponry. Remorselessly they advance, unleashing precision volleys while remaining virtually impervious to return fire. Even those that fall rise again to join the silent march. Amidst the phalanxes drift giant mechanoid arachnids and vehicles of strange, macabre design. Canoptek Scarabs – metal insects that phase in and out of reality – descend in great swarms, while talon-limbed horrors and spectral assassins emerge from the shadows. Looming over all are the Monoliths, Obelisks and Tesseract Vaults, great floating engines of destruction. Even the shards of old star gods, the C'tan, now serve the Necrons. Beneath the direction of their Overlords, the Necrons remain single-mindedly focussed on one purpose – to reclaim the stars.

SAUTEKH DYNASTY

There are many dynasties of Necrons, some of which have not yet reawoken. The greatest of the arisen Necron empires is that of the Sautekh Dynasty. They are led by Imotekh the Stormlord, a peerless warrior and pitiless commander. Beneath his tactical mastery, the Sautekh legions have mercilessly carved themselves a new empire. Under Imotekh's aggressive strategies, his dynasty has reclaimed dozens of systems and united many disparate Necron worlds under its glorious banner. The crownworld – the phaeron's seat of power – is Mandragora, on the Eastern Fringe. It has always been Imotekh's wish to reunite all tomb worlds beneath his rule and nothing can deter his plans, not even rampant Daemon incursions. As the Great Rift opened, the Stormlord launched his Absorption Wars, a many-pronged campaign to seize dozens of tomb worlds awakened by the warp influx. Imotekh sought to conquer them before they could fully rise from their stasis slumber, ensuring the continued rise of the Sautekh.

DYNASTIES

For millennia, the Necron dynasties ruled the galaxy. Time and the Great Sleep, however, have taken an inevitable toll. Those dynasties that have managed to wake seek a new age of Necron domination.

Mephrit

The star-killers. Exotic energies are boldly displayed by the ranks of the soldiery of the Mephrit Dynasty. The captive light of suns burns within all of the weapons they unleash upon their foes.

Nihilakh

In times of antiquity, this dynasty built treasure worlds filled with wealth plundered from a thousand civilisations. Regal in war, the warriors of Nihilakh wear turquoise and gold as their dynastic colours.

Novokh

The crimson armour of Novokh is a legacy of many bloody victories. The dynasty's symbol reflects the core system cluster of their territory and the six wars of conquest that spread out from its heart.

Charnovokh

Ravaged by Tyranid hive fleets and with their tomb worlds defiled by the Imperium, the legions of Charnovokh cling defiantly to the edges of the Eastern Fringe, their dynasty hanging in the balance.

NECRON WARGEAR

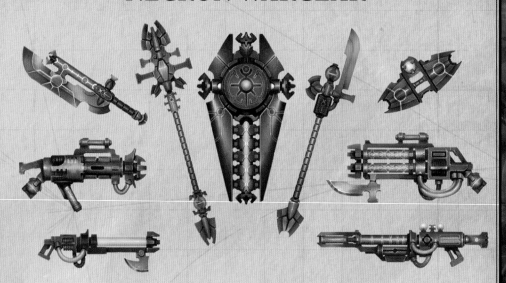

Necron technology is even less fathomable to Imperial Tech-Priests than the wonders wrought by the Aeldari. Gauss weapons are the most commonly carried weapon of the Necron soldiery. Unlike conventional Imperial energy weapons, a gauss projector does not deliver a laser burst or bolt of force, but instead emits a molecular disassembling beam capable of reducing flesh or armour to its constituent atoms. Other examples of Necron war-tech – quantum shielding, tesla and particle weaponry – are equally inexplicable in their operation.

ORKS

Over the long millennia the Orks have proven to be the most prolific and frequent threat to the Imperium. They can be found in warbands, clans and tribes spread across countless planets and space-borne fleets, sometimes even forming their own volatile empires.

Orks are a barbaric xenos race that infests the galaxy. No matter how far Mankind has travelled, they have found that Orks are either already there waiting for them or arrive soon after to launch their characteristically crude but devastating attacks. Orks are brutal, green-skinned creatures that revel in violence. So great is their need for conflict that, without a more obvious opponent with whom to do battle, the Orks will gladly fight amongst themselves. Their species is so numerous that, if the disparate groups were ever to cease hostilities with their own kind, the Orks would swiftly overrun the galaxy.

Size dominates Ork society, and the largest of their kind invariably lead them. On occasion, an especially hulking Ork Warboss will conquer several rival groups, forming the survivors into a massive army. What follows is known as a Waaagh! – part invasion and part holy war. During a Waaagh!, the greenskins will continue to flock to the leader's banner so long as they have something to conquer. Each new victory calls yet more greenskins from the surrounding region to join. A powerful Ork can lead a Waaagh! for a while, but to string together many victories and keep finding worthy targets to occupy the hordes takes an Ork with extreme cunning. Luckily, the combination of brawn and brains is rare in Orks, although when such a leader rises, the whole galaxy trembles.

THE CLANS

GOFFS

Orks of the Goff Clan are traditionalists in the greenskin fashion. They respect violence, especially at close quarters, and do not care for any frills or flash. Goff warbands are infantry-minded, and view other clans as soft. They dress predominantly in black decorated with dags or checks, and think camouflage fit only for cowards. Why hide from a foe?

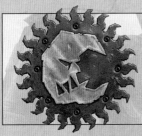

BAD MOONS

The richest of the Ork clans, the Bad Moons are known for having the best gear of war. Bad Moons Nobz tote gaudy back-banners and massive, kustomised weapons, and are followed around by mobs of scurrying grot servants. If it is loud and flashy, the ostentatious Bad Moons want it – they bristle with gold-plated firepower and shiny flair.

DEATHSKULLS

Plunderers without equal, the Deathskulls are noted for their ability to scrounge. They'll fight whole wars just so they can strip the battlefield clean. The salvage is then beaten into (or out of) shape by Meks, who then cobble it back together to create deadly new weaponry. A superstitious lot, Deathskulls believe blue is a lucky colour.

EVIL SUNZ

Orks belonging to the Evil Sunz Clan are irresistibly attracted to every conceivable kind of fast vehicle. Warbike mobs are especially popular, as are jetcraft pilots and super-charged Trukk crews. Evil Sunz wear red armour and often paint their machines red too, firmly believing in the old Ork adage that 'red ones go fasta'.

BLOOD AXES

Because of their habits of trading for Imperial wargear, wearing camouflage and using battle tactics, other Orks often distrust the Blood Axes. To add further contention, this clan favours the use of Kommandos, elite fighters that use dirty tricks like sneaking up on foes. Blood Axes ignore this derision, caring only for victory.

SNAKEBITES

Those Orks in the Snakebites Clan scorn technology, preferring 'da old ways'. Other clans consider them backward, but despite their feral, warpaint-wearing ways, the ferocity of the Snakebites' assaults is second to none. No clan breeds more dangerous squigs or grots than the Snakebites, and their camps teem with such creatures.

ODDBOYZ

PAINBOYZ

Part doctor, part dentist and part butcher, Painboyz are driven to perform exploratory surgery on living creatures. Sometimes they even do such operations when it is required. It is the Painboyz that 'fix' injuries to fellow greenskins (who luckily are quite hardy). The 'Doks', as they are also referred to, are often called upon to fuse the mechanical contraptions made by Mekboyz onto Orks. They work with a range of pincers, 'stabby bits', crude sawing instruments and rusty syringes that work as well in close combat as they do in operations. Indeed, most often it is all one and the same.

WEIRDBOYZ

The most deranged of all the greenskins are the Weirdboyz. These Orks are the most psychically attuned of their kind, and can absorb the wild mental energies of nearby Orks. They must find ways (often quite quickly) to vent the build-up of these volatile forces, resulting in Weirdboyz vomiting dangerous blasts of warp energy. It is on the battlefield where Ork emotions run highest, meaning Weirdboyz dragged to battle become infused with power of titanic proportions. If they can remain coherent (or are pointed in the right direction by their minders) this energy is unleashed upon the foe, bursting them apart.

MEKBOYZ

Ork Mekboyz inherently know how to fix all things mechanical using only the crudest of tools, a few well-placed kicks, and occasionally some mad gubbinz of their own invention. They are tinkerers extraordinaire, and they use a method of jury-rigging that is impossible for non-Orks to decipher. Rarely are inventions, war machines, or ramshackle vehicles built the same way twice. They go to war clanking with contraptions thought up by the Mekboyz – extra-shooty weapons, kustom force fields, or even the bizarre teleportation weapon known as the shokk attack gun.

ORK WEAPONS OF WAR

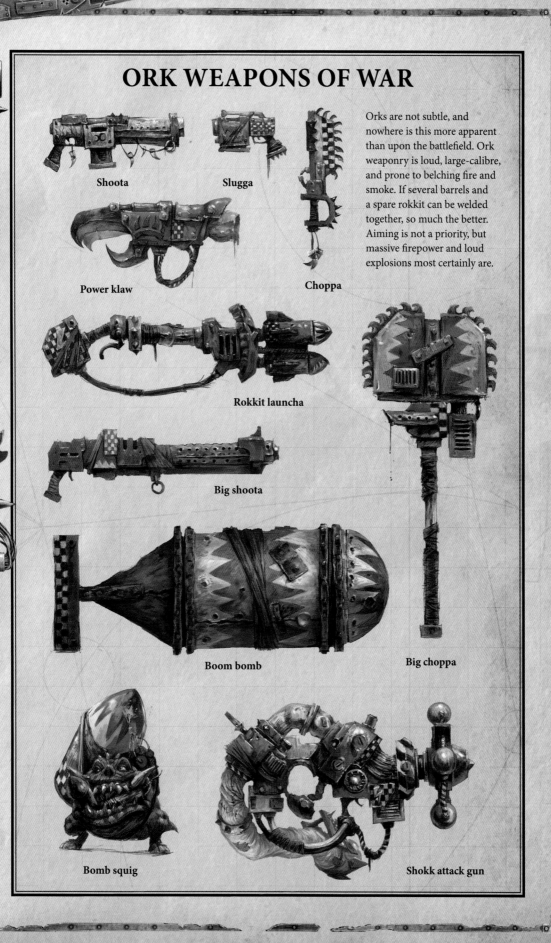

Shoota

Slugga

Power klaw

Choppa

Orks are not subtle, and nowhere is this more apparent than upon the battlefield. Ork weaponry is loud, large-calibre, and prone to belching fire and smoke. If several barrels and a spare rokkit can be welded together, so much the better. Aiming is not a priority, but massive firepower and loud explosions most certainly are.

Rokkit launcha

Big shoota

Boom bomb

Big choppa

Bomb squig

Shokk attack gun

T'AU EMPIRE

The T'au are an alien race that seeks to carve an empire into the havoc-filled Eastern Fringe. They mean to bring a new and enlightened way to a barbaric and unordered universe. Many races have already joined their cause and, in time, even those that resist are shown the benefits of T'au'va – the Greater Good.

On the Eastern Fringe of the galaxy, a new empire is growing. Ambitious and united in purpose, the xenos race known as the T'au has spread its 'enlightenment' across the stars. Although barely registering as a blip against the size of the sprawling Imperium, the rapid expansion of the T'au has drawn a predictably brutal response from the High Lords of Terra. As the T'au encroached on Imperial territory, several vast crusades were sent to halt the aggressive xenos colonisation. After purging the T'au colonies nearest their worlds, the Imperial forces crossed the Damocles Gulf, a space anomaly that had long formed a barrier to T'au expansion, to confront their foes. The relentless T'au, however, surprised the Imperial commanders with the strength of their defence, forcing a retreat. The T'au are a practical people, devoid of religion or psychic ability. Instead, they adhere to a rigid caste system, with each of the five castes (Fire, Earth, Air, Water and Ethereal) forming a subspecies within the race. Such segregation provides the clarity of purpose that allows

each member to fulfil their role within society – be it warrior, worker, pilot, or bureaucrat. The members of the ruling caste, the Ethereals, bind the other castes towards a common goal. It is they who steer the course of the T'au expansions, deciding which planets will be colonised, which aliens will be absorbed and which will be eliminated. Unlike the Imperium, the T'au attempt to sway other cultures, using diplomatic ploys to show the plentiful benefits of the Greater Good. Those who refuse to join the growing T'au Empire are quickly shown the error of their ignorance. The T'au military is fast, flexible, and well equipped with technologically advanced weaponry and agile battlesuits. With their organised methods of war and sophisticated weaponry, the T'au believe there is no foe they cannot defeat. Many aliens have already been conquered, and some, like the carnivorous Kroot and the insectoid Vespid, have been so enlightened they now send troops to assist further T'au expansions. The T'au hope to bring a progressive new age of light to the dark and savage galaxy.

'Our conquest is
inevitable, our ascension
a matter of time. Let
none who are wise deny
our destiny.'

- Aun'Va, Ethereal Supreme

SPHERES OF EXPANSION

The T'au Empire launched a new venture – the Fifth Sphere Expansion – as soon as the warp storms dissipated along the Eastern Fringe enough to allow such a thing. This endeavour followed hard on the heels of the ill-fated Fourth Sphere Expansion, which was lost at the time of the Great Rift.

The T'au are a dynamic race that have grown an empire in a relatively short time period. Their history – though merely a blink compared to that of the Imperium – has been marked by relentless colonisation efforts, known to them as spheres of expansion. Each of these great pushes ripples outwards from their core worlds, known as sept worlds, to colonise new systems. They conquer through trade and coercion, their battle-honed military always ready to step in as the final negotiators. The First Sphere Expansion ended when the T'au reached the limits of their ability to traverse space. Being a non-psychic race, the T'au have no understanding of the warp, so their star fleets travel at sub-light speeds. New technological innovations have steadily increased their range, allowing them to press ever further into the galaxy. Their Second and Third Spheres of Expansion were halted only due to the barrier of the Damocles Gulf and increased resistance from the Imperium of Mankind.

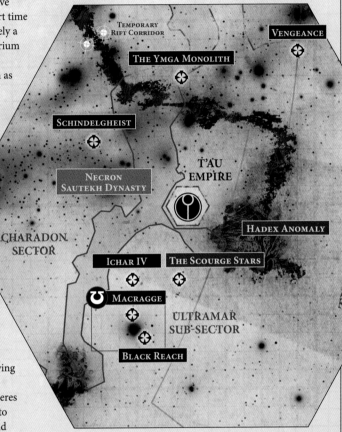

CONTINUOUS ADVANCEMENT

Unlike the Imperium of Mankind, the T'au Empire embraces new technology. Developed by the Earth caste, the Fire caste are supplied with advanced wargear, often further augmented with special-issue prototype weapons. T'au pulse, ion, and rail weapon technologies give their warriors a firepower advantage, both in terms of range and hitting power. All who choose to oppose the Greater Good learn to fear the deadly efficiencies of such weapons.

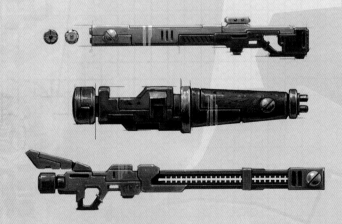

Vior'la Sept

One of the major first-phase septs, Vior'la is best known for its aggressive Fire Warriors.

T'au Sept

Home world of the T'au, this sept remains the capital and is the political centre of the T'au Empire.

Sa'cea Sept

Sa'cea is the most densely populated sept world. Its warriors are experts in urban warfare.

T'AU BATTLESUITS

At the apex of the advanced weaponry designed by the T'au are their battlesuits. Equipped with a wide variety of deadly weapon loadouts, the battlesuits combine offensive capability, armoured protection, and high manoeuvrability. Some bear repulsor jet engines granting them the ability to strike anywhere on a battlefield. Piloting such a battlesuit is the greatest honour for a Fire caste warrior, and before they are allowed to do so they must pass many trials.

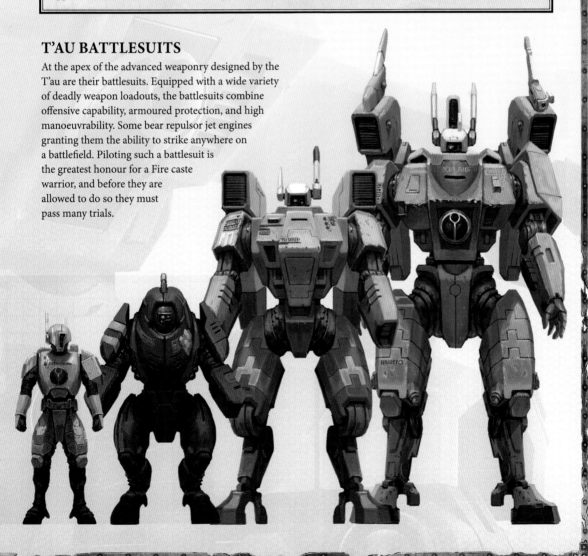

TYRANID HIVE FLEETS

Driven by an insatiable hunger, they come from beyond. They are drawn to galaxies teeming with life like predators on a blood scent. In their wake, they leave nothing behind. They are the Great Devourer, the Tyranids – a xenos race that seeks to strip down and absorb all living matter they come into contact with.

Beyond the edges of the Imperium lies the unspeakable cold of the intergalactic void. It is the great barrier that divides galaxy from galaxy, where grand vistas of space conspire to hold their secrets with inconceivable distances. Yet the void is not empty. An immeasurably ancient and exceedingly alien intelligence has emerged from that darkness, its many eyes drawn towards the bountiful lifeforms of the galaxy. From the void come the hive fleets, stretching out like impossibly vast tendrils, drifting in brooding silence. Once the remorseless shoals of the bio-ships detect a prey world, they close upon their target. There is no escape. When the Tyranids depart, they leave behind a barren rock scoured of anything that lives.

The Tyranid race comprises many different creatures all functioning as one, coordinated by the gestalt consciousness that is the Hive Mind. Each creature is linked by that monolithic sentience. On the battlefield, leader creatures serve as hubs to channel connections to the lesser swarms, synchronising their movements. It is this central intelligence that guides the Tyranid fleets towards prey planets, but it does more. So powerful are the emanations from the Hive Mind that they are accompanied by a smothering psychic phenomenon known to the Imperium's Astropaths as the Shadow in the warp. It is as if the darkness of the void is actively isolating worlds about to be consumed. The sight of an oncoming Tyranid invasion is one that few have witnessed and survived. Gigantic spores plummet down, splitting open to reveal broods of ferocious beasts. Swarms of scythe-limbed aliens move across the ground as one. Some carry grotesque living weapons capable of firing parasitic projectiles that chew into their targets' flesh. Stalker-organisms use perfect camouflage to ambush prey, winged monstrosities rain death, and the ground quakes as burrowing beasts tunnel up from below. Above all, towering behemoths stride upon multiple sets of legs unleashing bio-cannon blasts. Every Tyranid creature is a perfectly evolved killing machine, adapted for its role. Thus far, only their vanguard has reached the galaxy – the greater mass is still on its way.

A NEW MENACE

As the years pass, more Tyranid threats continue to enter the war-torn galaxy. Hive Fleets Hydra, Scylla, Charybdis and Kronus have thrust tendrils from out of the intergalactic void. Strangely, the initial invasions of Hydra seem to have bypassed other, more likely targets, instead seeking out splinters of previous Tyranid invasions in order to cannibalise them. Why the hive fleet would be adding to its growing biomass in this way remains a mystery.

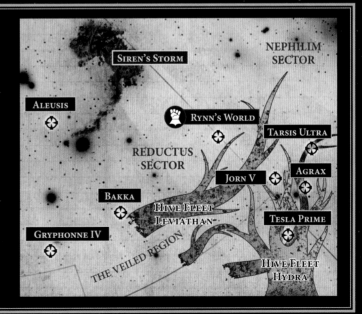

SIREN'S STORM

NEPHILIM SECTOR

ALEUSIS

RYNN'S WORLD

TARSIS ULTRA

REDUCTUS SECTOR

AGRAX

JORN V

BAKKA

HIVE FLEET LEVIATHAN

TESLA PRIME

GRYPHONNE IV

THE VEILED REGION

HIVE FLEET HYDRA

GENESTEALER CULTS

Insidious. Infectious. Hidden from sight, and walking openly, the Genestealer Cults have grown. They have spread their xenos corruption throughout the underbelly of the Imperium. They are patient, they bide their time – but when the moment is right, the uprising is as swift as it is merciless.

Sent out on seeding imperatives, Genestealers haunt space hulks, clamber aboard shuttles, and secrete themselves beneath the shadowy bulkheads of enormous starships. Many a crammed transport has unknowingly carried such lethal cargo, and in their hibernatory state, a Genestealer can even survive the cold vacuum of outer space. When a Genestealer reaches a world ripe for infection, it unfolds and begins its deadly work. Genestealers prefer heavily populated planets, especially hive worlds, where they can go into hiding, emerging from dark sewers to attack one human at a time. They do not kill, but implant a portion of their own biomass into their chosen host like a virus, turning them into xenos-worshipping followers. Soon, hybrids follow, monstrous crosses between Genestealers and humankind. So the cult grows. In the final stages, some hybrids – known as Neophytes – are merely pallid and bald, passing easily through the unhealthily overcrowded confines of their hive like wolves in sheep's clothing. Only when the brotherhood is strong enough do they strike. On the day of the great insurrection, secrecy is cast aside and the cult banners are lifted high. Surging from ambush, the Genestealer Cult attacks – inhumanly strong Aberrants, swarms of weapon-bearing Acolytes, and scuttling Purestrain Genestealers. Genestealer Cultists also usurp tanks and armoured vehicles to use against the foe. They are all led by the Genestealer Patriarch – the creature who started it all, since grown to gargantuan size and power. The slaughter that ensues is dreadful to behold.

SYMBOLS OF THE CULT UPRISINGS

Though only a handful of cults have been codified by the Ordo Xenos, data-harvests taken from Ghosar Quintus imply the presence of hundreds, perhaps thousands, in Ultima Segmentum alone. Each cult identifies its members by secret colours and hidden tattoos. By the time the cult banners are revealed, it is already too late.

ALIEN MENACE

From the lithe and deadly Aeldari to the ancient terror of the Necrons, from the technological supremacy of the T'au to the blade-limbed swarms of the Tyranids and the ramshackle savagery of the Orks, the xenos races of the Warhammer 40,000 galaxy are diverse and spectacular.

The Visarch

Yvraine, leader of the Ynnari

Combining the unparalleled discipline of the craftworld Aeldari with the depthless cruelty of the Drukhari, Ynnari warhosts bring the full fury of their ancient race to bear against their foes.

Eldrad Ulthran is amongst the greatest of his race's ancient Farseers. At the head of the warhosts of Ulthwé, this prescient arch-manipulator seeks to turn back the looming darkness and save his people from their final end.

Though their craftworld was fractured during the birth of Ynnead, the Swordwind of Biel-Tan still fight to eradicate the taint of the lesser races from a galaxy they believe to be theirs, and theirs alone.

The Wild Rider clans of Saim-Hann swoop into battle on skimming jetbikes, supported by squadrons of swift grav-tanks and agile combat aircraft. Speed and ferocity are their primary weapons, and they wield them with expert skill.

Alaitoc is famed for its Rangers, courageous Aeldari warriors who have strayed from the well-trodden paths of their people and journeyed far and wide across the stars.

Though they have common origins, the Aeldari of the craftworlds and those of Commorragh are still splintered parts of a once-great whole, and their irreconcilable differences often bring them into conflict with one another.

Breathtakingly swift, surpassingly deadly, the Harlequins of the Laughing God follow veiled agendas as they perform their deadly dances of war across the far-flung stars.

The Archons rule over the Drukhari Kabals, basking in the fear and pain of their unfortunate victims.

Monstrous and deformed, the warriors of the Haemonculus Covens are stitch-fleshed horrors from a madman's nightmare.

The soulless legions of the Nihilakh Dynasty advance towards the beleaguered Imperial lines, unleashing ancient weapons of incredible power designed to scour the lesser races from existence.

Commander Farsight is one of the greatest T'au war heroes who has ever lived. He is also hunted as a rebel by his own people.

Trazyn the Infinite is both a powerful war leader and an obsessive collector of esoteric weaponry and living curios.

The Fire caste are the warriors of the T'au Empire, fighting in close-knit infantry teams or piloting armoured battlesuits that possess the firepower to obliterate armies wholesale. The white-armoured warriors of Vior'la Sept are known for being especially hot-blooded examples of their already warlike caste.

Attacking in overwhelming waves of chitinous war-beasts, Hive Fleet Kraken seeks to bury the courageous T'au Fire Warriors in seething masses of slashing, biting monstrosities.

All-consuming tides of bio-engineered killing machines, the Tyranid hive fleets devour everything in their path and leave only death in their wake. Hive Fleet Leviathan is one of the most recent of these apocalyptically destructive swarms.

Upon the war-ravaged world of Armageddon, endless hordes of Orks followed Ghazghkull Thraka into battle. Though the Imperial defenders fought bravely, the ramshackle war engines and bellowing hordes of the greenskins won victory after victory.

ETERNITY OF WAR

In the grim darkness of the far future, there is only war. Like the players of some enormous game, the Dark Gods look out from the Realm of Chaos and move their pieces. Giants once more walk the stars, as the greatest of Daemons and Fallen Primarchs stride forth to do their masters' bidding. The very gates of hell have been opened, and the galaxy burns…

Everywhere, the foes of Humanity gathered, steeping themselves in the growing apocalypse. The Emperor's Realm was surrounded, besieged. No sub-sector, system or planet was immune from conflict. When all went dark, those planets fortunate enough to avoid invasion still felt war's touch. As Imperial citizens watched the stars disappear, rebellions rose. Some were led by those corrupted by Chaos, insidious traitors awaiting a sign from the Dark Gods. They betrayed their own species for false promises of power or material gain. Not all uprisings were the product of Chaos, however. On some Imperial worlds, fearful of sedition, the rulers became so repressive that civil strife was inevitable. Once the flickering beam of the Astronomican had returned to some parts of the galaxy, it brought with it another threat. As the Imperium broke down, aliens – whether barbaric plunderers, ancient powers, upstart usurpers, or voracious monsters – all came forwards. They too clamoured for the chance to tear their hunk of flesh from the carcass that was the Realm of Mankind.

Entities not seen, or glimpsed but briefly, during the long millennia stalked the stars once more. The most powerful Greater Daemons need to draw so much energy from the warp to stay manifest in reality that their presence in realspace tends to be relatively brief. The Great Rift's eruption, however, had sent tidal waves of unnatural energies to the furthest reaches of the galaxy, empowering even the greatest Daemons for longer and longer periods. And more terrors from beyond followed.

A new age of war and darkness was entered, plunging the Imperium and the entire galaxy into levels of war not seen since the zenith of the Horus Heresy. These campaigns, however, did not move in battlefronts, but erupted out of the roiling warp storms to wreak havoc before disappearing and turning up elsewhere, often halfway across the galaxy. Seeking to divide and conquer, the Chaos factions isolated swathes of the Imperium to pluck them off at their leisure. Old grudges were settled, while others used the mayhem to despoil the Imperium of Mankind for their own needs. Without plan or agenda beyond slaughter, the Red Tide – a carnage-filled crusade of wanton slaughter – launched a bloody path across the galaxy. Upon infernal battleships, the fallen Tech-Priests of the Dark Mechanicum stole forth from their hell-forge planets to scour the crippled Imperium for ancient archeotech, seeking the missing pieces to complete an unholy weapon of war, a terror not seen since the Age of Technology. Ahriman, Arch-Sorcerer of the Thousand Sons, brought terror raids to over three dozen planets, robbing their datascribes of precious knowledge before disappearing once again. From out of the Great Rift, each of the Dark Gods established their own strongholds, for secretly (and sometimes not so secretly) each coveted the whole of the galaxy for their own.

As hopeless as it seemed, the Imperium was not yet defeated. As the minions of the Dark Gods squabbled among themselves, bringing their endless battles from the Realm of Chaos with them into realspace, not all was lost. Eventually, the Emperor's Light could be seen once again, perhaps not as clearly, but it was visible nonetheless. And rumours of Primarchs returned to the galaxy gave many a sliver of hope – for his truest sons might yet bring victory as they had in days of legend.

RUTHLESSNESS IS THE KINDNESS OF THE WISE.

WAR ZONE: ULTRAMAR

Greedy eyes looked out from the roiling warp. They lingered long over the southern reaches of Ultima Segmentum. Nurgle wanted them for his own. He wished to lavish his gifts upon them, to watch their citizens sprout new growths and lament while other parts rotted and sloughed off.

The worlds of Ultramar were prosperous, well governed and aesthetically beautiful. It is no wonder that such a gem drew the eager eye of Nurgle. Wishing to annex those worlds directly into his own Garden in the Realm of Chaos, the Father of Plagues set his minions to the task. After the Great Rift tore reality and flooded warp energies into the galaxy, Nurgle deemed the time was ripe.

Where seeds of corruption had been planted, where the Plague That Walks, the Oozing Pox, and the Eyerot had decimated overcrowded hive worlds, there did Nurgle put forth his greatest efforts. As darkness closed over those worlds, new, virulent strains of those dreadful diseases started the cycle of death anew. This time, however, the cycle was completed, for there was life also. From the corpses of

the fallen burst countless Nurglings. In the devastation that ensued, Cults of Corruption summoned further aid. The following battles – known by the Imperium as the Plague Wars – ended when three systems to the galactic north of Ultramar were corrupted and turned into the Scourge Stars. Calling upon three of his greatest commanders, Nurgle tasked them with next conquering Ultramar.

ULTRAMAR INVADED

The first invaders to issue forth from the Scourge Stars were the Death Guard, led by their grim Primarch, Mortarion. His meticulously planned seven-part campaign would bring untold ruination to all of Ultramar. So began the first part – the War of Flies – including the assault of the Three Planets, the besieging of the hive world of Ardium, and

the Creeping Doom offensive against Espandor and Drohl. Virus bombardments preceded the Death Guard. Once-gloried hive cities became pits, and agri worlds became flyblown wastes. The attacks were slow but relentless, wearing down the Ultramarines and their auxilia. With communications severed and relief forces cut off by fresh warp storms, the defenders

were hard-pressed in a hundred locations across Ultramar. Then, Roboute Guilliman returned from his galaxy-spanning crusade. Tactically, Mortarion and his fellow commanders now found themselves evenly matched, their offensives blocked at every turn by the Ultramarines and their Primarch's precise counter-attacks. A new stage of the war had begun.

MACRAGGE

In the early stages of the invasion of Ultramar, many different strikes were levelled at the capital world of Macragge. Whether Mortarion planned these events to probe the defences of the Ultramarines' home world, or merely aimed to tie down as many of the Imperial forces as he could, is unknown. All of the battles were short, sharp affairs, such as rapid strikes from Plague Drone forces, or cultist attacks attempting to deliver pox bombs into the heavily guarded defence networks. Whatever Mortarion's intent, the number and variety of the attacks steadily drained both morale and resources from Macragge until Primarch Guilliman returned and seized the initiative with his own strikes into Chaos-held territories.

THE REALM OF ULTRAMAR

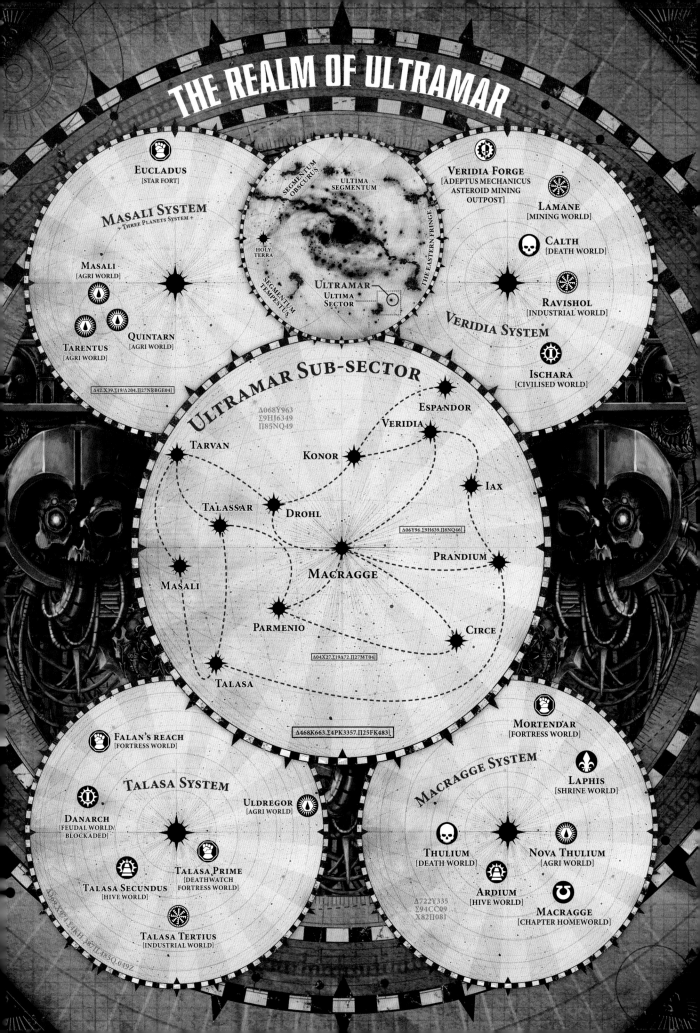

EUCLADUS
[STAR FORT]

MASALI SYSTEM
+ THREE PLANETS SYSTEM +

SEGMENTUM OBSCURUS
ULTIMA SEGMENTUM

HOLY TERRA

SEGMENTUM TEMPESTUS

ULTRAMAR
Ultima Sector

THE EASTERN FRINGE

VERIDIA FORGE
[ADEPTUS MECHANICUS ASTEROID MINING OUTPOST]

LAMANE
[MINING WORLD]

MASALI
[AGRI WORLD]

TARENTUS
[AGRI WORLD]

QUINTARN
[AGRI WORLD]

CALTH
[DEATH WORLD]

RAVISHOL
[INDUSTRIAL WORLD]

VERIDIA SYSTEM

ISCHARA
[CIVILISED WORLD]

Δ42.X39.Σ19/Δ204.Π27NRBGE04

ULTRAMAR SUB-SECTOR

Δ068Ϋ963
Σ9HJ6349
Π85NQ49

TARVAN

KONOR

ESPANDOR

VERIDIA

TALASSAR

DROHL

IAX

Δ06Y96.Σ9H639.Π8NQ46

MACRAGGE

MASALI

PRANDIUM

PARMENIO

CIRCE

Δ04X27.Σ19Δ72.Π27MT04

TALASA

Δ468K663.Σ4PK3357.Π25FK483

FALAN'S REACH
[FORTRESS WORLD]

MORTEND'AR
[FORTRESS WORLD]

TALASA SYSTEM

ULDREGOR
[AGRI WORLD]

MACRAGGE SYSTEM

LAPHIS
[SHRINE WORLD]

DANARCH
[FEUDAL WORLD/
BLOCKADED]

TALASA SECUNDUS
[HIVE WORLD]

TALASA PRIME
[DEATHWATCH FORTRESS WORLD]

THULIUM
[DEATH WORLD]

NOVA THULIUM
[AGRI WORLD]

ARDIUM
[HIVE WORLD]

Δ722Ϋ335
Σ94CC09
X82Π081

MACRAGGE
[CHAPTER HOMEWORLD]

TALASA TERTIUS
[INDUSTRIAL WORLD]

Δ362X974.Σ9H.Π38.Π-185Q.049Z

THE MARCH OF PLAGUES

In attacking Ultramar, Mortarion was not alone. Two other commanders led massive armies out from the Scourge Stars, each seeking to win the contaminated glory of Nurgle's favour.

Ku'gath Plaguefather, a favoured Great Unclean One, led the Bubonicus legions into Ultramar. Typhus, First Captain of the Death Guard, commanded a Plague Fleet, a dilapidated rot-armada packed with Renegades, cultists and his own loyal Death Guard. Ku'gath's Daemon legions ravaged the Tartella System, which lay between the Scourge Stars and Ultramar, before manifesting on the garden world of Iax, an ideal place to nurture new diseases. The Plague Fleet, meanwhile, destroyed three of the six massive star fortresses that stood sentinel over Ultramar's shipping lanes. Even with Guilliman's return, the attacks were too many and too widespread for the defenders to contain. The timely arrival of the Ultramarines' successor Chapters, however, along with reinforcements from several forge worlds, allowed the Primarch to attempt to regain the initiative. Guilliman launched the Spear of Espandor counter-attack, hoping to buy the forces of the Imperium more time.

ESPANDOR

Mortarion's Creeping Doom offensive on the cardinal world of Espandor initially made great advances. When Guilliman returned, however, he ordered a new defensive plan to slow the attacks. As the battle turned into a stalemate, the Primarch launched a series of system-wide counter-attacks.

DEADLOCKED

Across Ultramar, the Plague Wars escalated. Guilliman's brilliant counter-attacks staved off defeat, allowing him to stabilise fronts across several systems. The largest battles of the war, however, were still to come.

With Mortarion's Creeping Doom offensive mired in continent-spanning trench warfare in the Espandor System, the Daemon Primarch shifted his focus, joining forces with Ku'gath. Together, they sent their surviving forces to Parmenio and Iax simultaneously. On Parmenio, the largest armour and Titan battle of the war took place over the shell-ridden Plains of Hecatone. At the battle's height, Roboute Guilliman struck against Ku'gath's vanguard, slaying his lieutenant, Septicus, and shattering his Plague Guard. In space, Galatan – Ultramar's largest star fortress – attempted to provide support but was boarded by the Plague Fleet. Massive casualties ensued, including the loss of the Novamarines' Chapter Master. The Ultramarines and their auxilia made gains on Parmenio, and Guilliman led a relief force to Iax. Once a verdant garden world, it was in ruins when Primarch met Primarch. Guilliman confronted Mortarion, fighting to a deadlock before the Death Guard withdrew under cover of a virus bomb.

IAX BEFOULED

The final battle of the Plague War was fought at First Landing, on Iax. Before the ruined citadel the Death Guard held the upper hand, their relentless assault all but unstoppable, when Mortarion was summoned back to the Scourge Stars to defend his holdings at the onset of the War in the Rift.

FORCES OF THE IMPERIUM

The defence of Ultramar was really a tale of three parts: the initial losses, where the defenders gave ground before the Death Guard onslaught; the stabilisation with the return of Primarch Guilliman; and finally, the seizing of the initiative with the Primarch's counter-attacks along with the final battle.

DEFENDERS OF ULTRAMAR

SPEAR OF ESPANDOR

Ultramarines	7 Companies
Genesis Chapter	6 Companies
Aurora Chapter	5 Companies
Silver Eagles	5 Companies
Sons of Orar	3 Companies
Mortifactors	3 Companies
Knights Cerulean	3 Companies
Varied Astartes Chapters*	14 Companies
Ultramar Auxilia	9 Regiments
Order of the Valorous Heart	2 Preceptories
Grey Knights	Unknown
Sisters of Silence	Unknown

*Many Chapters arrived to lend aid to Ultramar and to fight beneath Roboute Guilliman. The Primarch and Lord Commander of the Imperium organised those Adeptus Astartes in less-than-company numbers into battle-brother battalions, using them for special missions and to shore up the Ultramar Auxilia.

THE PLAINS OF HECATONE

Varied Astra Militarum	18 Regiments
Ultramar Auxilia	21 Regiments
Ultramar Super-heavy Armour	3 Regiments
Ultramarines	3 Companies
Ultramarines Neophytes	Unknown
White Scars	3 Companies
Legio Oberon	Demi-Legion
Legio Atarus	Demi-Legion
Legio Fortis	Demi-Legion
House Terryn	3 Households
House Hawkshroud	2 Households
House Konor	2 Households
Legio Cybernetica	3 Cohorts
Skitarii	5 Legions

DEFENCE OF GALATAN

Novamarines	5 Companies
Ultramar Auxilia	12 Regiments
Deathwatch	21 Kill Teams
Grey Knights	Unknown

BATTLE OF FIRST LANDING

Roboute Guilliman	Primarch
Ultramarines	8 Companies
Novamarines	3 Companies
Silver Eagles	3 Companies
Howling Griffons	6 Companies
Libators	2 Companies
Ultramar Auxilia	21 Regiments
Astra Militarum	15 Regiments
Legio Praetor	Demi-Legion
Skitarii	5 Legions

'Let them flee beneath cover of their virus bomb. By the Emperor, they shall be repaid tenfold for the evils they have wrought upon Ultramar.'

- Roboute Guilliman

FORCES OF CHAOS

The invasion of Ultramar began as separate spearheads, but as the campaigns slowed, Mortarion and Ku'gath formed an alliance. Unlike the Champions of the other Dark Gods, Nurgle's lieutenants were more capable of cooperation. This was not the case, however, between Typhus and Mortarion.

INVADERS OF ULTRAMAR

BUBONICUS FORCE INFECTUS (IAX)

Ku'gath Plaguefather	Greater Daemon
Septicus	Greater Daemon
Plague Guard	Legion
Legions of the Three-Eyed Fly	7 Legions
Poxdroners	7 Legions
Bouncing Tide	Nurgling Horde
Slimepack	Beast of Nurgle Warherd
Sporewalker	Colossal Beast
Cult of Renewal	Seercult
Cult of Blessed Protrusion	Warcult

SIEGE BRINGERS (ARDIUM)

Poxguard	7 Companies
Dontorian Heavy Artillery	4 Batteries
Chem Squads	3 Companies
Contamination Corp	2 Companies
Dark Magi	Coven
Legio Pestis	Demi-Legion
Infernal Devices	3 Engines
Plague Zombies	Unknown

WAR OF FLIES CAMPAIGN

Death Guard	5 Plague Companies
Drudgewalkers	7 Plaguebearer Legions
Zzzzartap's Circus	7 Drone Wings
Flylords	4 Companies
Winged Rotflies	Mutated Fly Swarm

THE PLAINS OF HECATONE

Death Guard	4 Plague Companies
Children of Blight	12 Companies
Befoulers	7 Claw Corps
Rot Reapers	4 Companies
Blight Guard	14 Regiments
Filth Engines	7 Regiments
Steel Tide	15 Companies
Ironhulks	12 Regiments
Plaguereapers	3 Companies
Dontorian Heavy Artillery	2 Batteries
Seven Blights	7 Blight Towers
Legio Mortis	Demi-Legion
House Slughorn	3 Households

FINAL BATTLE OF IAX

Mortarion	Daemon Primarch
Death Guard	Traitor Legion
The Scabbed	Chapter
Heltrenchers	5 Companies
Epidemius	Proctor of Pestilence
Sloughskins	7 Plaguebearer Legions
Carrion Legion	7 Plaguebearer Legions
Talliers of the Dead	7 Plaguebearer Legions
House Drear	3 Households
The Anointed	Warcult
Keepers of the Cauldron	Seercult
Infumers	3 Chem Legions
Slimehorn Legions	7 Pestigor Legions

'Bursting with life. Bursting with life. Bursting with life.'

- War Drone of the Sloughskins

THE FALL OF CADIA

At the culmination of Abaddon's Thirteenth Black Crusade, the Cicatrix Maledictum had all but consumed Cadia. With the great pylons toppled by Abaddon's conquering hordes and the colossal warp storm of the Eye of Terror no longer held at bay, the dread powers of Chaos ravaged the planet beyond recovery. And still the neighbouring worlds and systems were defiant.

Had Cadia not been famous for holding so long against the odds, it is likely the other planets in the system would have capitulated or given up almost immediately. No normal world could stand in the face of the horrendous, sanity-devouring armies that descended upon the Cadian Gate in such terrifying measure. However, the wider systems of Cadia, Belis Corona, and Agripinaa stood fast.

Perhaps, just as a veteran can lead lesser men to deeds of great heroism, Cadia had inspired those worlds around it to defend every nation and city to the last bullet. Perhaps Cadia's surviving soldiery lent strength through their hunger for retribution. Perhaps those battered by the storm simply fought for survival. Whatever the reason, the defenders of the Cadian Gate resolved to uphold the virtues of its lynchpin world come what may.

In the confusion of outright war, the hordes of Chaos began to turn upon themselves. Though they were ascendant, their ultimate conquest had yet to be clinched. Rival warlords, both mortal and daemonic, clashed over the spoils of victories not yet won. The Imperial defenders were quick to capitalise on each strategic misstep,

for many were veterans of the wars upon Cadia, and they knew how to goad a fractious enemy into overextending its reach. From dissolution came destruction. Day by day the Imperial armies clawed back a semblance of control. Soon the war zone was in contention once more, the dread stranglehold of Chaos loosened by the sheer determination of the Astra Militarum and the vengeful fury of the Space Marines. Each new dawn was greeted by a scattering of ships from the Great Exodus, those fortunate souls who had braved the empyrean tempests and lived to tell of it. Again and again the fighting escalated, the fires of war that had burned Cadia to cinders roaring to life anew upon the other worlds of the Cadian System, as well as those of the Belis Corona and Agripinaa Systems.

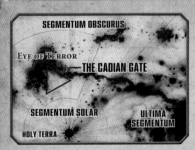

CADIAN SYSTEM

SEGMENTUM OBSCURUS

EYE OF TERROR

THE CADIAN GATE

SEGMENTUM SOLAR

ULTIMA SEGMENTUM

HOLY TERRA

KASR PARTOX (FORTRESS WORLD)

MACHARIA (MILITARISED HIVE WORLD)

SOLAR MARIATUS (FORTRESS WORLD)

CADIA (LYNCHPIN FORTRESS WORLD)

KOROLIS (PROMETHIAN PRODUCTION FACILITY)

PROSAN (HOSTILE ENVIRONMENT TRAINING FACILITY)

KASR SONNEN (FORTRESS WORLD)

KASR HOLN (FORTRESS WORLD)

VIGILATUM (NAVAL TRAINING WORLD)

ST. JOSMANE'S HOPE (DESTROYED)

THE CADIAN GATE

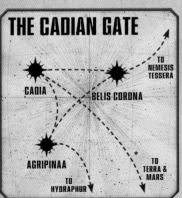

TO NEMESIS TESSERA

CADIA

BELIS CORONA

AGRIPINAA

TO TERRA & MARS

TO HYDRAPHUR

BELIS CORONA SYSTEM

GELDARIS (PURGED)

BELIS CORONA (NAVAL DOCK)

CORWYN BELT (RADIOACTIVE ASTEROID FIELD)

MALUSOIR (DEATH WORLD)

LAURENTIX (CONTACT LOST)

ANTAR (FIRE WORLD)

BELISIMAR (CLASSIFIED)

BAIRSTEN PRIME (DURALIUM ORE MINING WORLD)

AGRIPINAA SYSTEM

CHAEROS (INDUSTRIAL WORLD)

AGRIPINAA (FORGE WORLD)

NARSINE (HIVE WORLD)

ORAX (MINING WORLD)

AURENT (NAVAL WAY STATION)

URATH (DEATH WORLD)

[AGRIPINAA SYSTEM CORE WORLDS SHOWN]

While the planet Cadia was the main target of Abaddon's invasion, the region was heavily built-up with defences. Every planet was heavily garrisoned and well equipped with orbital sentry stations and vast arrays of defence lasers, rockets and ion shields. Yet with innumerable warp storms raging, the systems around the Cadian Gate found it extremely risky to deploy reinforcements to aid one another, or even to use their many war fleets to drive off the attacking hordes. Still, despite being outnumbered many times over, each of the fallen systems and planets reaped a heavy toll upon the Chaos attackers, none more so than the fortress worlds of Solar Mariatus, Partox, and finally Cadia herself.

ARMIES OF THE IMPERIUM

The final battles of Cadia had prevented the disaster from being total. Though Cadia itself was lost, the defence of Kasr Kraf held up Abaddon's final assault, and the mayhem that followed allowed a great number of troops and military assets to reach the Imperial evacuation zone and depart.

THE LAST DEFENCE OF CADIA

DEFENCE OF KASR TRUNCH

Cadian Shock Troops	127 Regiments
Cadian Kasrkin	65 Regiments
Cadian Youth Corp	12 Regiments
Tithed Astra Militarum	18 Regiments
Skitarii	5 Legions
Siege Auxilia Corps	528 Batteries
Legio Metalica	Demi-Legion
Order of the Bloody Rose	2 Preceptories
Angels of Absolution	3 Companies
Black Consuls	4 Companies
Varied Astartes Chapters*	4 Companies

TRUNCH COUNTER-ATTACK

Black Consuls	6 Companies
Watchguards	6 Companies
Varied Astartes Chapters*	12 Companies
Officio Assassinorum	Classified

The Cadian Gate was guarded by the Astartes Praeses but also by elements of 21 other Chapters deployed across the sector.

THE LONG RETREAT

Cadian Shock Troops	41 Regiments
Cadian Kasrkin	16 Regiments
Zenonian Free Companies	9 Companies
Tithed Astra Militarum	12 Regiments
Dhonovar Heavy Armour	5 Companies
Legio Cybernetica	3 Cohorts
Order of the Ebon Chalice	3 Preceptories
Hallicon Armoured	5 Regiments
Ordo Reductor	Demi-Legion
Legio Ignatum	Legion

HIGH-ORBIT OFFENSIVE

Novamarines	4 Companies
Reclaimers	3 Companies
Excoriators	3 Companies
Cerulean Guard	3 Companies
Iron Hands	2 Companies
Varied Astartes Chapters*	7 Companies

All the Adeptus Astartes assets were stripped from Mos Khazner's defence in an attempt to retake the orbital batteries. Their success allowed the Long Retreat.

CASTELLAN'S LAST STAND

Cadian Shock Troops	99 Regiments
Cadian Kasrkin	6 Regiments
Brazen Claws	3 Companies
Black Consuls	2 Companies
Centurio Ordinatus	4 Ordinatus
Legio Gryphonicus	Demi-Legion
Freeblades	Unknown
Skitarii	3 Legions
Fort Drokz Penal Legions	4 Legions
House Krast	2 Households
Legion of the Damned	Unknown
Relictors	2 Companies
Masque of the Hidden Path	9 Troupes
Varied Astartes Chapters*	5 Companies

++Transmission: The last ship – *Pride of Cadia* – is away. Repeat, the last transport is away. May the Emperor protect us.++

FORCES OF CHAOS

Abaddon led the final assault force against Cadia in person. With him came the legions of the hellish Eye of Terror, the manifold hosts of the Dark Gods amassed under a single banner. The cause that united them was not just the destruction of the Imperium, but the demise of the material realm itself.

FINAL ASSAULT UPON CADIA

ABADDON'S VANGUARD

Black Legion	Traitor Legion
Iron Warriors	Traitor Legion
World Eaters	5 Warbands
Emperor's Children	5 Hedonistic Hosts
Night Lords	3 Warbands
Death Guard	3 Plague Companies
Alpha Legion	Unknown
Word Bearers	5 Companies
Legio Mortis	Demi-Legion

RED LEGIONS

Khan'zhar the Red	Exalted Greater Daemon
Bloodguard	8 Greater Daemons
Redhost	8 Legions
Fellblades	8 Legions
Kaghrexx's Destroyers	8 Legions
Khârn the Betrayer	Legend
Gorehands	5 Companies
Blood Engines	Armour Battalion
Skullcorps	18 Regiments
Bloodemption	Cult

PLAGUE ARMIES

Slogoth Poxbelly	Exalted Greater Daemon
Drub'sla Plaguehost	7 Legions
Three-Eyed Tolltakers	7 Legions
Blightwalkers	7 Legions
Nurgling Tide	Uncountable
The Tainted	7 Companies
The Horned	Pestigor Legion
The Risen	Plague Zombies
Ogryn Brutepox	3 Companies
The Stigmatus Convent	Entire Cult
The Viscous	Entire Cult

THE HOST IRIDESCENT

M'katchnar	Exalted Greater Daemon
Triumvirate of Arcanzarr	Daemon Coven
Scintillating Host	9 Legions
Legions of Shimmerlak	9 Legions
Unkbolt Conflock	9 Tzaangor Warflocks
The Scourged	4 Companies
Eagles Iridescent	3 Companies
Kabal of Umbra	Entire Cult

THE DECADENT HORDE

Sidroh the Sinuous	Exalted Greater Daemon
The Writhing Host	6 Legions
The Undulators	6 Legions
Violators	5 Warbands
Children of Torment	3 Warbands
Pain Armoured Brigade	2 Sonic Companies
The Hedonastic	Entire Cult
Tentacled Behemoth	Warp Monster

THE DAMNED

As befits Abaddon's cruelty and meticulous planning, thirteen massive transports of combat-drugged mutants, wretches, zombies and Chaos Spawn were crash-landed into the ruined city of Kasr Kharkovan, ensuring that many of the final assaults were performed by the least storied among his armies.

'Destroy it all. Do not stop until it is ruins. Let it become a monument to death.'

WAR ZONE: STYGIUS

In the wake of the Great Rift, Tzeentch looked upon his brothers. Without plan or agenda, Khorne and Slaanesh were glutting themselves on slaughter and torment, consumed by their rampages, but when Tzeentch saw Nurgle corrupting a whole realm, he grew jealous, seeking as ever to conspire against him, but also wishing to seize star systems for his own. So did the Architect of Fate put a million plans in motion. The Crystal Stars intrigued Tzeentch, as did the Shrouded Zone. It was the Stygius Sector, however, that he would attempt to claim first. It was in Segmentum Obscurus, near the Eye and cut off from the Emperor's Light. There, entropy raged the fiercest, and amidst the maelstrom of unnatural energies the tightly packed pattern of nine-times-nine star systems called out irresistibly to Tzeentch.

OPENING PHASES

The war began with cult uprisings across a score of planets. Although the Noctis Aeterna had long since ended in the galactic south, the sectors of the Imperium Nihilus were still wracked with frequent warp storms. Each planet was isolated, a perfect atmosphere for the Changeling to play his many duplicitous roles. Only when each world was seething with rebellion did invasion follow. Sweeping out of the warp rifts came Magnus the Red and his Thousand Sons, the Greater Daemon M'Kachen and its Great Changehost, and the Coven of Nine, each leading an army of Renegades, Daemons, and cultists. Three of the star systems were swiftly conquered, as the arcane assaults were too much for the Imperial defenders. Of those worlds attacked, only the benighted hive world of Mordian held out.

COUNTER-ATTACK

As storms shifted and revealed the weakest flickering of the Astronomican, relay networks sent out a slew of distress signals. Several Chapters of Adeptus Astartes and Skitarii Legions answered. Daring only short jumps through the warp, these forces arrived too late – seven sub-sectors had already fallen into Chaos hands. The battles to stave off the invasion and retake the fallen planets were epic in size and savagery. In a long campaign, the siege of Mordian was finally relieved. This was followed by six major clashes in the Dhobash System, where the Thousand Sons met the Space Wolves amidst crystal terraforming on Tarkan. Initial Imperial gains were soon offset, however, and only the unlooked-for arrival of an Aeldari warhost on the ice world of Rimenok staved off further Imperial disaster.

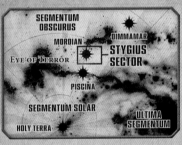

STYGIUS SECTOR

TO CYPRA MUNDI
TO DIMMAMAR
KHRAVOS
MORDIAN
URTEK
DHOBASH
PRISMATA
SALAMAR
TO PISCINA

MORDIAN SYSTEM

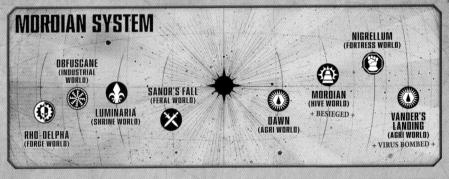

NIGRELLUM
(FORTRESS WORLD)

OBFUSCANE
(INDUSTRIAL WORLD)

LUMINARIA
(SHRINE WORLD)

SANOR'S FALL
(FERAL WORLD)

MORDIAN
(HIVE WORLD)
+ BESIEGED +

DAWN
(AGRI WORLD)

VANDER'S LANDING
(AGRI WORLD)
+ VIRUS BOMBED +

RHO-DELPHA
(FORGE WORLD)

DHOBASH SYSTEM

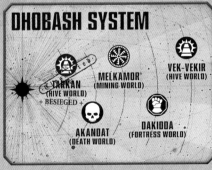

TARKAN
(HIVE WORLD)
+ BESIEGED +

MELKAMOR
(MINING WORLD)

VEK-VEKIR
(HIVE WORLD)

AKANDAT
(DEATH WORLD)

DAKIODA
(FORTRESS WORLD)

PRISMATA SYSTEM

HUYGEN
(MINING WORLD)

HELIOTRAX
(ARCHIVE WORLD)

SAPHYRE
(AGRI WORLD)

KALIDOS
(HIVE WORLD)

CHROMA
(DEATH WORLD)

AMARANTHUS
(FACTORY WORLD)

War in the Stygius Sector was rendered hellish by the waxing power of Tzeentch. Temporal anomalies flowed from the roiling storms of the Great Rift, hurling entire warfleets far into the past or future. Worlds shifted place or even disappeared – the 44th Necromundan 'Spirehawks' were lost when they commenced a combat drop on the world of Dakidda, only for it to vanish into a sucking empyric vortex. Even on the ground, day became night, gravity and time writhed like pained animals, and the dead rose as ghosts to torment the living.

ARMIES OF THE IMPERIUM

A hastily prepared relief effort, the Stygius Crusade was not well enough supplied nor of sufficient numbers to defeat the combination of Daemon and Traitor Legions arrayed against them. The initial headway won by the ferocity of the Adeptus Astartes' assaults could not be sustained.

STYGIUS CRUSADE

MORDIAN DEFENDERS

Mordian Iron Guard	26 Regiments
Tetrarchs Guard	12 Regiments
Mordian Defence Force	18 Regiments
Mordian Penal Battalions	3 Regiments
Mordian Super-heavy Battalion	5 Companies
Astropathic Corps	3 Companies
Pressed Hive Gangs	Unknown
Nigrellum Guard	8 Regiments
The Ordo Xenos Contingent	Unknown
The Ordo Hereticus Contingent	Unknown
The Ordo Malleus Contingent	Unknown

MORDIAN RELIEF FORCE

Space Wolves	9 Great Companies
Iron Hands	7 Companies
Dark Angels	6 Companies
Angels of Redemption	3 Companies
Skitarii	5 Legions
Legio Cybernetica	2 Cohorts
House Mundast	2 Households

ASSAULT ON TARKAN

Space Wolves	7 Great Companies
Iron Hands	5 Companies
Dark Angels	4 Companies
Sons of Medusa	3 Companies
Tarkan Longrifles	10 Regiments
Tarkan Roughriders	1 Company
Mordian Iron Guard	7 Regiments
Varied Astra Militarum	12 Regiments
Tarkan Brutes	Manufactorum Enforcers

OPERATION PRISMATA

Space Wolves	2 Great Companies
Iron Hands	5 Companies
Brazen Claws	4 Companies
Dark Angels	4 Companies
Angels of Vengeance	5 Companies
Consecrators	5 Companies
Sisters of Silence	Unknown
Grey Knights	Unknown

DISASTER AT RIMENOK

Rimenok Ice Warriors	12 Regiments
Rimenok Heavy Armour	3 Companies
Rimenok Beast Trainers	1 Company
The Faithful	Zealot Mob
Mordian Iron Guard	5 Regiments
Space Wolves	4 Great Companies
Iron Hands	3 Companies
Dark Angels	3 Companies

ALLIES FROM ULTHWÉ

Seer Council	Coven
Black Storm	4 Warhosts
Lileath's Blade	1 Skyhost
Serpent Striking	1 Aspect Warhost
Duality of Purpose	2 Revenant Titans

++Transmission: Attention Men of the Imperium. We are the Seer Council of Ulthwé. We broadcast on these frequencies to tell you the future. Your foe Magnus has read it also. There can be no victory here. Our Strike Force will cover your retreat. Martyrdom here serves no purpose save the enemy's.++

FORCES OF CHAOS

Charged with invading an entire sector of Imperial space, the eleven different army groups wove a pattern of attacks and advances that was well coordinated and seamless. Guided by mighty Sorcerers and oracles, it was not long before a new realm in realspace was carved out for Tzeentch.

CONQUERORS OF A NEW REALM

SIEGE OF MORDIAN

Coven of Nine	6 Exalted Sorcerers
Coven of Many Eyes	Sorcerer Coven
Benedictian Guard	13 Regiments
Nochfell Black Guard	Unknown
Night Lords	5 Warbands
Knights of the Silver Tower	3 Companies
Oracles of Change	Warband
Engines Arcana	12 Batteries
Spellcannon of Tlaxx	3 Batteries
Conflagral Host	Flamer Legion
Skyscreamers	3 Aerial Legions
Capering Cohorts	9 Legions
Cracklehost of T'zarr	9 Legions
Morphius Conflock	9 Tzaangor Warflocks
Pact of Nine Promises	Seercult
Masked Brotherhood	Warcult
Warpchild	Colossal Summoned Entity
Cult of the Whispered Word	Unknown
Reign of Lies	Subversive Division
The Grand Illusion	Planetwide Spell

CONQUERORS OF DHOBASH

Magnus the Red	Daemon Primarch
Thousand Sons	Traitor Legion
Host of a Thousand Names	9 Legions
Congregation of Flame	9 Legions
Unbound	9 Legions
House Chromatic	9 Households
Doom Wing	5 Wings
Talons Iridescent	5 Wings
Dark Mechanicum	6 Legions
Bastions Crystalline	9 Fortresses

PRISMATA RITUAL

Coven of Nine	2 Exalted Sorcerers
Cult of Bluefire	Seercult
Cult of Coldflame	Seercult
Changebringers	4 Companies
Ploggcha Conflock	9 Tzaangor Warflocks
Dark Mechanicum	3 Legions
Legio Proditor	Legion
House Arcanus	3 Households

SLAUGHTER AT RIMENOK

Thousand Sons	Traitor Legion
Kairos Fateweaver	Greuter Daemon
League of Fate	Lord of Change Coven
Banner of Many Eyes	9 Legions
Talons of Change	9 Legions
Mutagenics	9 Legions
House Chromatic	9 Households
Warriors Resplendent	5 Companies
Talons Iridescent	5 Wings
Traitors of Tarkan	5 Regiments
Coven of Disbelief	Warcult
Bolts Arcanite	Warcult
Conjurers of Fear	Seercult
Burning Idol	Arcane Effigy

++All things are mutable... Stars, Time, Vengeance. The Dark Stars shall be ours... And nine times nine are their number.++

- Regardless of what was sent, this was the only astropathic message receivable in the Stygius Sector

THE BLOOD CRUSADE

In celebration of the great conquests that were sure to come, Khorne bellowed. That roar shook the galaxy, sending further splits in reality cracking across its riven middle. His followers – from Daemon legions to brutish beasts to violent-minded hive cultists – all took up that call to arms. Riding new crests of the warp storms known as the Blood Waves, the Daemon legions erupted from the Cicatrix Maledictum, bringing new orgies of slaughter across the galaxy. Thus began the Blood Crusade. The red-raged armies did not seek out destinations. Instead, the gore-slavering fiends merely rode where the storms took them, materialising upon a planet to unleash carnage, and leaving when the tempests moved beyond. Eight distinct spearheads drove out into the galaxy in all directions, and as blood-trails draw in predators, so too did the Blood Crusade. Renegades, cultists, the criminally violent – all were drawn towards this unbound rage. Tomb worlds fell, Imperial forge worlds became abattoirs, and Tyranid hive fleets were eradicated. In some cases, entire populations were sacrificed to the Blood God, but in most instances the attack only lasted for a few hours, delivering its bloody decimation before the Slaughterhost was gone again. New forces joined, while others dropped off. In all the thousands of battles, only twice did the Blood Crusade meet its match. Only upon hearing the whispered words of his brother Tzeentch did Khorne finally halt his Blood Crusade, calling back his most fell-handed lieutenants for what was to be known as the War in the Rift.

FIRST WAVE OF FURY

THE FIRST BLADE
Skarbrand .... *The Living Rage*
Kharkexx........ *Greater Daemon*
Cult Risings .... *888 Cults*
Redblades................ *88 Legions*
Disembowelers............*8 Legions*
Bloodcrushers ....*8 Legions*
Gorefists .... *4 Blood Hosts*
Veindrinkers....... *4 Blood Hosts*
Ravagers .... *3 Blood Hosts*
Slaughterkin .... *8 Blood Hosts*
Brazen Beasts ..... *5 Blood Hosts*
Redhorn Bloodgors ... *Warherd*
Iron Brigade .... *War Engines*
Demolishers ... *8 Skull Batteries*

THE SECOND BLADE
Ka'Bandha......*Greater Daemon*
Doombreed .....*Daemon Prince*
Snarlpack .... *88 Legions*
Karanak's Hunt........ *88 Legions*
Doom Battery.*8 Lords of Skulls*
Slaughterkin .... *8 Blood Hosts*
Khârn the Betrayer....... *Legend*
World Eaters...... *Traitor Legion*
Red Redemption .... *Warcult*
Dhorexx Fiend .... *Warp Beast*
Malcrusher ....*Warp Beast*
Maulers .... *6 Companies*
Shredblades ....*Warcult*

ARMIES OF OCTARIUS

GHAZGHKULL'S GREENSKIN HORDE
Ghazghkull ....*Ork Warlord*
Iron Mountains ...*Gargant Mob*
Goffguard...............*15 Big Mobs*
Stompa Mobs ....*6 Big Mobs*
Blitz Brigade ....*33 Big Mobs*
Freebooterz............*28 Big Mobs*
Speed Freeks.........*15 Big Mobs*
Dread Mob ....*19 Big Mobs*
Trukk Brigade ....*15 Big Mobs*
Waaagh! Core......*126 Big Mobs*
Goff Killmob ....*12 Mobs*
Air Skwadrons...........*27 Flights*
Grot Hordes......................*Lotz*

HIVE FLEET LEVIATHAN
Swarmlord ....*Leader*
Bio-Titans ....*48 Creatures*
Subterranean Swarm *Unknown*
Gaunt Swarm ....*Unknown*
Hive Broods...............*Unknown*
Crone Armada ....*Unknown*

The combined might of Ghazghkull's greenskins and the Tyranid hordes of Hive Fleet Leviathan fought the Blood Crusade to a standstill on Octarius before the Daemons left via warp storm.

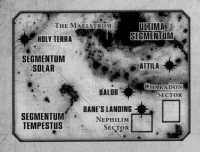

BALOR SYSTEM

BANE'S LANDING

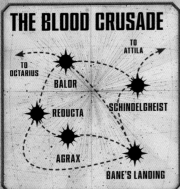

THE BLOOD CRUSADE

OCTARIUS SYSTEM

ATTILA SYSTEM

CRAFTWORLD IYANDEN

In the starless gloom of the Noctis Aeterna, Craftworld Iyanden was assaulted by the greatest of the Aeldari's foes. A Slaaneshi Daemon host, led by the Keeper of Secrets N'Kisha, channelled a warp storm to break through the craftworld's formidable protections. Once more, fighting took place beneath the domes and among the splendours of that majestic craftworld. Were it not for the sudden appearance of warhosts from all the Aeldari factions – craftworlds, Drukhari, Corsairs, Harlequins, Exodites and Ynnari – then all would have been lost. Despite the common-cause victory, however, the Aeldari remained fractured.

ARMAGEDDON

Through the influx of warp energies, the planet of Armageddon had been transformed into a hellscape. Daemon armies swept across battlefields no longer chained to the laws of reality. Luckily for the remaining Imperial armies (twenty-five regiments of Imperial Guard and elements of nine Adeptus Astartes Chapters) and the Orks (a variety of unknown clans), the Daemon legions were just as content to battle amongst themselves as to hunt down and eradicate the survivors. Due to communication difficulties, the exact numbers of extracted Imperial defenders are unknown.

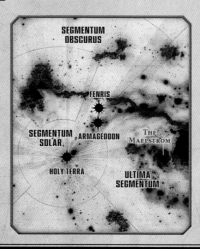

WAR IN THE RIFT

Ever jealous of one another, the Dark Gods began to war amongst themselves in realspace. The opening campaign saw Tzeentch and Khorne send legions to the Scourge Stars seeking to destroy Nurgle's growing foothold. War spread as Nurgle recalled his lieutenants from Ultramar and counter-attacked the realspace strongholds of his rivals. Slaanesh allied with all sides at different times, always furthering his own gains. The greatest of Daemons met in grinding clashes of attrition at the titanic Battle of Vigrid, the fighting only ending when all agreed to Tzeentch's proposal to settle the war via a contest of champions.

THERE IS ONLY WAR

Identify your target.
Concentrate your fire on it to
the exclusion of all else. When
it is destroyed, choose another
target. That is the way to
secure victory!

- *The* Tactica Imperium

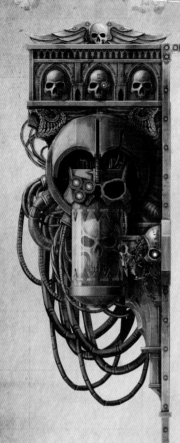

PLAYING THE GAME

Welcome to the rules section of Warhammer 40,000 – a guide to playing games in the war-torn galaxy of the Dark Millennium. As well as including the core rules for engaging in tabletop warfare with your miniatures, this section is packed with different ways to enjoy games of Warhammer 40,000, crammed with inspiration and brimming with battles.

Throughout the following pages you'll find an array of different rules and guidelines to suit all hobbyists, from casual collectors who play occasional games with their friends, to veteran warriors who've spent years honing their forces for competitive tournaments. The core rules are everybody's starting point, but as everyone enjoys the Games Workshop hobby in different ways, this section of the book also introduces three different ways to approach your games: open play, narrative play, and matched play. Each offers a different experience but it's important to note that elements of each can be mixed and matched to create whatever kind of gaming experience you want – they are a gaming toolbox, providing inspiration and options to

get the dice rolling and allow you to play with your collection of Citadel Miniatures on the tabletop.

You will also find a guide to building battlefields, the rules for forming a Battle-forged army, and an introduction to advanced rules, which explore additional ways to fight your battles. So whether you are looking to wage war in one of the myriad deadly environments of the galaxy, play a team game, or fight battles as part of an escalating narrative campaign, there is an expansion to enable you to do so. A universe of war awaits you – read on to see short explanations of what you will find on these pages and how to use them in your games, starting with the essential core rules.

CORE RULES (PG 176)

Start here! Whatever type of game you want to play, you'll need the core rules, which form the essential foundation for playing games of Warhammer 40,000. These rules show you how to move, use psychic powers, shoot, charge and fight with your models – basically everything you need to start waging miniature war! They provide the key mechanics for everything from foot-slogging infantry to gigantic monsters and armour-clad war machines, allowing you to quickly build up from your first few simple games to grand spectacles of all-out war.

The core rules also provide plenty of helpful clarifications, hints and tips, along with a single mission (the suitably titled 'Only War'), which serves as a perfect introduction to gaming in the Warhammer 40,000 universe. Wherever you go with your games, the core rules will provide the foundation you need to get started, and be your constant gaming companion.

Before trying too many of the diverse options offered by the Warhammer 40,000 gaming hobby, it's recommended that you play a few games using just these rules. This will build a great grounding for what comes after.

ADVANCED RULES (PG 238)

At its heart, Warhammer 40,000 is a game that pits one army of warriors against another in tabletop conflict to the death. Beyond that core premise, it is a hobby of vast and thrilling variation that allows you to depict everything from breakneck aerial dogfights and orbital drop-assaults to war across hostile alien environments between multiple different armies at once and close-run battles through the war-torn streets of an Imperial hive – all encompassed by the advanced rules.

Whether you choose to introduce any advanced rules to your games, or even combine several different aspects in a single game, all of these optional mechanics build upon the core rules – they add to or provide variation on the core rules, rather than requiring you to learn a whole new game system! From huge multiplayer battles and sprawling sieges, to campaigns fought over strange alien worlds, the advanced rules will provide you with exciting new gaming experiences to suit whatever type of game you want to play for years to come.

OPEN PLAY (PG 188)

The first of the three distinct ways to play Warhammer 40,000, open play is the most free-form and adaptable. It can be as simple or as complex as you like – you can literally just pick any Citadel Miniatures you have and start playing. It's as easy as that, and playing games this way can lead to extraordinary battles as players are free to put their entire collections on the battlefield to get the dice rolling started! Whether this leads to titanic clashes between huge armies that last entire weekends, or desperate and dramatic battles against the odds, the emphasis in open play is firmly on playing a fun wargame with whatever parts of your collections you wish, in whatever fashion you so choose.

This section also contains a selection of story hooks, to use as inspiration for your games. With a little prior thought and discussion, your Warhammer 40,000 battles can take on a thrilling, story-driven aspect, transcending the simple rules of the game and becoming something altogether more dramatic and involving. Desperate last stands, vendettas between mighty heroes, courageous rescue missions and endless other characterful conflicts can easily be brought to life on the tabletop in an open play game.

Open play is also an ideal way of gaming when you have multiple players who want to get involved in a battle all at once. Allowing for all kinds of variation in terms of team gaming, outnumbered players fighting against the odds, or whatever other scenario you can envision, this section provides you with the help you need to get the most out of your multiplayer games.

NARRATIVE PLAY (PG 192)

AN EVOLVING EXPERIENCE

With three different styles of play to explore, dozens of missions to play, and an ever-expanding array of armies and Detachments to collect, Warhammer 40,000 could potentially seem intimidating to a new player. Fortunately, by starting with the core rules and building up at an appropriate pace, you can enjoy your hobby in whatever way suits you. By taking your time and trying things out, you'll soon find the combination that best fits your play style, and if things ever start to feel a little bit routine, just try out some new rules!

Narrative play is based around the stories embedded in the background of Warhammer 40,000, either those in our books or those you write yourself. You'll often find that reading up on the history of a particular Faction, hero or battle is all the inspiration you need to set up a game and play it.

Perhaps you enjoyed the story of a bitter rivalry between two characters in the background, whether it be the ongoing feud between Commissar Yarrick and Ghazghkull Thraka or Wolf Lord Logan Grimnar's quest for revenge upon the Daemon Primarch Magnus the Red. Maybe tales of strategy and massed battle bring you inspiration, stories of sudden ambushes, sweeping flank attacks and meat-grinder offensives through the smoke and fire of no man's land. Whatever the case, narrative play provides guidelines and structured scenarios that allow you to recreate your favourite war stories on the tabletop.

There are many places to find these sorts of exciting tales, from the histories and backgrounds provided in this book and in codexes to the dramatic stories in Black Library's Warhammer 40,000 novels.

Unlike open play, which leaves the impetus on the players to determine their own story and victory conditions, narrative play gives a somewhat tighter framework to operate in. Examples of this can be found in the seven new missions found in this section of rules. Going beyond the straightforward battle fought in the Only War scenario, games such as Patrol and Ambush alter the parameters of your games and provide players with differing roles and objectives where one plays as the attacker and the other as the defender.

The additional rules provided in this section are intended to help with your own battlefield storytelling, and with a little experience and imagination, you and your opponents can quickly piece together your own exciting narrative play missions to depict whatever deadly scenario you wish.

BATTLE-FORGED ARMIES (PG 240)

While open play encourages gamers to place whatever models they want to on the tabletop, in whatever quantities they choose, both narrative and matched play tend to use Battle-forged armies. These forces bring additional structure and balance to the gaming experience.

When selecting a Battle-forged army, you will find that there are greater restrictions and considerations of structure placed upon you. Some people will intentionally build their collections using the Battle-forged template to ensure that they can easily assemble a Battle-forged force for any game they play. Others prefer to collect however the mood takes them, and then simply form models from their collection into a Battle-forged army when their games require them to do so. Either method is equally valid, and both allow you to build exciting and impressive miniatures collections.

Battle-forged armies must be organised into Detachments (groupings of units with specific strategic roles), twelve of which are presented in this book. With your army fully made up of Detachments, you will gain access to Command Points (pg 242), which unlock Stratagems that can be used in all Warhammer 40,000 missions.

MATCHED PLAY (PG 212)

As the name would suggest, tabletop wargames are just that: games to be enjoyed by all players involved. For some, this enjoyment is derived from assembling Battle-forged armies that they believe provide the optimal combination of units, and then pitting these armies against one another in balanced contests of strategy and skill.

Matched play allows for armies of this sort to be tested against each other under conditions that give no particular advantage to either side, in order to see which army is strongest and which general is canniest. It's a more balanced and controlled way of playing games, often favoured by those collectors who engage in gaming tournaments and similar events. Matched play is also a fantastic way to ensure a relatively balanced gaming experience for those who like playing at local gaming clubs or stores, where they may find themselves

having pick-up games against opponents they have never faced before.

This section of the rules includes a further twelve missions that are designed to compliment the rules for Battle-forged armies and create a gaming experience where both players have as equal a chance of securing victory as possible.

The six Eternal War missions are the most stable and straightforward in this rulebook. Typically based around both players attempting to break into the other's territory, secure control of objectives, or eliminate particular enemy targets, each one is an exciting tactical challenge every time you play.

By comparison, the six Maelstrom of War missions are more unpredictable. These games use dynamic Tactical Objectives to randomise players' victory conditions and keep games hanging in the balance.

WHERE TO PLAY

There are lots of places to play Warhammer 40,000, and opponents are normally easy to find. If you are lucky enough to have a local gaming club or gaming store nearby, these can be great places to play and to meet new opponents and favourite rivals in the making. Alternatively, many collectors enjoy playing games with their friends, often building gaming tables at home to play on. Still others involve themselves in campaign events and tournaments, spending whole weekends playing game after game against many opponents.

DATASHEETS

The warriors, monsters and war machines that fight for control of the galaxy are incredibly diverse, each with their own style of waging war. Each unit has a datasheet that lists the characteristics, wargear and abilities of the models in that unit – here we explain what some of it means, while the core rules (over the page) explain how it's all used in the game.

1. Unit Name

Models move and fight in units, which can have one or more models. Here you'll find the name of the unit.

2. Battlefield Role

This is typically used when making a Battle-forged army (pg 240).

3. Power Rating

The higher this is, the more powerful the unit! You can determine the Power Level of your entire army by adding up the Power Ratings of all the units in your army.

4. Profiles

These contain the following characteristics that tell you how mighty the models in the unit are:

Move (M): This is the speed at which a model moves across the battlefield.

Weapon Skill (WS): This tells you a model's skill at hand-to-hand fighting. If a model has a Weapon Skill of '-' it is unable to fight in melee and cannot make close combat attacks at all.

Ballistic Skill (BS): This shows how accurate a model is when shooting

with ranged weapons. If a model has a Ballistic Skill of '-' it has no proficiency with ranged weapons and cannot make shooting attacks at all.

Strength (S): This indicates how strong a model is and how likely it is to inflict damage in hand-to-hand combat.

Toughness (T): This reflects the model's resilience against physical harm.

Wounds (W): Wounds show how much damage a model can sustain before it succumbs to its injuries.

1 LORD OF CONTAGION **2** ☠ **3** 8 POWER

PROFILES **4**

NAME	M	WS	BS	S	T	W	A	Ld	Sv
Lord of Contagion	4"	2+	2+	4	5	6	4	9	2+

UNIT COMPOSITION **5**

A Lord of Contagion is a single model.

WARGEAR **6**

A Lord of Contagion is armed with a plaguereaper.

ABILITIES **7**

Disgustingly Resilient (pg 17)

Nurgle's Gift: All **DEATH GUARD** models within 7" of a Lord of Contagion are surrounded by a deadly aura of plague and disease. Roll a dice for each enemy unit that is within 1" of such a model at the start of your turn. On a roll of 4+, that unit suffers a mortal wound.

Cataphractii Armour: A Lord of Contagion has a 4+ invulnerable save, but you must halve the result of the dice rolled when determining how far this model Advances.

Teleport Strike: When you set up a Lord of Contagion during deployment, he can be set up in a teleportarium chamber instead of being placed on the battlefield. If he does so, he can use a teleport strike to arrive on the battlefield at the end of any of your Movement phases; when he does so set him up anywhere that is more than 9" from any enemy models.

WEAPONS **8**

WEAPON	RANGE	TYPE	S	AP	D	ABILITIES
Plaguereaper	Melee	Melee	+2	-3	3	Plague Weapon (pg 17)

FACTION KEYWORDS	CHAOS, NURGLE, HERETIC ASTARTES, DEATH GUARD	**9**
KEYWORDS	INFANTRY, CHARACTER, LORD OF CONTAGION	

A SMALL MIND HAS NO ROOM FOR DOUBT.

Attacks (A): This tells you how many times a model can strike blows in hand-to-hand combat.

Leadership (Ld): This reveals how courageous, determined or self-controlled a model is.

Save (Sv): This indicates the protection a model's armour gives.

5. Unit Composition

This tells you what models are in the unit.

6. Wargear

This covers the basic weapons and equipment the models are armed with.

7. Abilities

Many units have exciting special abilities that are not covered by the core rules; these will be described here.

8. Weapons

The weapons that a unit comes equipped with are described using a set of characteristics as follows:

Range: How far the weapon can shoot. Weapons with a range of 'Melee' can only be used in hand-to-hand combat. All other weapons are referred to as ranged weapons.

Type: These are all explained under the Shooting and Fight phases of the core rules.

Strength (S): How likely the weapon is to inflict damage. If a weapon's Strength lists 'User', it is equal to the wielder's current Strength. If a weapon lists a modifier such as '+1' or 'x2', you should modify the user's current Strength characteristic as shown to determine the weapon's Strength. For example, if a weapon's Strength was 'x2', and the user had a Strength characteristic of 6, that weapon has Strength 12.

Armour Penetration (AP): How good it is at getting through armour.

Damage (D): The amount of damage inflicted by a successful hit.

Other weapons, for example those a unit may take as an optional choice, are typically described elsewhere, such as in a codex.

9. Keywords

All datasheets have a list of keywords, sometimes separated into Faction keywords and other keywords. The former can be used as a guide to help decide which models to include in your army, but otherwise both sets of keywords are functionally the same. Sometimes a rule will say that it applies to models that have a specific keyword. For example, a rule might say that it applies to 'all **ADEPTUS ASTARTES** models'. This means it would only apply to models that have the Adeptus Astartes keyword on their datasheet.

MODIFYING CHARACTERISTICS

Some large models' characteristics can change as the model suffers damage – look at such a model's remaining wounds and consult the appropriate row of the chart on their datasheet to determine its current characteristics.

You may also encounter abilities and rules that modify a characteristic. All modifiers are cumulative, though you should apply any multiplication or division to the characteristic (rounding fractions up) before applying any addition or subtraction.

You may encounter a characteristic that is a random value instead of a number. For example, a Move characteristic might be 2D6", or an Attacks value might be D6. When a unit with a random Move characteristic is selected to move, determine the entire unit's move distance by rolling the indicated number of dice (pg 176). For all other characteristics, roll to determine the value on an individual – per-model – basis each time the unit makes attacks, inflicts damage, and so on. Note that, regardless of the source, characteristics of '-' can never be modified, and the Strength, Toughness and Leadership characteristics of a model can never be modified below 1.

WARHAMMER 40,000 CODEXES

So now you know what a datasheet is and how it works – in conjunction with the core rules that follow (plus your Citadel Miniatures, battlefield, dice and tape measure, of course!), you've got everything you need to start playing games of Warhammer 40,000 and dive into epic battle.

But where do you find datasheets? Well, when you buy a box of Citadel Miniatures they'll be in the box with them, and they are also present in codexes. A codex is the ultimate resource for your chosen army (or armies!), containing datasheets for all the miniatures that are part of a particular Faction. But that's not all – in codexes you'll also find army-specific special rules that reflect the character of the army, exciting Warlord Traits, Stratagems, wargear, and even unique relics.

Each codex is also filled with a wealth of inspirational background material, organisational information, stunning art and miniatures photography, colour guides and heraldry, all of which provide context for how a Faction works in the Warhammer 40,000 universe. Head over to games-workshop.com to find out more.

CORE RULES

Warhammer 40,000 puts you in command of a force of mighty warriors and war machines. The core rules on these pages contain everything you need to know in order to use your Citadel Miniatures collection to wage glorious battle across the war-torn galaxy.

MODELS & DATASHEETS

The rules and characteristics for all models, and some terrain features, are presented on datasheets, which you will need in order to use the models in battle.

UNITS

Models move and fight in units, made up of one or more models. A unit must be set up and finish any sort of move as a group, with every model within 2" horizontally, and 6" vertically, of at least one other model from their unit: this is called unit coherency. If anything causes a unit to become split up during a battle, it must re-establish its unit coherency the next time it moves.

TOOLS OF WAR

In order to fight a battle, you will require a tape measure and some dice.

Distances in Warhammer 40,000 are measured in inches (") between the closest points of the bases of the models you're measuring to and from. If a model does not have a base, such is the case with many vehicles, measure to and from the closest point of that model's hull instead. You can measure distances whenever you wish.

Warhammer 40,000 uses six-sided dice, sometimes abbreviated to D6. Some rules refer to 2D6, 3D6 and so on – in such cases, roll that many D6s and add the results together. If a rule requires you to roll a D3, roll a dice and halve the total. When halving any dice roll, round fractions up before applying modifiers (if any) to the result. All modifiers are cumulative. If a rule requires a dice roll of, for example, 3 or more, this is often abbreviated to 3+.

THE BATTLE ROUND

Warhammer 40,000 is played in a series of battle rounds. During each battle round, both players have a turn. The same player always takes the first turn in each battle round – the mission you are playing will tell you which player this is. Each turn consists of a series of phases, which must be resolved in order. The phases are as follows:

1. **MOVEMENT PHASE**
   Move any units that are capable of doing so.

2. **PSYCHIC PHASE**
   Psykers can use powerful mental abilities.

3. **SHOOTING PHASE**
   Your units may shoot enemy units.

4. **CHARGE PHASE**
   Your units may move into close combat against enemy units.

5. **FIGHT PHASE**
   Both players' units pile in and attack with melee weapons.

6. **MORALE PHASE**
   Test the courage of depleted units.

Once a player's turn has ended, their opponent then starts their turn. Once both players have completed a turn, the battle round has been completed and the next one begins, and so on, until the battle is concluded.

1. MOVEMENT PHASE

The ground shakes to the tread of marching feet and the growl of engines as armies advance across the battlefield and vie for advantageous positions.

Start your Movement phase by picking one of your units and moving each model in that unit until you've moved all the models you want to. You can then pick another unit to move, until you have moved as many of your units as you wish. No model can be moved more than once in each Movement phase.

Moving

A model can be moved in any direction, to a distance, in inches, equal to or less than the Move characteristic on its datasheet. No part of the model's base (or hull) can move further than this. It cannot be moved through other models or through terrain features such as walls, but can be moved vertically in order to climb or traverse any scenery.

If the datasheet for a model says it can **FLY**, it can move across models and terrain as if they were not there.

Minimum Move

Some models that can **FLY** have a Move characteristic consisting of two values. The first is the model's minimum speed – in the Movement phase, all parts of the model's base must end the move at least that far from where they started. The second is its maximum speed – no part of the model's base can be moved further than this. If a model cannot make its minimum move, or is forced to move off the battlefield because of its minimum speed, it is destroyed and removed from the battlefield – the model has either stalled and crashed or been forced to abandon the battle.

Enemy Models

All models in the same army are friendly models. Models controlled by an opposing player are enemy models. When you move a model in the Movement phase, it may not be moved within 1" of any enemy models.

Falling Back

Units starting the Movement phase within 1" of an enemy unit can either remain stationary or Fall Back. If you choose to Fall Back, the unit must end its move more than 1" away from all enemy units. If a unit Falls Back, it cannot Advance (see below), or charge (pg 182) later that turn. A unit that Falls Back also cannot shoot later that turn unless it can **FLY**.

Advancing

When you pick a unit to move in the Movement phase, you can declare that it will Advance. Roll a dice and add the result to the Move characteristics of all models in the unit for that Movement phase. A unit that Advances can't shoot or charge later that turn.

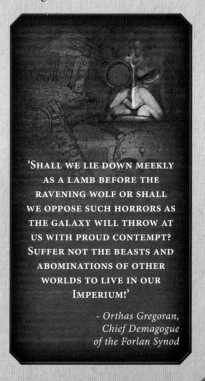

'SHALL WE LIE DOWN MEEKLY AS A LAMB BEFORE THE RAVENING WOLF OR SHALL WE OPPOSE SUCH HORRORS AS THE GALAXY WILL THROW AT US WITH PROUD CONTEMPT? SUFFER NOT THE BEASTS AND ABOMINATIONS OF OTHER WORLDS TO LIVE IN OUR IMPERIUM!'

- *Orthas Gregoran, Chief Demagogue of the Forlan Synod*

WOBBLY MODEL SYNDROME

Sometimes you may find that a particular piece of terrain makes it hard to put a model exactly where you want. If you delicately balance it in place, it is very likely to fall as soon as somebody nudges the table, leaving your painted model damaged or even broken. In cases like this, we find it is perfectly acceptable to leave the model in a safer position, as long as both players have agreed and know its 'actual' location. If, later on, your enemy is considering shooting the model, you will have to hold it back in the proper place so they can check if it is visible.

REINFORCEMENTS

Many units have the ability to be set up on the battlefield mid-turn, sometimes by using teleporters, grav chutes or other, more esoteric means. Typically, this happens at the end of the Movement phase, but it can also happen during other phases. Units that are set up in this manner cannot move or Advance further during the turn they arrive – their entire Movement phase is used in deploying to the battlefield – but they can otherwise act normally (shoot, charge, etc.) for the rest of their turn. Units that arrive as reinforcements count as having moved in their Movement phase for all rules purposes, such as shooting Heavy weapons (pg 180). Any unit that has not arrived on the battlefield by the end of the battle counts as having been destroyed.

Some rules allow you to re-roll a dice roll, which means you get to roll some or all of the dice again. You can never re-roll a dice more than once, and re-rolls happen before modifiers (if any) are applied.

Roll-offs

Some rules instruct players to roll off. To do so, both players roll a D6, and whoever scores highest wins the roll-off. In the case of a tie, both players re-roll their D6; this is the only time players can re-roll a re-roll – if the second and subsequent rolls are also tied, keep on rolling until a winner is decided.

Sequencing

While playing Warhammer 40,000, you'll occasionally find that two or more rules are to be resolved at the same time – normally 'at the start of the Movement phase' or 'before the battle begins'. When this happens during the game, the player whose turn it is chooses the order. If these things occur before or after the game, or at the start or end of a battle round, the players roll off and the winner decides in what order the rules are resolved.

2. PSYCHIC PHASE

Warrior mystics and sorcerers wield the strange power of the warp to aid their allies and destroy their foes. Harnessing this force is not without risk, however, and with the smallest mistake, the effort can spell doom for all nearby.

> **PSYCHIC SEQUENCE**
> 1. Choose psyker and power
> 2. Make Psychic test
> 3. Enemy takes Deny the Witch test
> 4. Resolve psychic power

1. Choose Psyker and Power

Some models are noted as being a **PSYKER** on their datasheet. Psykers can manifest their otherworldly abilities and attempt to deny enemy sorceries. The powers a psyker knows, and the number of powers they can attempt to manifest or deny each Psychic phase, are detailed on their datasheet.

Psychic Powers

Unless stated otherwise, all psykers know the *Smite* psychic power, listed below. Some know other powers instead of, or in addition to, *Smite* – the model's datasheets and other supplementary rules you are using will make it clear which powers each psyker knows. If a psyker generates their powers before the battle, do so immediately before either player starts to deploy their army.

> **Smite**
>
> *Smite* has a warp charge value of 5. If manifested, the closest visible enemy unit within 18" of the psyker suffers D3 mortal wounds (pg 181). If the result of the Psychic test was more than 10, the target suffers D6 mortal wounds instead.

2. Make Psychic Test

A psyker can attempt to manifest a psychic power they know by taking a Psychic test. To do so, roll 2D6. If the total is equal to or greater than that power's warp charge value, the power is successfully manifested. A psyker cannot attempt to manifest the same psychic power more than once in a turn.

Perils of the Warp

If you roll a double 1 or a double 6 when taking a Psychic test, the psyker immediately suffers Perils of the Warp. The psyker suffers D3 mortal wounds as the forces of the Daemon-haunted warp claw at their mind. If the psyker is slain by Perils of the Warp, the power they were attempting to manifest automatically fails and each unit within 6" immediately suffers D3 mortal wounds, as the psyker is dragged into the warp or else detonates in a burst of empyric feedback.

3. Deny the Witch Tests

A psyker can attempt to resist a psychic power that has been manifested by an enemy model within 24" by taking a Deny the Witch test – this takes place immediately, even though it is not your turn. To do so, roll 2D6. If the total is greater than the result of the Psychic test that manifested the power, it has been resisted and its effects are negated. Only one attempt to deny each successfully manifested psychic power can be made each turn, regardless of the number of psykers you have within 24" of the enemy model manifesting the psychic power.

4. Resolve Psychic Power

So long as the Psychic test was successful, the psyker did not die as a result of the Perils of the Warp, and the attempt was not thwarted by a Deny the Witch test, then you may resolve the effect of the psychic power, which will be described in the power itself.

3. SHOOTING PHASE

Guns thunder and shrapnel falls from the sky. Muzzle flare shines through the gloom in bursts, beams of las-fire illuminate the fog of war, and spent ammunition cartridges and power cells are left discarded across the battlefield.

SHOOTING SEQUENCE

1. Choose unit to shoot with
2. Choose targets
3. Choose ranged weapon
4. Resolve attacks
   - Make hit roll
   - Make wound roll
   - Enemy allocates wound
   - Enemy makes saving throw
   - Inflict damage

1. Choose Unit to Shoot With

In your Shooting phase you can shoot with models armed with ranged weapons. First, you must pick one of your units to shoot with. You may not pick a unit that Advanced or Fell Back this turn, or a unit that is within 1" of an enemy unit. Unless otherwise stated, each model in the unit attacks with all of the ranged weapons it is armed with. After all of the unit's models have fired, you can choose another unit to shoot with, until all eligible units that you want to shoot with have done so.

2. Choose Targets

Having chosen a shooting unit, you must pick the target unit, or units, for the attacks. In order to target an enemy unit, a model from that unit must be within the Range of the weapon being used (as listed on its profile) and be visible to the shooting model. If unsure, stoop down and get a look from behind the shooting model to see if any part of the target is visible. For the purposes of determining visibility, a model can see through other models in its own unit.

Models cannot target enemy units that are within 1" of friendly models – the risk of hitting your own troops is too great.

3. Choose Ranged Weapon

The weapons a model has are listed on its datasheet. If a model has several weapons, it can shoot all of them at the same target, or it can shoot each at a different enemy unit. Similarly, if a unit contains more than one model, they can shoot at the same, or different targets as you choose. In either case, declare how you will split the shooting unit's shots before any dice are rolled, and resolve all the shots against one target before moving on to the next.

Number of Attacks

Each time a model shoots a ranged weapon, it will make a number of attacks. You roll one dice for each attack being made. The number of attacks a model can make with a weapon, and therefore the number of dice you can roll, is found on the weapon's profile, along with the weapon's type. A weapon's type can impact the number of attacks it can make (see overleaf).

Characters

Some models are noted as being a **CHARACTER** on their datasheet. These heroes, officers, prophets and warlords are powerful individuals that can have a great impact on the course of a battle. The swirling maelstrom of the battlefield can make it difficult to pick out such individuals as targets, however. A **CHARACTER** can only be chosen as a target in the Shooting phase if they are the closest visible enemy unit to the model that is shooting. This does not apply to **CHARACTERS** with a Wounds characteristic of 10 or more, due to their sheer size.

FAST DICE ROLLING

The rules for resolving attacks (pg 181) have been written assuming you will make them one at a time. However, it is possible to speed up your battles by rolling the dice for similar attacks together. In order to make several attacks at once, all of the attacks must have the same Ballistic Skill (if it's a shooting attack) or the same Weapon Skill (if it's a close combat attack). They must also have the same Strength, Armour Penetration and Damage characteristics, and they must be directed at the same unit. If this is the case, make all of the hit rolls at the same time, then all of the wound rolls. Your opponent can then allocate the wounds one at a time, making the saving throws and suffering damage each time as appropriate. Remember, if the target unit contains a model that has already lost any wounds, they must allocate further wounds to this model until either it is slain, or all the wounds have been saved or resolved.

AURA ABILITIES

Some units – usually **CHARACTERS** – have abilities that affect certain models within a given range. Unless the ability in question says otherwise, a model with a rule like this is always within range of the effect.

For example, a Lord of Contagion has the Nurgle's Gift ability, which affects all **DEATH GUARD** models within 7" of him. As the Lord of Contagion is also a **DEATH GUARD** model, he benefits from this ability as well.

Weapon Types

There are five types of ranged weapon: Assault, Heavy, Rapid Fire, Grenade and Pistol. A model shooting one of these weapons can make a number of attacks equal to the number written on its profile after its type. For example, a model firing an 'Assault 1' weapon can make 1 attack with that weapon; a model firing a 'Heavy 3' weapon can make 3 attacks, etc.

If a weapon has more than one attack, it must make all of its attacks against the same target unit.

Each type of ranged weapon also has an additional rule that, depending upon the situation, might affect the accuracy of the weapon or when it can be fired. These are as follows:

ASSAULT

Assault weapons fire so rapidly or indiscriminately that they can be shot from the hip as warriors dash forwards into combat.

A model with an Assault weapon can fire it even if it Advanced earlier that turn. If it does so, you must subtract 1 from any hit rolls made when firing that weapon this turn.

HEAVY

Heavy weapons are the biggest and deadliest guns on the battlefield, but require reloading, careful set-up or bracing to fire at full effect.

If a model with a Heavy weapon moved in its preceding Movement phase, you must subtract 1 from any hit rolls made when firing that weapon this turn.

RAPID FIRE

Rapid Fire weapons are versatile weapons capable of aimed single shots at long range or controlled bursts of fire at close quarters.

A model firing a Rapid Fire weapon doubles the number of attacks it makes if its target is within half the weapon's maximum range.

GRENADE

Grenades are handheld explosive devices that a warrior throws at the enemy while their squad mates provide covering fire.

Each time a unit shoots, a single model in the unit that is equipped with Grenades may throw one instead of firing any other weapon.

PISTOL

Pistols are carried one-handed and can even be used in a melee to shoot at point-blank range. Many warriors carry one as a sidearm, alongside their primary weapon.

A model can fire a Pistol even if there are enemy units within 1" of its own unit, but it must target the closest enemy unit. In such circumstances, the model can shoot its Pistol even if other friendly units are within 1" of the same enemy unit.

Each time a model equipped with both a Pistol and another type of ranged weapon (e.g. a Pistol and a Rapid Fire weapon) shoots, it can either shoot with its Pistol(s) or with all of its other weapons. Choose which it will fire (Pistols or non-Pistols) before making hit rolls.

4. Resolve Attacks

Attacks can be made one at a time, or, in some cases, you can roll for multiple attacks together. The following sequence is used to make attacks one at a time:

1. **Hit Roll:** Each time a model makes an attack, roll a dice. If the roll is equal to or greater than the attacking model's Ballistic Skill characteristic, then it scores a hit with the weapon it is using. If not, the attack fails and the attack sequence ends. A roll of 1 always fails, irrespective of any modifiers that may apply.

2. **Wound Roll:** If an attack scores a hit, you will then need to roll another dice to see if the attack successfully wounds the target. The roll required is determined by comparing the attacking weapon's Strength characteristic with the target's Toughness characteristic, as shown on the following table:

WOUND ROLL	
ATTACK'S STRENGTH VS TARGET'S TOUGHNESS	**D6 ROLL REQUIRED**
Is the Strength TWICE (or more) than the Toughness?	2+
Is the Strength GREATER than the Toughness?	3+
Is the Strength EQUAL to the Toughness?	4+
Is the Strength LOWER than the Toughness?	5+
Is the Strength HALF (or less) than the Toughness?	6+

If the roll is less than the required number, the attack fails and the attack sequence ends. A roll of 1 always fails, irrespective of any modifiers that may apply.

3. **Allocate Wound:** If an attack successfully wounds the target, the player commanding the target unit allocates the wound to any model in the unit (the chosen model does not have to be within range or visible to the attacking unit). If a model in the target unit has already lost any wounds, the damage must be allocated to that model.

4. **Saving Throw:** The player commanding the target unit then makes a saving throw by rolling a dice and modifying the roll by the Armour Penetration characteristic of the weapon that caused the damage. For example, if the weapon has an Armour Penetration of -1, then 1 is subtracted from the saving throw roll. If the result is equal to, or greater than, the Save characteristic of the model the wound was allocated to, then the damage is prevented and the attack sequence ends. If the result is less than the model's Save characteristic, then the saving throw fails and the model suffers damage. A roll of 1 always fails, irrespective of any modifiers that may apply.

5. **Inflict Damage:** The damage inflicted is equal to the Damage characteristic of the weapon used in the attack. A model loses one wound for each point of damage it suffers. If a model's wounds are reduced to 0, it is either slain or destroyed and removed from play. If a model loses several wounds from a single attack and is destroyed, any excess damage inflicted by that attack is lost and has no effect.

Invulnerable Saves

Some models possess supernatural reflexes or are protected by force fields that grant them an invulnerable save. Each time a wound is allocated to a model with an invulnerable save, you can choose to use either its normal Save characteristic or its invulnerable save, but not both. If a model has more than one invulnerable save, it can only use one of them – choose which it will use. If you use a model's invulnerable save, it is never modified by a weapon's Armour Penetration value.

Terrain and Cover

The battlefields of the far future are littered with terrain features such as ruins, craters and twisted copses. Models can take shelter within such terrain features to gain protection against incoming weapons' fire.

If a unit is entirely on or within any terrain feature, add 1 to its models' saving throws against shooting attacks to represent the cover received from the terrain (invulnerable saves are unaffected). Units gain no benefit from cover in the Fight phase (pg 182).

Mortal Wounds

Some attacks inflict mortal wounds – these are so powerful that no armour or force field can withstand their fury. Each mortal wound inflicts one point of damage on the target unit. Do not make a wound roll or saving throw (including invulnerable saves) against a mortal wound – just allocate it as you would any other wound and inflict damage to a model in the target unit as described above. Unlike normal attacks, excess damage from attacks that inflict mortal wounds is not lost. Instead keep allocating damage to another model in the target unit until either all the damage has been allocated or the target unit is destroyed.

4. CHARGE PHASE

Warriors hurl themselves into battle to slay with blade, hammer and claw.

CHARGE SEQUENCE
1. Choose unit to charge with
2. Choose targets
3. Enemy resolves Overwatch
4. Roll 2D6 and make charge move

1. Choose Unit to Charge With

Any of your units within 12" of the enemy in your Charge phase can make a charge move. You may not choose a unit that Advanced or Fell Back this turn, nor one that started the Charge phase within 1" of an enemy.

2. Choose Targets

Once you have chosen an eligible unit, select one or more enemy units within 12" of them as the target(s) of the charge. Each target unit can then attempt to fire Overwatch.

3. Overwatch

Each time a charge is declared against a unit, the target unit can immediately fire Overwatch at the would-be attacker. A target unit can potentially fire Overwatch several times a turn, though it cannot fire if there are any enemy models within 1" of it. Overwatch is resolved like a normal shooting attack (albeit one resolved in the enemy's Charge phase) and uses all the normal rules except that a 6 is always required for a successful hit roll, irrespective of the firing model's Ballistic Skill or any modifiers.

4. Make Charge Move

After any Overwatch has been resolved, roll 2D6. Each model in the charging unit can move up to this number of inches – this is their charge distance this turn. The first model you move must finish within 1" of an enemy model from one of the target units. No models in the charging unit can move within 1" of an enemy unit that was not a target of its charge. If this is impossible, the charge fails and no models in the charging unit move this phase. Once you've moved all the models in the charging unit, choose another eligible unit and repeat the above procedure until all eligible units that you want to make charge moves have done so. No unit can be selected to charge more than once in each Charge phase.

Heroic Intervention

After the enemy has completed all of their charge moves, any of your **Characters** that are within 3" of an enemy unit may perform a Heroic Intervention. Any that do so can move up to 3", so long as they end the move closer to the nearest enemy model.

5. FIGHT PHASE

Carnage engulfs the battlefield as the warring armies tear each other apart.

FIGHT SEQUENCE
1. Choose unit to fight with
2. Pile in up to 3"
3. Choose targets
4. Choose melee weapon
5. Resolve close combat attacks
   - Make hit roll
   - Make wound roll
   - Enemy allocates wound
   - Enemy makes saving throw
   - Inflict damage
6. Consolidate up to 3"

1. Choose Unit to Fight With

Any unit that charged or has models within 1" of an enemy unit can be chosen to fight in the Fight phase. This includes all units, not just those controlled by the player whose turn it is. All units that charged this turn fight first. The player whose turn it is picks the order in which these units fight. After all charging units have fought, the players alternate choosing eligible units to fight with (starting with the player whose turn it is) until all eligible units on both sides have fought once each. No unit can be selected to fight more than once in each Fight phase. If one player runs out of eligible units, the other player completes all of their remaining fights, one unit after another. A fight is resolved in the following steps:

2. Pile In

You may move each model in the unit up to 3" – this move can be in any direction so long as the model ends the move closer to the nearest enemy model.

3. Choose Targets

First, you must pick the target unit, or units, for the attacks. To target an enemy unit, the attacking model must either be within 1" of that unit, or within 1" of another model from its own unit that is itself within 1" of that enemy unit. This represents the unit fighting in two ranks. Models that charged this turn can only target enemy units that they charged in the previous phase.

If a model can make more than one close combat attack (see right), it can split them between eligible target units as you wish. Similarly if a unit contains more than one model, each can target a different enemy unit. In either case, declare how you will split the unit's close combat attacks before any dice are rolled, and resolve all attacks against one target before moving on to the next.

VICTORY IS THE PROMISE OF THE EMPEROR'S COMMAND.

Number of Attacks

The number of close combat attacks a model makes against its target is determined by its Attacks characteristic. You roll one dice for each close combat attack being made. For example, if a model has an Attacks characteristic of 2, it can make 2 close combat attacks and you can therefore roll 2 dice.

4. Choose Melee Weapon

Each time a model makes a close combat attack, it uses a melee weapon – the weapons a model is equipped with are described on its datasheet. If a datasheet does not list any melee weapons, the model is assumed to fight with a close combat weapon, which has the following profile:

WEAPON	RANGE	TYPE	S	AP	D
Close combat weapon	Melee	Melee	User	-	1

If a model has more than one melee weapon, choose which it will use before rolling the dice. If a model has more than one melee weapon and can make several close combat attacks, it can split its attacks between these weapons however you wish – declare how you will divide the attacks before any dice are rolled.

5. Resolve Close Combat Attacks

Close combat attacks can be made one at a time, or in some cases you can roll the dice for a number of attacks together. The attack sequence for making close combat attacks is identical to that used for shooting attacks (pg 181) except you use the model's Weapon Skill characteristic instead of its Ballistic Skill to make hit rolls.

6. Consolidate

You may move each model in the unit up to 3" – this move can be in any direction so long as the model ends the move closer to the nearest enemy model.

6. MORALE PHASE

Even the bravest heart may quail when the horrors of battle take their toll.

In the Morale phase, starting with the player whose turn it is, players must take Morale tests for units from their army that have had models slain during the turn.

To take a Morale test, roll a dice and add the number of models from the unit that have been slain this turn. If the result of the Morale test exceeds the highest Leadership characteristic in the unit, the test is failed. For each point that the test is failed by, one model in that unit must flee and is removed from play. You choose which models flee from the units you command.

TRANSPORTS

Some models are noted as being a **TRANSPORT** on their datasheet – these vehicles ferry warriors to the front line, providing them with speed and protection. The following rules describe how units can embark and disembark from transports, and how they are used to move their passengers across the battlefield. Note that a unit cannot both embark and disembark in the same turn.

Transport Capacity: All transports have a transport capacity listed on their datasheet. This determines how many friendly models, and of what type, they can carry. A model's transport capacity can never be exceeded.

When you set up a transport, units can start the battle embarked within it instead of being set up separately – declare what units are embarked inside the transport when you set it up.

Embark: If all models in a unit end their move within 3" of a friendly transport, they can embark within it. Remove the unit from the battlefield and place it to one side – it is now embarked inside the transport.

Embarked units cannot normally do anything or be affected in any way whilst they are embarked. Unless specifically stated, abilities that affect other units within a certain range have no effect whilst the unit that has the ability is embarked.

If a transport is destroyed, any units embarked within it immediately disembark (see below) before the transport model is removed, but you must then roll one dice for each model you just set up on the battlefield. For each roll of 1, a model that disembarked (your choice) is slain.

Disembark: Any unit that begins its Movement phase embarked within a transport can disembark before the transport moves. When a unit disembarks, set it up on the battlefield so that all of its models are within 3" of the transport and not within 1" of any enemy models – any disembarking model that cannot be set up in this way is slain.

Units that disembark can then act normally (move, shoot, charge, fight, etc.) during the remainder of their turn. Note though, that even if you don't move disembarking units further in your Movement phase, they still count as having moved for any rules purposes, such as shooting Heavy weapons (pg 180).

EXAMPLE TURN

On these pages you will find an example turn of Warhammer 40,000. All six phases of a player's turn are described. In the examples shown below, it is the Death Guard player's turn, and we join the battle just as they are about to launch an assault upon a force of Space Marines.

1. MOVEMENT PHASE

The Death Guard player starts by moving their unit of Plague Marines. They have a Move characteristic of 5", and so are moved as close as possible towards the Space Marines.

The Death Guard player then moves their Malignant Plaguecaster, and decides this model should Advance...

The player rolls a D6, scoring a 4. The Malignant Plaguecaster (Move 5"), can therefore move up to 9".

2. PSYCHIC PHASE

The Death Guard only has a single psyker – the Malignant Plaguecaster. This model attempts to manifest the Smite power.

The Death Guard player takes a Psychic test by rolling 2D6, and scores a total of 6. This is greater than the power's warp charge value of 5, so the test is passed.

 + =6

The closest enemy unit are the Intercessors. They suffer D3 mortal wounds. The Death Guard player rolls a 5, which means the Intercessor Squad loses 3 wounds, enough to kill one Intercessor and wound another.

÷ 2 rounds to 3

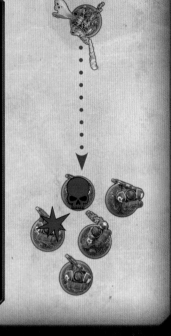

3. SHOOTING PHASE

The Death Guard player selects the unit of Plague Marines to shoot with. The Plague Marines will shoot with their boltguns, while the Plague Champion will throw a krak grenade.

The targets are 6" away, which is within range of the Plague Marines' boltguns. These are Rapid Fire 1 weapons, and so each fires twice at half range or less. The Death Guard player therefore rolls 8 dice to see if the shots hit. The Plague Marines' Ballistic Skill is 3+, so 6 shots hit and the others miss.

The Death Guard player then makes a wound roll for each hit. A boltgun's Strength of 4 equals the target's Toughness of 4, meaning a roll of 4+ is required to successfully wound the target. The Death Guard player rolls for each shot, four of which are successful. The Space Marine player will now need to make a saving throw for each.

One of the rolls is less than the Intercessor's Save characteristic of 3+, so the wound is allocated to the wounded Intercessor. A boltgun inflicts 1 point of damage on this model, which removes its last wound and it is slain. The other wounds are saved and bounce off the Space Marines' power armour.

4. CHARGE PHASE

The Death Guard player chooses the Plague Marines to charge the Intercessors.

The Space Marine player fires Overwatch and makes 4 hit rolls. Models only hit on 6s when firing Overwatch, however both hits go on to wound, and then both saving throws are failed – two models are slain!

After resolving Overwatch, the Death Guard player rolls 2D6, scoring 7. The Plague Marines can charge 7" – enough to move within 1" of the Intercessors.

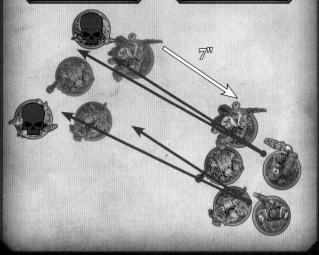

The Plague Champion then throws a krak grenade, which hits. This grenade has a Strength of 6, which wounds the Intercessors on a roll of 3+ as its Strength is greater than the Intercessors' Toughness. The Space Marine player then rolls a 3 for their saving throw, but must subtract 1 from the roll because the krak grenade has an AP characteristic of -1. The final result of 2 fails to protect the Space Marines.

 -1 = 2 ✗

A krak grenade inflicts D3 damage; the Death Guard player rolls a 6, inflicting 3 points of damage. This causes an Intercessor to lose both its wounds. As it is slain by this attack, the other point of damage is discarded and has no effect.

 ÷ 2 = 3

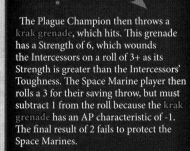

5. FIGHT PHASE

Units that charged always resolve their fights first. In this case, that means the Plague Marines unit fights first.

They start by piling in, each model moving up to 3" closer to the nearest model. All are now within 1" of an enemy.

The Plague Marines will use their plague knives to make their close combat attacks against the Intercessor unit, but the Plague Champion, who has an Attacks characteristic of 2, chooses to make 1 close combat attack using his plague sword, and 1 using his power fist. The Death Guard player rolls 2 hit rolls for the plague knives (rolling a 3 and a 5), 1 for the plague sword (rolling a 3), and 1 for the power fist (rolling a 2).

Plague sword   *Power fist*

The Plague Marines and the Plague Champion both have a Weapon Skill characteristic of 3+, so the attack made with the power fist misses, but all the others hit. After wound rolls and saving throws are taken, another Intercessor has been slain. The Plague Marine unit then **consolidates**, one of its models moving closer to the nearest enemy model.

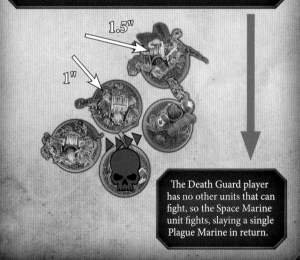

The Death Guard player has no other units that can fight, so the Space Marine unit fights, slaying a single Plague Marine in return.

6. MORALE PHASE

Both the Plague Marine unit and the Intercessors have suffered casualties during the turn, and so both have to take a Morale test.

The Death Guard player goes first, rolling a 6. Three Plague Marines died this turn, so 3 is added to the roll, for a total of 9. This exceeds the highest Leadership in the unit by 1 (the Plague Champion has a Leadership characteristic of 8), so 1 of the remaining models flees the battlefield.

The Space Marine player then takes a Morale test for the Intercessors, rolling a 3. When the number of casualties is added they have a total of 7. This is less than the unit's highest Leadership of 8 – the test is passed and no models flee.

The Death Guard turn is now complete, and the Space Marine player can now start their turn.

FIGHTING A BATTLE

THE MISSION

Before you can wage war in a game of Warhammer 40,000, you must select a mission. The core rules include a single mission – Only War – which is ideal to get the action started quickly. Others can be found elsewhere in this book, in other books, or you could play a mission of your own creation. If you and your opponent can't agree on which mission to play, both players should roll a dice, re-rolling ties, and whoever rolls the highest decides on the mission.

THE BATTLEFIELD

In the far future, battles are fought across an infinite variety of strange and alien planets where no land is left untouched by the blight of war. Crystal moons, derelict space hulks, carnivorous death worlds and nightmarish Daemon worlds are just a few of the fantastical landscapes that can be recreated whenever you play a game of Warhammer 40,000.

A battlefield can be any surface upon which the models can stand – a dining table, for example, or the floor. We typically assume a battlefield is 6' by 4' (although some missions will state other dimensions), but it should always be large enough to accommodate all your models – if it is not, simply increase the size of the battlefield.

Unless the mission you are playing instructs you otherwise, you should then feel free to create an exciting battlefield using any terrain features from your collection that you wish. In general, we recommend having one or two features in each 2' by 2' area. Don't worry if your battlefield doesn't match these requirements, but keep in mind that playing on very small or very large battlefields, or ones that are either a barren wasteland or filled to overflowing with terrain features, may give an advantage to one side or the other.

BATTLEZONES & EXPANSIONS

If you are battling in a specific battlezone, or if you are using a particular expansion, there might be additional rules pertaining to setting up the battlefield, and special rules that alter how some terrain interacts with your warriors. Bear these in mind when creating your battlefield.

THE WARLORD

Once you have mustered your army, nominate one of your models to be your Warlord.

If your Warlord is a **CHARACTER**, it can use a Warlord Trait – a preferred tactic or personal ability that marks them out amongst their peers. Immediately before either player starts to deploy their army, you can roll on the Warlord Trait table here to determine what Warlord Trait your Warlord has. Alternatively, choose the trait that most suits your Warlord's temperament or style of war.

WARLORD TRAITS

03	WARLORD TRAIT
1	**Legendary Fighter:** If this Warlord charges in the Charge phase, add 1 to their Attacks characteristic until the end of the ensuing Fight phase.
2	**Inspiring Leader:** Friendly units within 6" of this Warlord can add 1 to their Leadership characteristic.
3	**Tenacious Survivor:** Roll a dice each time this Warlord loses a wound. On a 6, the Warlord shrugs off the damage and does not lose the wound.

ONLY WAR

The time has come to prove your worth as the greatest warlord in the galaxy! All that stands between you and ultimate glory is an enemy army bent upon your destruction.

THE ARMIES

In order to play this mission, you must first muster an army from the miniatures in your collection. You can include any models in your army.

Sometimes you may find that you do not have enough models to field a minimum-sized unit (this can be found on each unit's datasheet); if this is the case, you can still include one unit of that type in your army with as many models as you have available.

THE BATTLEFIELD

Create the battlefield and set up terrain. The players must then place objective markers to represent sites of tactical or strategic import that one or both armies are attempting to secure. Objective markers can be represented by any suitable marker or piece of terrain. Each player must place two objective markers anywhere on the battlefield, so long as they are each at least 10" away from any other objective marker. We suggest taking turns to place these, starting with whichever player wins a roll-off. A player controls an objective marker if there are more models from their army within 3" of it than there are enemy models (measure to the centre of the marker).

PRIMARY OBJECTIVES

Before setting up their armies, both players roll off. The player who rolls higher then rolls on the primary objectives table (see right) to determine which are used during the mission.

DEPLOYMENT

Once the victory conditions have been determined, the player who did not roll on the primary objectives table then divides the battlefield into two equal-sized halves. Their opponent then decides which half is their own deployment zone, and which half is the other player's deployment zone.

The players then alternate deploying their units, one at a time, starting with the player who did not pick their deployment zone. Models must be set up in their own deployment zone, more than 12" from the enemy deployment zone. Continue setting up units until both players have set up all the units in their army, or you have run out of room to set up more units.

POWER LEVEL

Before battle begins, determine each army's Power Level by adding together the Power Ratings of all the units set up in that army; whichever player has the lowest is the Underdog. If both have the same Power Level, the player who assigned the deployment zones is the Underdog.

If the difference between the Power Levels of the two armies is 10 to 19, the Underdog receives one Command re-roll; if the difference is 20 to 29, the Underdog receives two Command re-rolls, and so on. Each Command re-roll can be used once, at any point during the battle, to re-roll a single dice.

FIRST TURN

The Underdog chooses who has the first turn.

BATTLE LENGTH

The battle lasts for five battle rounds, or until one army has slain all of its foes.

VICTORY CONDITIONS

If one army has slain all of its foes, it immediately wins a major victory. Otherwise, at the end of the battle, the player who has the most victory points wins a major victory. If both players have the same number of victory points at the end of the battle, the Underdog wins a minor victory.

PRIMARY OBJECTIVES	
D3	**VICTORY CONDITIONS**
1	**Slay and Secure:** At the end of the battle, each objective marker is worth 2 victory points to the player who controls it. Players also earn D3 victory points if the opposing army's Warlord was slain during the battle.
2	**Ancient Relic:** At the start of the first battle round, but before the first turn begins, randomly select one objective marker; remove the other objective markers from the battlefield. At the end of the battle, the remaining objective marker is worth 6 victory points to the player who controls it.
3	**Domination:** At the end of each turn, each objective marker is worth 1 victory point to the player who controls it. Keep a running score from turn to turn.

OPEN PLAY

Are you new to tabletop wargaming? Or are you a grizzled veteran looking for a new challenge? Either way, open play games are one of the best ways to get started, providing you with almost limitless options and flexibility.

Brilliant ideas are sometimes the simplest, and open play games of Warhammer 40,000 epitomise this. Open play is a style of gaming that allows you to take to the battlefield with any army, made up of any Citadel Miniatures from your collection – no restrictions. It's as straightforward and streamlined as wargaming gets, and it's a great way to begin.

Many players love the deep and complex rules that have traditionally defined tabletop wargaming, and if that's your preferred style, then you'll find plenty of support and guidance right here in this book. However, there's also a lot of fun to be found in a more flexible approach. All you need to play an open play game are your painted miniatures, their datasheets, the core rules, a set of dice, a tape measure, a surface on which to play and a willing opponent. Then, just set up your models and start having fun! You can add extra dimensions to your open play games by incorporating any of the rules or guidelines that appear in this and other Warhammer 40,000 books, such as rules for Detachments, battlezones and battlefield terrain. Alternatively, you can devise your own missions, creating entirely new objectives or special rules, or you could adapt any existing mission to better suit your needs.

The flexible nature of open play means that you can spend as much or as little time as you like reading rules, and it's a great introduction to the world of tabletop games. This style of gaming is perfect for beginners, who may not yet own a complete collection of miniatures. It's also ideal for veterans thinking of starting a new collection, and allows battles to be fought with just a few units of the models you plan to collect, so that you can see how they perform and what tactics work best with them.

Open play games allow the broadest choice of army selection, providing the greatest degree of freedom for collecting miniatures and putting together an army. Rather than structuring your collection around a particular Faction (pg 240), you can be inspired by any facet of the diverse and brutal galaxy, or simply by the models you most admire. If you're the proud owner of a varied collection of warriors, war machines and monstrous creatures, there's nothing to stop you fielding all of them in a single game. You can even deploy every last miniature you own in a battle of apocalyptic proportions, or set yourself unusual challenges. For instance, you could discover how many Space Marine Intercessors it takes to bring down your friend's Khorne Bloodthirster, or see how long a heroic Terminator Captain could fight off a Nurgling horde.

While there are no restrictions or requirements placed on the models you can use in open play games, it's best to have a chat with your opponent before the game begins to discuss what models you will each be taking in your armies. You can even make use of elements of matched play, like points, if you wish, but it is entirely up to you.

Besides giving you freedom to do more with your collection, open play games are also perfect for battles between multiple players. For example, there's a great fight to be had where a third player brings their Drukhari raiders to the battlefield. The piratical xenos strike from the shadows, preying on targets from the other armies, or perhaps even forging fleeting alliances with one side or the other. In open play, the types of battles you fight are limited only by your imagination.

You should feel free to tinker with any aspect of playing a game of Warhammer 40,000 that appeals to you. You could, for example, devise other methods of deploying your forces. You might place a screen across the centre of the table so that the armies can deploy in secret, or you and your opponent might each draw a map showing where you plan to deploy your units, and so on.

With so much scope for fun and creativity, open play is one of the most accessible and enjoyable gaming styles, for beginners and veterans alike. So what are you waiting for? Grab your miniatures collection, however large or small, and give open play a try!

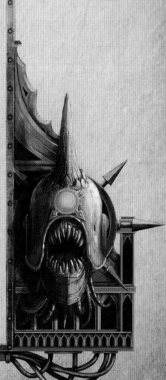

'SICKNESS, DISEASE, PLAGUE AND POX, SUFFERING AND THE SLOW, LIVING ROT. SUCH WONDROUS GIFTS DOES NURGLE SEEK TO BESTOW UPON THE UNWORTHY HUMAN CATTLE OF THE IMPERIUM. WE ARE MERELY THE VECTORS BY WHICH HIS VIRULENT BENEFICENCE MAY BE SPREAD TO THE UNDESERVING MASSES.'

- Urgloth Rotheart, Plague Champion of the Death Guard

*Warhammer 40,000 battles
are conventionally fought
between two players, but
battling it out with three
or more lends the game
a different dynamic and
ensures that no one has to sit
out. Of course, the real joy
of team games is the social
aspect, and you'll discover
true camaraderie with your
fellow gamers over salvoes of
good-natured banter aimed
across the battlefield, making
it clear that this gaming style
is fun for friend and foe alike.*

*It couldn't be easier to play a
team game. Once all players
have assembled with their
armies, simply split into
two teams – how you divide
the players is entirely up to
you. Having done so, select
one model on each team to
be their Warlord and then
play the battle exactly as
you normally would, using
the same rules but replacing
terms like 'player' and
'opponent' with 'team' or
'opposing team'.*

WAR WITHOUT END

**No form of war is unknown in the galaxy. On these pages you will find three examples
of open play missions – Annihilation, Hold at all Costs and Death or Glory – that you
can use to start waging war right away. You will also find a few ideas below to spark
your imagination for other open play battles; you should feel free to use these hooks as
the basis of your battles, or simply create ones of your own.**

- An elite force strikes behind enemy lines
  to assassinate the foe's commanders.

- An evil ritual is nearing completion – fight
  to prevent its culmination, or bring about
  its fruition.

- A group of sappers attempts to sabotage a
  mighty war machine or fortress before it,
  and its terribly powerful weapons, become
  fully operational.

- A convoy is ambushed – how many of its
  vital supplies can it escape with?

- You and your opponent(s) are trying to
  reach a powerful relic; use your fastest
  units to race across the long battlefield and
  be first to claim the prize!

- As you signal the attack, your own allies
  suddenly reveal their traitorous intent and
  open fire upon your lines. Can you rally to
  wage a war on two fronts and prevail?

- Your enemy believes their position
  unassailable. Lead the forlorn attempt to
  create a breach and bring victory!

- A band of operatives must silence sentries
  and enable their army's approach.

- A priceless piece of archeotech is lost
  within these war-torn ruins – your forces
  must be the ones to discover its location
  and take it back to your headquarters.

- A beleaguered army must hold out long
  enough for reinforcements to relieve them.

- You have been entrusted with the life of
  a dignitary – you must escort them safely
  across the war zone.

- Snipers and close-quarters fighters come
  into their own in a claustrophobic battle
  through the ruins of a fallen hive city.

- After months of fighting, the enemy army
  is on the verge of routing. Break their
  morale and victory will be assured.

ANNIHILATION

Two warlords face each other, intent on destroying all that stand before them. Each must attempt to annihilate their opponent, whilst minimising their own losses.

THE ARMIES

In order to play this mission, you must first muster an army from the miniatures in your collection. You can include any models in your army, but this mission works especially well when both armies have a roughly equal Power Level.

THE BATTLEFIELD

Create the battlefield and set up terrain.

DEPLOYMENT

Once the battlefield has been created, the players roll off. The player who rolled highest divides the battlefield into two equal-sized halves. Then, the player who rolled lowest chooses a half to be their deployment zone; the opposite half is their opponent's deployment zone. The players then alternate deploying their units, one at a time, starting with the player who did not pick their deployment zone. Models must be set up in their own deployment zone, more than 12" from the enemy deployment zone. Continue setting up units until both players have set up all the units in their army, or you have run out of room to set up more units.

FIRST TURN

The player who finished setting up their army first can choose whether to have the first or second turn.

BATTLE LENGTH

The battle lasts for five battle rounds, or until one army has slain all of its foes.

VICTORY CONDITIONS

If one army has slain all of its foes, it immediately wins a major victory. Otherwise, at the end of the battle, the player who has the most models remaining wins a minor victory.

HOLD AT ALL COSTS

The battlefield lies at a crossing of key strategic importance. A defending army stands ready to hold it at all costs in the face of a superior foe that surrounds them.

THE ARMIES

In order to play this mission, you must first muster an army from the miniatures in your collection. You can include any models in your army, but this mission works especially well when the Power Level of one army is between a third higher and double that of the other. In this mission, the player whose army has the higher Power Level is the Attacker; their opponent is the Defender.

THE BATTLEFIELD

Create the battlefield and set up terrain. The centre of the battlefield should contain at least one terrain feature, such as a hill, a building or a large ruin that the Defender's units can begin the battle holding.

DEPLOYMENT

Once the battlefield has been created, the Defender sets up their entire army anywhere that is within 18" of the centre of the battlefield. The Attacker then sets up their entire army anywhere that is more than 12" from any enemy model.

FIRST TURN

The players should roll off, and whoever rolls highest can choose whether to have the first or second turn.

BATTLE LENGTH

The battle lasts for five battle rounds, or until one army has slain all of its foes.

VICTORY CONDITIONS

If one army has slain all of its foes, it immediately wins a major victory. Otherwise, at the end of the battle, the player whose model is closest to the centre of the battlefield wins a major victory.

DEATH OR GLORY

An outnumbered army faces inevitable defeat, but if they sell their lives dearly, and even a single warrior survives, they will have earned a heroic death.

THE ARMIES

In order to play this mission, you must first muster an army from the miniatures in your collection. You can include any models in your army, but this mission works especially well when the Power Level of one army is at least twice that of the other. In this mission, the player whose army has the higher Power Level is the Attacker, and their opponent is the Defender.

THE BATTLEFIELD

Create the battlefield and set up terrain.

DEPLOYMENT

Once the battlefield has been created, the players should roll off. The player who rolled lowest chooses a half to be their deployment zone; the opposite half is their opponent's deployment zone. The Attacker sets up their entire army first, and the Defender sets up their entire army second. Models must be set up in their own deployment zone, more than 12" from the enemy deployment zone.

FIRST TURN

The Defender can choose whether to have the first or second turn.

BATTLE LENGTH

The battle lasts for five battle rounds, or until one army has slain all of its foes.

VICTORY CONDITIONS

If one army has slain all of its foes, it immediately wins a major victory. Otherwise, at the end of the battle, the Defender wins a heroic victory if they have even a single model remaining on the battlefield.

NARRATIVE PLAY

With a cast of indomitable heroes, diabolical villains and enigmatic xenos, a plot of system-spanning conflicts, unshakeable loyalty and ruthless betrayals, and of course spectacular battles, every Warhammer 40,000 story is an epic in itself. Narrative play is all about enacting such tales on your own battlefield.

All across the galaxy, relentless battles of conquest and survival are being fought between the forces of the Imperium, Chaos, and the disparate xenos races. Just as you might expect, recreating these sprawling conflicts on the tabletop is a hugely popular part of the Games Workshop hobby, allowing you to make these stories your own. Put simply, narrative play is a gaming style that ties the battles you play on your tabletop to the stories of the Imperium and its foes.

Most games of Warhammer 40,000 tell a story. Every time players get together and talk about why their armies might be fighting each other, they are working out a narrative game. Once objectives have been decided, there are endless ways to build that story into the game. Armies might be modified to better reflect the protagonists of the story, specific scenery might play a part in recreating the landscape, 'house rules' might be invented to represent the consequences of victory and defeat – even the paint schemes can be developed to reflect the

narrative the players are trying to create. This element of planning and storytelling sets narrative play apart from open play, embedding the games firmly in the worlds of Warhammer 40,000.

Narrative play can be further enhanced through the use of Battle-forged armies (pg 240). In these armies, your units are organised into Detachments, which not only allows your armies to better reflect the background of their Faction, but also awards Command Points, giving you access to general and mission-specific Stratagems which you can use to shape the battle.

The stories set out in the various Warhammer 40,000 publications are there to provide a setting for your collections of Citadel Miniatures. By their very nature, these tales describe battles fought by named individuals and specific armies, such as the Ambush at Dhorak Pass, when the Cadian regiments commanded by Commissar Odoski came under attack from the Alpha Legion.

We have included a mission at the end of this section that allows you to refight that battle, as well as a general guide on how to create your own missions based on historical events. These kinds of battles are referred to as 'Echoes of War' missions.

Most of the missions presented in this section take a more flexible approach to war in the far future, however. We've included six missions, each representing a classic type of battle that you can easily adapt to suit your own narrative should you so choose – we call these 'Crucible of War' missions. The Meat Grinder mission, for example, centres around a desperate defence against a foe who throws his forces at the enemy in ceaseless waves. It is representative of a thousand such conflicts in the Dark Millennium, and is ideal for recreating classic battles such as Ghazghkull Thraka's assault on Hades Hive, or the Ultramarines' ill-fated defence of Macragge's polar fortresses during the First Tyrannic War.

Narrative games are typically asymmetrical, with one player taking the role of the attacker and the other taking the role of the defender. Each player's army might be composed according to these different roles, with access to different abilities, and one player will often have an advantage over the other. These types of narrative games present a whole new challenge to a general, and require different skills and stratagems if you are to succeed.

Narrative games also tend to have more bespoke rules than either open play or matched play games. This is simply because narrative missions are more detailed in the way they try to recreate the stories, events and strategies of particular battles. Planning a narrative game, and working out which special rules you will use, is often just as fun as playing the game itself, as it lets you really unleash your imagination.

All of the missions and rules in this section can be used to provide inspiration for battles of your own creation. Recreating a battle just as it happened is great fun, and as we provide many missions that do this, it's very easy as well. With only a little effort, however, it is just as satisfying to use these missions as the framework for making up your own stories, tailored to your own collections. The only limitations to a narrative game are those of the story itself – which you get to create! Small and large armies, one-off games or campaigns (pg 272), simple or complex additional rules – all of the parameters are up to you and your opponent, ensuring that the games you play build on and support the legends of your collections.

'TO HUNT THE FALLEN, WE MUST BE STRONG, SWIFT AND SILENT. WE MUST PLACE TRUST IN OUR SWORN BROTHERS ALONE, AND SHOW NEITHER MERCY NOR HESITATION TO ANY WHO SEEK TO OBSTRUCT OR BETRAY US.'

- Sergeant Zamorael, Dark Angels Ravenwing

NARRATIVE PLAY MISSION RULES

Most narrative play missions use one or more additional special rules to better represent the different tactics and strategies used by attackers and defenders. Some of the more in-depth mission special rules are collected below and referenced by the missions that appear later in this section.

CONCEALED DEPLOYMENT

In some battles, commanders have had time to conceal the positions of their forces from the enemy.

If a mission uses Concealed Deployment, the Defender will need a set-up marker for each unit in their army that they intend to start the battle deployed on the battlefield. You do not need any markers for units that will start the battle embarked on a **TRANSPORT**, only a marker for the transport itself. Each marker needs to be distinct (for example by having a different number) so it can correspond to a specific unit. The Defender must write down which unit each marker represents and keep this information secret from his opponent.

When the Defender deploys their army, they set up the markers instead of their models. Once the Defender has set up all their markers, the Attacker deploys all their forces. Once this has been done, the Defender then reveals which marker corresponds to which unit, setting up the appropriate models as they do so. The first model in each unit must be placed exactly where the unit's set-up marker was placed, and the entire unit must be set up wholly within the player's own deployment zone.

DAWN RAID

Cunning commanders may attack under cover of darkness to conceal their advance from the foe.

If your mission uses Dawn Raid, both players must subtract 1 from all hit rolls made in the Shooting phase during the first battle round of the game.

PRELIMINARY BOMBARDMENT

In a major offensive, the attacker will often launch a heavy bombardment prior to the main attack.

If your mission uses Preliminary Bombardment, then at the start of the first battle round, but before the first turn begins, the Attacker should roll a dice for each enemy unit that is on the battlefield (do not roll for units that are embarked inside **TRANSPORTS**). On a roll of 6, that unit has been hit by a Preliminary Bombardment; that unit suffers D6 mortal wounds. **INFANTRY** units that are hit by a Preliminary Bombardment can choose to go to ground before the damage is determined – if they do, they only suffer D3 mortal wounds, but cannot take any actions during their first turn.

RANDOM BATTLE LENGTH

War is rarely predictable, and the time available to achieve your objectives is never certain.

If your mission uses Random Battle Length, at the end of battle round 5, the player who had the first turn must roll a D6. On a roll of 3+, the game continues, otherwise the game is over. At the end of battle round 6, the player who had the second turn must roll a D6. This time the game continues on a roll of 4+, otherwise the game is over. The battle automatically ends at the end of battle round 7.

RESERVES

Reserves are forces which are not directly present at the start of an engagement but are available as reinforcements during battle.

If a mission uses Reserves, it will detail which units in your army start the game in Reserve – these units are not deployed with the rest of your army.

The mission will usually state when the units placed in Reserve arrive on the battlefield – this is typically at the end of a particular Movement phase. If the mission does not specify when units arrive, roll for each unit at the end of your second Movement phase (and at the end of each of your Movement phases thereafter) – this is called a Reserve roll. On a 3+, the unit being rolled for arrives from Reserve. Note that if a unit placed into Reserve is embarked within a **TRANSPORT**, they will arrive when their transport does, not separately (if rolling, make a single roll for the transport and the units embarked in it).

The mission will explain how and where to set up units when they arrive from Reserve – typically within a short distance of a specified edge of the battlefield.

SENTRIES

Many commanders use sentries to guard vital locations and raise the alarm if intruders are spotted.

If your mission uses Sentries, the Defender will need one extra unit to act as their Sentries. Unless otherwise stated, this unit should have the Troops Battlefield Role, contain up to 10 models and have a Power Rating of 10 or less. The Sentries' Power Rating is excluded when you are calculating the total Power Level of your army.

The mission rules will detail where Sentries are set up, but it should be noted that each Sentry model moves and acts as a separate, individual unit throughout the battle. At the start of each of the Defender's Movement phases, both players roll a dice for each Sentry model, in an order chosen by the Defender. The player who rolled the highest can move the model the distance indicated on their dice in any direction (a Sentry cannot Advance as part of this move). If the rolls are tied, the Sentry does not move.

At the start of the game, all is quiet and the alarm has yet to be sounded, but it is raised if any of the following occur:

- A model from the Attacker's army fires a ranged weapon or manifests a psychic power.
- A model from the Attacking player's army attacks a Sentry in the Fight phase but fails to kill them. Note that Sentries cannot fire Overwatch until after the alarm is raised.
- A model from the Attacking player's army is spotted by a Sentry. An enemy unit is spotted if it is within a certain range of any Sentry at the end of any Movement phase (irrespective of whether or not that unit is visible to the Sentry). The spotting range depends upon the Power Rating of the Attacker's unit, as detailed below:

POWER RATING	SPOTTED WITHIN
5 or less	3"
6-10	6"
11-19	9"
20 or more	12"

If the alarm is raised during the Attacker's turn, their turn ends after the action that raised the alarm has been completed. If the alarm is raised during the Defender's turn, the Defender immediately starts a new turn in which they can typically set up response forces or reinforcements; this will be detailed in the mission itself. In either case, the Sentries are now under full control of the Defender.

SUSTAINED ASSAULT

Occasionally, an army will possess overwhelming superiority in numbers, with wave upon wave of its troops hurling themselves forward.

If your mission uses Sustained Assault, any of the Attacker's units that are destroyed can be brought back into play later in the battle, to represent their almost limitless supply of reinforcements. At the end of each of the Attacker's Movement phases, roll a dice for each of their destroyed units, adding 2 to the result if that unit has the Troops Battlefield Role. On a 4+, immediately set up that unit within 6" of a battlefield edge – the mission will specify which.

The Attacker can also, at the end of any of their turns, remove any of their units from the battlefield that have a quarter or less of their starting number of models (or, in the case of single-model units, a quarter or less of its starting number of wounds). This unit then counts as having been destroyed for all purposes, and so can be brought back into play later as described above.

CRUCIBLE OF WAR
MEAT GRINDER

The enemy forces arrayed against you are the last stubborn defenders of this war zone, grimly holding out despite being overwhelmingly outnumbered. You have been committed to lead an all-out attack to annihilate them in their entirety. Friendly casualties are of no concern – no enemy must survive!

THE ARMIES

Each player must first muster an army from the miniatures in their collection. A player can include any models in their army, but if their army is Battle-forged (pg 240) they will also be able to use the appropriate Stratagems included with this mission. Once the armies have been chosen, the players must then decide who will be the Attacker and who will be the Defender. If the Power Levels of the two armies are different, then the player whose army has the higher Power Level should be the Attacker and their opponent should be the Defender. Otherwise the players can roll off to decide.

THE BATTLEFIELD

Create a battlefield using the deployment map below and then set up terrain. The Defender's deployment zone should contain several defensible pieces of terrain, such as ruins or obstacles, from which they can make their defiant last stand. The Attacker's deployment zone should be more sparse by comparison, to better represent the no man's land they are crossing.

DEPLOYMENT

After terrain has been set up, the players then deploy their armies using the Concealed Deployment rules (pg 194). None of the Defender's units can use abilities that allow them to arrive on the battlefield mid-battle – such units must be set up on the battlefield during deployment, using the Concealed Deployment rules.

PRELIMINARY BOMBARDMENT

Once both sides have been set up, the Attacker launches a Preliminary Bombardment (pg 194).

FIRST TURN

The Attacker rolls a dice. On a 1, 2 or 3, the Attacker has the first turn, and on a 4, 5 or 6, the Defender has the first turn.

SUSTAINED ASSAULT

The Attacker can use the Sustained Assault rules (pg 195) to represent their overwhelming superiority in numbers. Each time one of the Attacker's replacement units arrives, set up the models in that unit within 6" of the Attacker's battlefield edge.

BATTLE LENGTH

The players should use the Random Battle Length rules (pg 194) to determine how long the battle lasts.

VICTORY CONDITIONS

If at the end of the battle the Defender has any models remaining on the battlefield, they win a major victory. Any other result is a major victory for the Attacker.

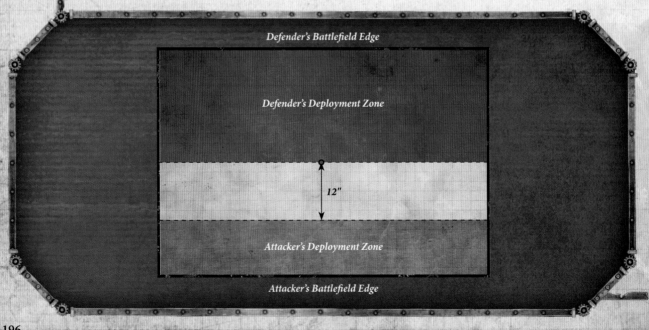

Defender's Battlefield Edge

Defender's Deployment Zone

12"

Attacker's Deployment Zone

Attacker's Battlefield Edge

STRATAGEMS

In this mission, the players can use Command Points (CPs) to use the following bonus Stratagems:

1CP | **SUSTAINED BOMBARDMENT**
Attacker Stratagem
Use this Stratagem immediately before rolling to see if a unit is hit by your Preliminary Bombardment. Roll 3 dice instead of 1.

1CP | **DECOYS**
Defender Stratagem
Use this Stratagem immediately before placing your set-up markers. You can place two extra set-up markers as decoys. When a decoy is revealed, simply remove the marker.

1CP | **SPIES**
Attacker Stratagem
Use this Stratagem immediately after the Defender has finished placing their set-up markers. Select one of the markers – the Defender must reveal which unit is hiding there and immediately set the unit up (the first model in that unit must be set up on the marker as normal).

1CP | **FOXHOLES**
Defender Stratagem
Use this Stratagem when one of your **INFANTRY** units is hit by a Preliminary Bombardment, but before the number of hits is determined. Halve the number of hits (rounding up) suffered by that unit.

1CP | **TRAPS**
Defender Stratagem
Use this Stratagem when a replacement unit arrives on the battlefield. Roll a dice for each model in that unit – for each roll of 6, one model in that unit is slain (controlling player's choice).

2CP | **OUTFLANKING REINFORCEMENTS**
Attacker Stratagem
Use this Stratagem when a replacement unit arrives on the battlefield. That unit can be set up anywhere within 6" of any battlefield edge other than the Defender's battlefield edge.

CRUCIBLE OF WAR
AMBUSH!

Under cover of darkness, the attacker's forces have prepared a deadly trap and are even now lying in wait for a convoy of enemy reserves heading for the front line. They hope to catch their foe unawares and destroy them utterly before they can escape or mount a retaliatory counter-strike.

THE ARMIES

Each player must first muster an army from the miniatures in their collection. A player can include any models in their army, but this mission works especially well with ground-based armies that contain few, if any, units that can **FLY**. If a player's army is Battle-forged (pg 240) they will also be able to use the appropriate Stratagems included with this mission. Once the armies have been chosen, the players must then decide who will be the Attacker and who will be the Defender. If the Power Levels of the two armies are different, then the player whose army has the higher Power Level should be the Attacker and their opponent should be the Defender. Otherwise the players can roll off to decide.

THE BATTLEFIELD

Create a battlefield using the deployment map below and then set up terrain. The Defender's deployment zone represents a thoroughfare leading towards the front line and should be exposed. The Attacker's deployment zone should be covered in dense terrain such as woods or ruins, making it a perfect ambush site.

DEPLOYMENT

After terrain has been set up, the players set up their armies using the Concealed Deployment rules (pg 194). However, for this mission, the roles are reversed; the Attacker uses set-up markers to deploy their army first, and the Defender then sets up as normal.

FIRST TURN

The Attacker has the first turn.

DAWN RAID

This mission uses the Dawn Raid rules (pg 194).

ESCAPE ROUTE

The Defender's units can move off the battlefield edge labelled 'Escape Route' so long as all of their models are able to make it off the board in the same phase. Any that do so have escaped the ambush – they are removed from the battlefield and take no further part in the battle.

BATTLE LENGTH

The players should use the Random Battle Length rules (pg 194) to determine how long the battle lasts.

VICTORY CONDITIONS

At the end of the battle, add up the Power Ratings of all the Defender's escaped units (see Escape Route, above) and compare this to the Power Level of their army (count the entire unit's Power Rating, even if only a single model escaped). If the combined Power Rating of the escaped units is one third or more of the army's Power Level, the Defender wins a major victory. Any other result is a major victory for the Attacker.

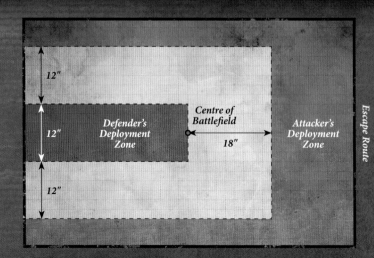

STRATAGEMS

In this mission, the players can use Command Points (CPs) to use the following bonus Stratagems:

NIGHT RAIDER
1+CP

Attacker Stratagem

Use this Stratagem immediately after deployment. For each Command Point you spend, the Dawn Raid rules apply for one additional battle round. For example, if the Attacker uses 2 Command Points on this Stratagem, both players must subtract 1 from all hit rolls made in the Shooting phase during the first three battle rounds of the game.

SPECTRUM-ENHANCEMENT WARGEAR
1CP

Attacker Stratagem

Select one of your own units immediately before it makes its shooting attacks. That unit can shoot without penalties from Dawn Raid this phase.

PRELIMINARY BOMBARDMENT
3CP

Attacker Stratagem

Use this Stratagem immediately after both sides have deployed. You can launch a Preliminary Bombardment (pg 194).

THE TABLES TURNED
1CP

Defender Stratagem

Use this Stratagem immediately after both sides have deployed, but before the first turn begins. The Defender rolls a dice – on a 6, they get the first turn instead.

RETURN FIRE
2CP

Defender Stratagem

Use this Stratagem at the end of your opponent's first Shooting phase. Select a unit in your army that was the target of at least one shooting attack; that unit can make a shooting attack at the enemy as if it were your own Shooting phase.

IRON DISCIPLINE
1CP

Defender Stratagem

Use this Stratagem after the Attacker has resolved a Preliminary Bombardment. Roll a dice for each of your units that went to ground; on a 2+ they can act normally during their first turn.

CRUCIBLE OF WAR
PATROL

You have been detailed to patrol no man's land and drive off any enemy forces encountered. Additional forces are near at hand to secure victory, but be warned – the enemy have their own reserves and will attempt to do the same to you.

THE ARMIES

Each player must first muster an army from the miniatures in their collection. A player can include any models in their army, but if their army is Battle-forged (pg 240) they will also be able to use the appropriate Stratagems included with this mission. Once the armies have been chosen, the players must then decide who will be the Attacker and who will be the Defender. If the Power Level of one of the armies is a third or more higher than the opposing army's Power Level, then the player whose army has the higher Power Level should be the Attacker and their opponent should be the Defender. Otherwise the players can roll off to decide.

THE BATTLEFIELD

Create a battlefield using the deployment map below and then set up terrain. Ruined buildings and craters litter the battlefield, the fallout from months of conflict.

DEPLOYMENT

After terrain has been set up, the Defender sets up any three of their units within their deployment zone – one of these units must have the Troops Battlefield Role. The Attacker then selects three of their units to serve as their patrol – one of these units must have the Troops Battlefield Role. All other units arrive later in the battle using the Reserves rules (pg 194).

FIRST TURN

Both players roll a dice, rolling again in the case of a tie. The player who rolls highest chooses who has the first turn.

DRAWN TO BATTLE

Starting from the second battle round, each player makes a roll for each of their units in Reserve at the end of their Movement phase. Attacking units arrive on a 4+, while Defending units arrive on a 3+. Units automatically arrive at the end of a player's fourth Movement phase if they have not already done so.

When a unit arrives, set it up anywhere within 6" of the controlling player's battlefield edge.

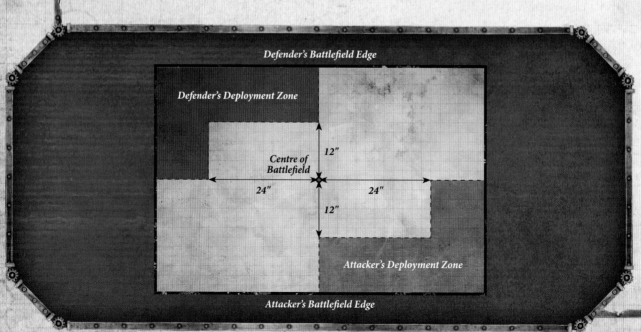

Defender's Battlefield Edge

Defender's Deployment Zone

Centre of Battlefield

12"

24"   24"

12"

Attacker's Deployment Zone

Attacker's Battlefield Edge

STRATAGEMS

In this mission, the players can use Command Points (CPs) to use the following bonus Stratagems:

2CP
ENCIRCLING REINFORCEMENTS
Attacker Stratagem
Use this Stratagem when one of your units arrives from Reserve. That unit can be set up anywhere within 6" of any battlefield edge other than the Defender's battlefield edge.

1CP
RAPID REINFORCEMENTS
Defender Stratagem
Use this Stratagem immediately before making a Reserve roll. The unit being rolled for automatically arrives – there is no need to make the Reserve roll.

2CP
SIGNAL THE ATTACK
Attacker Stratagem
Use this Stratagem at the end of your Movement phase, before making any Reserve rolls. Until the end of the turn you can add 1 to every Reserve roll you make.

1-2CP
DELAYED RESERVES
Defender Stratagem
Use this Stratagem immediately before your opponent makes a Reserve roll. If you spend 1 CP, your opponent must subtract 1 from the roll, but if you spend 2 CPs, they must subtract 2 instead.

2CP
PATROL IN FORCE
Attacker Stratagem
Use this Stratagem after the Defender has deployed their patrol. You can set up one additional unit during deployment – this unit must have the Troops Battlefield Role.

2CP
HOME ADVANTAGE
Defender Stratagem
Use this Stratagem immediately before rolling to determine who will have the first turn. You can roll two dice instead of one, and choose the highest result.

BATTLE LENGTH
The players should use the Random Battle Length rules (pg 194) to determine how long the battle lasts.

VICTORY CONDITIONS
At the end of the game, the player who has scored the most victory points wins a major victory. If both players have the same number of victory points, the game is a draw. Each player scores 1 victory point for each enemy unit that is destroyed (any unit not on the battlefield at the end of the game counts as having been destroyed).

> 'MERCY IS A WORD FOR TRAITORS AND COWARDS. IT IS A WORD FOR HERETICS. LET ALL WHO SPEAK IT BE STRUNG UP BY THEIR DUPLICITOUS TONGUES.'
>
> *- Confessor Belithael of the Dark Angels*

CRUCIBLE OF WAR
BLITZ

The war progresses and the offensive is pushing the enemy back all along the front. However, the foe has mustered a strong defence at a vital crossing, and thus far, all attempts to break through their lines have failed. You must attempt to smash the defenders aside and drive deep into enemy territory.

THE ARMIES

Each player must first muster an army from the miniatures in their collection. A player can include any models in their army, but this mission works especially well with ground-based armies that contain few, if any, units that can **FLY**. If a player's army is Battle-forged (pg 240), they will also be able to use the appropriate Stratagems included with this mission. Once the armies have been chosen, the players must then decide who will be the Attacker and who will be the Defender. If the Power Levels of the two armies are different, then the player whose army has the higher Power Level should be the Attacker and their opponent should be the Defender. Otherwise the players can roll off to decide.

THE BATTLEFIELD

Create a battlefield using the deployment map below and then set up terrain. The battlefield represents a well-defended and fortified position which the attackers are trying to break through. The Defender's Front Line and Second Line deployment zones should both feature plenty of dense terrain features, such as ruins, to shelter within, or even a series of obstacles, defence lines, razor wire and other defences with the potential to halt the Attacker's advance. The Attacker's deployment zone, by contrast, is a carefully prepared killing field, with relatively little cover available.

DEPLOYMENT

After terrain has been set up, the players set up their armies using the Concealed Deployment rules (pg 194). The Defender must attempt to place an equal number of set-up markers in their Front Line and Second Line deployment zones.

PRELIMINARY BOMBARDMENT

Once both sides have been set up, the Attacker launches a Preliminary Bombardment (pg 194).

FIRST TURN

The Attacker has the first turn.

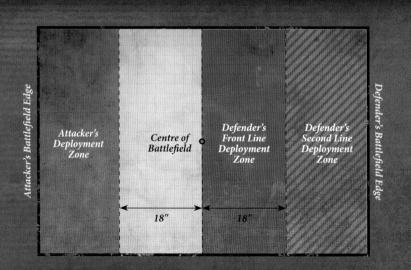

STRATAGEMS

In this mission, the players can use Command Points (CPs) to use the following bonus Stratagems:

1CP ### HEAVY BOMBARDMENT
Attacker Stratagem
Use this Stratagem immediately before rolling to see if a unit is hit by your Preliminary Bombardment. The unit being rolled for is hit on a 4+ instead of only a 6.

2CP ### DUG-IN DEFENCES
Defender Stratagem
Use this Stratagem immediately after setting up one of your units. Until that unit moves (for any reason) you can add 1 to that unit's saving throws against all shooting attacks.

1CP ### COVER GROUND
Attacker Stratagem
Use this Stratagem immediately before a unit rolls for its Advance distance – you count as having rolled a 6.

1CP ### PROXIMITY MINES
Defender Stratagem
Use this Stratagem the first time an enemy unit moves into or through your Front Line deployment zone. Roll a dice for each model in that unit – for each roll of 6, one model in that unit is slain (controlling player's choice).

2CP ### FORCED MARCH
Attacker Stratagem
Use this Stratagem when a replacement unit arrives on the battlefield. That unit can be set up anywhere within the Attacker's deployment zone that is more than 9" away from any enemy model.

1CP ### DECOYS
Defender Stratagem
Use this Stratagem immediately before placing your set-up markers. You can place two extra set-up markers as decoys. When a decoy is revealed, simply remove the marker.

SUSTAINED ASSAULT

The Attacker uses the Sustained Assault rules (pg 195) to represent their overwhelming superiority in numbers. Each time one of the Attacker's replacement units arrives, set up the unit wholly within 6" of the Attacker's battlefield edge. The Attacker must attempt to bring on units if they can – there can be no holding back.

BATTLE LENGTH

The players should use the Random Battle Length rules (pg 194) to determine how long the battle lasts.

VICTORY CONDITIONS

At the end of the game, the player who has scored the most victory points wins a major victory. If both players have the same number of victory points, the game is a draw. Victory points are achieved for the following:

Break Through: The Attacker scores 1 victory point for each of their units with at least one model completely within the Defender's Front Line deployment zone at the end of the battle. They score 2 victory points instead for each of their units with at least one model completely within the Defender's Second Line deployment zone at the end of the battle.

Destroy any Approach: Each time one of the Attacker's units is destroyed, the Defender scores 1 victory point.

CRUCIBLE OF WAR
SABOTAGE

The attacker is leading a force on a surprise raid deep in enemy territory. Their mission is to sneak past the sentries guarding an important installation and plant explosives to destroy it. The defender's main forces are on high alert, however, and should the alarm be raised, they will respond with deadly force.

THE ARMIES

Each player must first muster an army from the miniatures in their collection. A player can include any models in their army, but this mission works especially well with armies that have a Power Level of 50 to 100, and which do not include many (or any!) **VEHICLES** or **MONSTERS**. If a player's army is Battle-forged (pg 240), they will also be able to use the appropriate Stratagems included with this mission. Once the armies have been chosen, the players must then decide who will be the Attacker and who will be the Defender. If the Power Levels of the two armies are different, then the player whose army has the higher Power Level should be the Attacker and their opponent should be the Defender. Otherwise the players can roll off to decide. The Defender will need an additional unit to act as their Sentries (pg 195).

THE BATTLEFIELD

Create a battlefield using the deployment map below and then set up terrain. The Defender's deployment zone needs to include an objective marker or a suitable piece of scenery that is wholly within 12" of the centre of the battlefield to represent the target of the Sabotage (called the Objective)

DEPLOYMENT

After terrain has been set up, the Defender sets up their Sentries. At least half of the Sentries must be placed within 12" of the centre of the battlefield, but the remainder can be placed anywhere in the Defender's deployment zone. The Attacker then sets up as many of their units as they wish anywhere within their own deployment zone. All remaining units for both sides are placed in Reserve; they will arrive during the battle as described opposite.

FIRST TURN

The Attacker has the first turn.

ATTACKER'S RESERVES

The Attacker is allowed to bring on any Reserve units that they wish to at the end of each of their Movement phases. When a unit arrives from Reserve, they must be set up within 6" of their battlefield edge.

DEFENDER'S RESERVES

The Defender is allowed to bring on any Reserve units at the end of any of their Movement phases after the alarm has been sounded. On the first turn after the alarm is sounded, the Defender must roll a dice before bringing on a Reserve unit; it will only arrive on a roll of 3+. In subsequent turns, no roll is required. All models in the unit must be deployed wholly within 6" of one of the Defender's two battlefield edges, and with all models more than 9" from any enemy models.

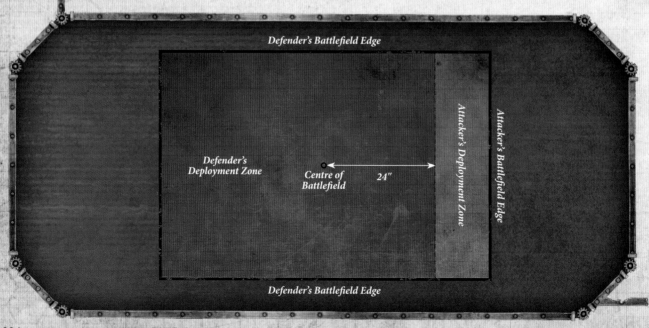

STRATAGEMS

In this mission, the players can use Command Points (CPs) to use the following bonus Stratagems:

1CP

SILENCED WEAPONS
Attacker Stratagem

Use this Stratagem when one of your units makes a shooting attack, immediately before the attack is resolved. The alarm is only sounded if the target of the shooting attack loses one or more wounds, but is not slain.

1CP

CAMOUFLAGE
Attacker Stratagem

Use this Stratagem when one of your units is set up during deployment. Halve that unit's Power Rating when working out the distance at which it can be spotted by Sentries.

1CP

EXTRA EXPLOSIVES
Attacker Stratagem

Use this Stratagem after a unit has made a Sabotage attempt. That unit can make one additional Sabotage attempt during the game (it cannot make another Sabotage attempt this turn, however).

2CP

SENSORS
Defender Stratagem

Use this Stratagem after you have set up your Sentries on the battlefield. All Sentries can add 3" to the distances at which they will spot an enemy model.

1CP

CUT THE WIRES
Defender Stratagem

Use this Stratagem if any of your units are within 3" of the Objective at the end of the game. Reduce the number of Sabotage attempts that have been made by 1, to a minimum of 0 attempts.

2CP

EXTRA SENTRIES
Defender Stratagem

Use this Stratagem immediately before setting up your Sentries. Two units can be set up as Sentries rather than only one unit.

SABOTAGE

Units from the Attacker's army can make a Sabotage attempt if they are within 3" of the Objective at the end of any of their turns. An individual unit cannot attempt to Sabotage the Objective more than once during the battle, but any number of different units from the Attacker's army can do so. **Vehicles** and **Monsters** cannot make Sabotage attempts.

Keep track of the number of Sabotage attempts that are made over the course of the mission. When the battle ends, the Attacker rolls a dice, adding the number of Sabotage attempts to the result. If the score is 7 or more, the Objective is destroyed in a massive explosion!

Proximity Alert: The alarm is automatically sounded from the end of the turn in which the first Sabotage attempt is made, even if no Sentries are left on the battlefield.

BATTLE LENGTH

The players should use the Random Battle Length rules (pg 194) to determine how long the battle lasts.

VICTORY CONDITIONS

If the Objective is destroyed (see Sabotage), the Attacker wins a major victory. Otherwise, the Defender wins a major victory.

CRUCIBLE OF WAR
RESCUE

A spy has narrowly evaded capture by the foe, but they are still trapped behind enemy lines. Your orders are to locate the spy, and then escort them from the battlefield before enemy reinforcements arrive to overwhelm your rescue force.

THE ARMIES

Each player must first muster an army from the miniatures in their collection. A player can include any models in their army, but this mission works especially well with armies that have a Power Level of 50 to 100, and which do not include many (or any!) **VEHICLES** or **MONSTERS**. If a player's army is Battle-forged (pg 240), they will also be able to use the appropriate Stratagems included with this mission.

Once the armies have been chosen, the players must then decide who will be the Attacker and who will be the Defender. If the Power Levels of the two armies are different, then the player whose army has the higher Power Level should be the Attacker and their opponent should be the Defender. Otherwise the players can roll off to decide. The Attacker will need a single **INFANTRY** model with a Wounds characteristic of no more than 4 to represent the Spy. The Defender will need an additional unit to act as their Sentries (pg 195).

THE SPY

The Spy model is not included in the Attacker's Battle-forged army, and does not contribute to the Attacking army's Power Level. It is treated as a unit consisting of a single model, that can only be attacked by enemy models if it is the closest target.

THE BATTLEFIELD

Create a battlefield using the deployment map below and then set up terrain. Once all the terrain has been set up, the players take it in turns, starting with the Attacker, to pick a piece of terrain in the Defender's deployment zone in which the Spy may be hiding, until a total of six terrain pieces have been chosen (alternatively, players can place six objective markers).

DEPLOYMENT

After terrain has been set up, the Defender sets up a unit of Sentries (pg 195). At least a third of the Sentries must be placed within 12" of the centre of the battlefield, but the remainder can be placed anywhere in the Defender's deployment zone. The Attacker then sets up as many of their units as they wish anywhere within their own deployment zone. All remaining units for both sides are placed in Reserve; they will arrive during the battle as described below.

FIRST TURN

The Attacker has the first turn.

ATTACKER'S RESERVES

The Attacker is allowed to bring on any Reserve units that they wish to at the end of each of their Movement phases. When a unit arrives from Reserve, they must be set up within 6" of their battlefield edge.

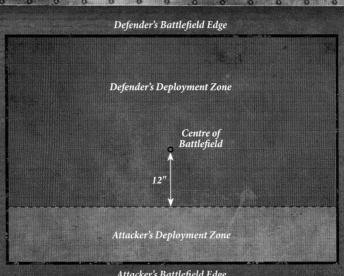

Defender's Battlefield Edge

Defender's Deployment Zone

Centre of
Battlefield

12"

Attacker's Deployment Zone

Attacker's Battlefield Edge

STRATAGEMS

In this mission, the players can use Command Points (CPs) to use the following bonus Stratagems:

1CP — SILENCED WEAPONS
Attacker Stratagem

Use this Stratagem when one of your units makes a shooting attack, immediately before the attack is resolved. The alarm is only sounded if the target of the shooting attack loses one or more wounds, but is not slain.

2CP — SENSORS
Defender Stratagem

Use this Stratagem after you have set up your Sentries on the battlefield. All Sentries can add 3" to the distances at which they will spot an enemy model.

2CP — NIGHT RAID
Attacker Stratagem

Use this Stratagem after both sides have deployed. The Dawn Raid rules (pg 194) are used in this mission and the spotting range for all Sentries is halved during the first battle round.

3CP — RAPID RESPONSE
Defender Stratagem

Use this Stratagem before rolling to see if a Reserve unit arrives on the turn after the alarm is sounded. The unit automatically arrives without the dice being rolled, and can arrive within 6" of any battlefield edge other than the Attacker's.

1CP — SCAN FOR DISTRESS BEACONS
Attacker Stratagem

Use this Stratagem at the end of your Movement phase if a model is within 12" of one of the pieces of terrain that may contain the Spy that has yet to be investigated. On a 6, you have found the Spy and it is placed using the rules below.

2CP — EXTRA SENTRIES
Defender Stratagem

Use this Stratagem immediately before setting up your Sentries. Two units can be set up as Sentries rather than only one unit.

DEFENDER'S RESERVES

The Defender is allowed to bring on any Reserve units at the end of any of their Movement phases after the alarm has been sounded. On the first turn after the alarm is sounded, the Defender must roll a dice before bringing on a Reserve unit; it will only arrive on a roll of 4+. In subsequent turns, no roll is required. All models in the unit must be deployed wholly within 6" of the Defender's battlefield edge, and with all models more than 9" from any enemy models.

FINDING THE SPY

Roll a dice the first time one of the Attacker's models finishes a move within 3" of a piece of terrain (or marker) that may contain the Spy. On a roll of 6, or if this is the last place the Spy could be, the model representing the Spy is set up by the Attacker within 3" of the terrain, more than 1" from any enemy models. If this is impossible, the Spy is slain and the Attacker loses the battle immediately.

The Spy cannot move in the Movement phase in which it is discovered. In addition, the alarm is automatically sounded at the end of the turn in which the Spy is discovered, even if no Sentries are left on the battlefield.

BATTLE LENGTH

The players should use the Random Battle Length rules (pg 194) to determine how long the battle lasts.

VICTORY CONDITIONS

If the Spy has been discovered and is still alive at the end of the game, the Attacker wins the battle. Otherwise the Defender wins the battle.

Across the worlds bordering the Damocles Gulf, the armies of the Imperium gather their full might to drive back the xenos foe. Against them stand the invading armies of the T'au, their ascendant technology as swift and lethal as any threat the Imperium has yet faced.

HISTORICAL BATTLES

The galaxy is replete with heroic deeds and legendary battles. With a little imagination, you can recreate these battles with your armies on the tabletop and find out if history will repeat itself, or if your command can alter the course of fate.

After reading about a specific battle, many players become inspired and wish to incorporate similar themes into their own games. Some players may even take their inspiration a step further, wanting to replicate not just the flavour of the battle that inspired them, but recreate the conflict exactly. Such 'historical' battles offer many unique and rewarding challenges.

There are myriad ways to approach recreating a historical battle. There is no right or wrong method, and players should experiment to find what works best for them. Unlike a pick-up-and-play match against a regular opponent, replaying a historical battle takes some degree of planning. How much depends on the scale and detail of the battle you are trying to bring to life. In some cases, there will already be an Echoes of War mission that represents the event. Effectively a ready-made historical battle, these narrative missions feature all you need to recreate the clash on the tabletop. We have provided one here as an example – Ambush at Dhorak Pass – including a brief summary of the events (below) and the mission that recreates it (right).

Conversely, if a battle is recounted in less detail, further research and perhaps a little innovation is called for. If there is no mission for the battle you wish to enact, you may want to make up your own rules. You could adapt an existing mission to better suit your needs or devise one completely from scratch. Read the source material again and study any artwork, both of which can give you glimpses into the circumstances of the battle. Look for any details that can be translated to the tabletop, such as mentions of the different types of units that were present, or of the heroes that led them into battle, the strategies they used, the terrain they fought over, and so on. The more you discover and translate into your rules, the more authentic and enjoyable your game will be. Inventing rules, army lists and a modelled battlefield for a historical re-fight is all part of the fun!

THE AMBUSH AT DHORAK PASS

The Cadian Dhorak front was beginning to crumble beneath the onslaught of relentless Chaos attacks. Yet this was Cadia – a fortress world as well prepared for war as any in the Imperium, honed by battles uncounted. Reinforcements were already en route – with tank columns of the Cadian 309th Armoured Regiment leading companies of the 822nd Infantry – 'The Sureshots' – to the aid of their beleaguered comrades. They did not make it. Waiting for them on the supply route was a carefully laid Alpha Legion ambush. Designed to deny Imperial reinforcements at the most critical junctures of the final battles, such ambushes had been set up all across the multiple fronts. Under cover of the unnatural darkness of violent warp storms, the Alpha Legion had laid a characteristically effective trap behind the Dhorak front. A series of quake-mines across the path stalled the lead Imperial

forces, their own wrecked vehicles blocking their route. Then, with perfect timing, hidden Chaos troops rose from concealment to lay down a deadly crossfire upon both flanks. In this way, the undersized strike force whittled down the Imperial forces' superior numbers. Cadians are born to fight, however. Under barked commands from their Commissar, they began to coolly lay down return fire while attempting to fall back in good order. Commissar Odoski knew he needed to extract himself from the immediate ambush, and that if he could set his firing line then his superior numbers and armour could make his foe pay for their daring. Unfortunately, this played right into the Alpha Legion's plan. Summoned Daemons materialized amidst the Cadians' rear ranks, and for the first time, panic began to set in amongst the battle-hardened Astra Militarum. In a few short moments,

only smoking wrecks and cruelly hewn corpses were left at the crossroads, the only sound the crackle of flames and a last few vox calls from the Dhorak front – still calling for aid that would never arrive.

ECHOES OF WAR
AMBUSH AT DHORAK PASS

The final battles of Cadia were marked not just by the terrible onslaught of Abaddon's assaults, but also by innumerable synchronised ambushes. The action at the Dhorak Pass crossroads is an example of how the smaller Alpha Legion strikes could eliminate larger Imperial forces.

THE MISSION

This mission is a variation of the Ambush! mission (pg 198). Select the armies and create the battlefield as described below, but otherwise use all the rules as listed in the Ambush! mission, along with the additional rules and modifications detailed here.

THE ARMIES

The Defender commands an Astra Militarum army; the Cadian 309th Armoured and 822nd Infantry under the Command of Commissar Odoski. The Attacker commands Alpha Legion Chaos Space Marines and a host of their Daemon allies. The Cadian forces outnumber the Alpha Legion forces.

THE BATTLEFIELD

Use the deployment map and set up terrain as shown below to create the Dhorak Pass battlefield.

DAEMONIC AMBUSH

The Alpha Legion player's **DAEMON** units are not set up during deployment, but will arrive later during the battle. At the end of the Alpha Legion player's third Movement phase, they set up all of their **DAEMON** units anywhere on the battlefield more than 9" from any enemy model.

UNNATURAL DARKNESS

Do not use the Dawn Raid rules. Instead, use all the rules from Battlezone: Night Fight (pg 252) to better reflect the darkness caused by the warp storms.

BLOCKED ROUTE

The wrecks in the middle of the battlefield have blocked the road. Models cannot move through or over them and must move around them.

QUAKE-MINES

Roll a dice each time an **ASTRA MILITARUM** unit Advances along the Dhorak Road (see map) – on a 1 it triggers quake-mines buried by the Alpha Legion and immediately suffers D6 mortal wounds.

THE SURESHOTS

To represent their disciplined firing lines, the Cadian player can re-roll any hit rolls of 1 in the Shooting phase for any of their **INFANTRY** units that remained stationary in their preceding Movement phase.

COMMISSAR ODOSKI

If Commissar Odoski exits the battlefield (see Escape Route, pg 198) then the battle immediately ends and the Cadian player wins a major victory.

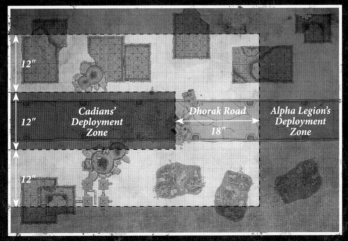

12"

12"

*Cadians'
Deployment
Zone*

Dhorak Road

18"

*Alpha Legion's
Deployment
Zone*

12"

Escape Route – Towards Dhorak Front

MATCHED PLAY

Armies come in all shapes and sizes, with unique strengths and weaknesses, but to test a general's mettle as a commander, there needs to be a level playing field. This is the goal of matched play.

Matched play games give you the option to fight battles with armies that are intentionally balanced against one another, allowing you to test not only your tactical skill on the battlefield, but also your strategic ability to choose an army that can defeat all opponents!

There are several ways to choose an army for matched play games. Typically, you and your opponent will build an army to an agreed points limit, but you could instead, for example, build armies that have a set number of units. Alternatively, you could use the Wounds characteristic or the Power Rating of each unit, either setting an upper limit for each unit or a fixed total for both armies. These are just a few examples of ways you can organise an army for matched play games – you and your opponent can use any system you like, as long as you both agree.

Forging an army for matched play is a more detailed process than it is for open and narrative play games. Firstly, it involves a conversation between you and your opponent in which you decide on the parameters of the battle. Whatever your chosen method of army selection, there will be some calculations to make as you select your forces to your agreed limits. Finally, you will need to organise your army into Detachments, as all matched play games use the Battle-forged army rules (pg 240). This is very straightforward and a fun process in its own right. It also means that, in matched play games, the game has essentially started before the first miniature is set up on the battlefield. Your knowledge of the units available to you and the wargear they use will be pivotal in this army-selection process, and knowledge of your opponent's force can be just as important.

BELLIGERENCE ALLIED TO FAITH CAN MOVE A MOUNTAIN.

Which combinations of units work best may not be obvious at first, but once you've played a few games, you will find the balance that works best for you.

When using Battle-forged armies, most Detachments will grant you Command Points (pg 242). These grant access to Stratagems, powerful tools that you can use to turn the tide of battle.

This section includes six Eternal War and six Maelstrom of War missions, which are designed to be played as part of matched play battles – the former use fixed ways of scoring victory points, the latter use dynamic Tactical Objectives which reflect changing orders. Unlike the missions presented in the narrative play section, where either the attacker or defender might have a slight advantage, in matched play missions both players share the same goal, providing them with an even chance of achieving victory.

There are several benefits to matched play. A battle between armies that are equally balanced makes for a decisive test of your strategic acumen, and the outcome of such a clash will always be hard to predict. Once you have settled on

an army configuration, you essentially have a pick-up-and-play force that you can bring to any table, against any opponent, and there's no need to agree on the setting and story of a battle as you would in a narrative play game. Matched play is ideal for school leagues and tournaments, as it provides clear guidelines on the size and strength of the armies taking part, as well as ensuring that all battles are as fair as they can be. Also, putting limits on an army makes it easier to control how long a game will last, and as such, matched play is perfect for a quick game in your local hobby store. Some tournaments or events apply extra rules which may affect the armies you can choose, creating new challenges for players. For example, they might limit Battle-forged armies to three Detachments, or introduce exclusive new Detachments for you to use.

The following pages offer more details on assembling matched play armies and playing matched play battles. But however enjoyable it is to design a perfect army, a true general will only be satisfied after their force has sallied forth and proven its worth on the battlefield. Matched play beckons – and glory awaits!

'TWIST YOUR ENEMY'S DEEDS. RENDER HIS VICTORIES YOUR OWN. WEAVE ABOUT HIM THE STRANDS OF FATE AND PROVIDENCE UNTIL, WITH BUT A TWITCH OF HIS STRINGS, YOU COMPEL YOUR PUPPET TO LIE, TO KILL, AND EVEN SACRIFICE HIS OWN LIFE, IN FURTHERANCE OF THE WILL OF TZEENTCH.'

- *Ezorath Qu'rastis, Sorcerer of the Thousand Sons*

CHOOSE ARMIES

The rules presented here are designed so that the opposing armies used in a matched play game have as equal a chance of winning as possible. Mustering an army for matched play is therefore a more detailed affair than it is for open play or narrative play style gaming.

When choosing an army for a matched play game, your army must be Battle-forged (pg 240) and its total points value cannot exceed the limit set for your game.

ARMY FACTION

All of the units in a matched play army, with the exception of those that are **Unaligned**, must have at least one Faction keyword in common (e.g. **Imperium** or **Chaos**), even though they may be in different Detachments.

POINTS LIMIT

In a matched play game, you will need to determine with your opponent the points limit for your game. Usually, both players will use the same limit, but this does not need to be the case.

To use a points limit, you will need to reference the points values, which are found in a number of Warhammer 40,000 publications, such as codexes. In these you will find the points costs for every model and weapon described in that book. Simply add up the points values of all the models and weapons in your army, and make sure the total does not exceed the agreed limit for the game.

REINFORCEMENT POINTS

Sometimes a psychic power or ability will allow you to add units to your army, or replace units that have been destroyed. One of the most common examples of such an ability might allow you to summon a unit of **Daemons** to the battlefield. In a matched play game, you must set aside some of your points in order to use these units. The points you set aside are called your reinforcement points, and need to be recorded on your army roster (see below).

Each time a unit is added to an army during battle, you must first subtract the number of points the unit would cost from your pool of reinforcement points. If there are not enough points in the pool to pay for the unit, you must either decrease the size of the unit (down to the minimum unit size) or the number of upgrades until you have enough points for it, or decide not to use it after all. If you decide not to use the unit, then the ability or psychic power that allowed you to take it in the first place is still considered to have been used, even though no unit actually arrived.

ARMY ROSTER

Once you have picked your army, record the details of it on a piece of paper (called your army roster). The roster must include the units in your army, details of the upgrades they have, and must also say which unit in the army will be the army's Warlord.

ORGANISED EVENTS

If you are using matched play for an organised event such as a tournament, we suggest using the table below as a helpful guideline. Of course, if you are organising such an event, you should feel free to modify these guidelines to better suit your event's own needs, schedule, etc.

ORGANISED EVENT GUIDELINES

POINTS LIMIT	NUMBER OF DETACHMENTS	BATTLEFIELD SIZE	GAME LENGTH
Up to 1,000	Up to 2 per army	4' x 4'	Up to 2 hours
1,001-2,000	Up to 3 per army	6' x 4'	2 to 3 hours
2,001-3,000	Up to 4 per army	8' x 4'	3 or more hours

CHOOSE MISSION

The only thing that remains to be done is to choose the mission you will use for the game. We have included two sets of matched play missions in this book: six Eternal War missions, and six Maelstrom of War missions. Each set has been devised to present different tactical challenges.

Matched play games use missions. You can simply agree with your opponent which set of matched play missions you wish to use, or you can roll off, and whoever rolls highest can choose which set to use.

Most matched play missions come in sets of six. Having picked the set you wish to use, you can either select one of the six missions, or roll a dice to randomly select one by using the appropriate table:

ETERNAL WAR TABLE

D6	MISSION
1	Retrieval Mission (pg 218)
2	No Mercy (pg 219)
3	The Scouring (pg 220)
4	Big Guns Never Tire (pg 221)
5	Secure and Control (pg 222)
6	The Relic (pg 223)

MAELSTROM OF WAR TABLE

D6	MISSION
1	Cleanse and Capture (pg 230)
2	Contact Lost (pg 231)
3	Tactical Escalation (pg 232)
4	Spoils of War (pg 233)
5	Cloak and Shadows (pg 234)
6	Deadlock (pg 235)

OBJECTIVE MARKERS

Many missions use objective markers – these represent sites of tactical or strategic import that both sides are attempting to secure. These can be represented by any appropriate markers, pieces of terrain or spare models that you have available, but nicely modelled bespoke ones are the most satisfying to use on your battlefield. When measuring distances involving objective markers, always measure to and from the centre of the marker.

SUDDEN DEATH

Generally a game will not finish before the agreed turn limit. However, it is possible to achieve a 'sudden death' victory in the following circumstances:

1. If one player concedes the battle, the game ends immediately and a crushing victory goes to their opponent.

2. If at the end of any turn after the first battle round, one player has no models on the battlefield, the game ends immediately and their opponent automatically wins a crushing victory. Do not include any Fortifications when determining if a player has any units on the battlefield unless they have a unit embarked inside – even the most formidable bastion requires a garrison if it is to pose a threat.

MATCHED PLAY MISSION RULES

The following three special rules apply to all matched play games:

PSYCHIC FOCUS

With the exception of *Smite*, each psychic power can be attempted only once per turn, rather than once per psyker per turn.

STRATEGIC DISCIPLINE

The same Stratagem cannot be used by the same player more than once during any single phase. This does not affect Stratagems that are not used during a phase, such as those used 'before the battle begins' or 'at the end of a battle round'.

TACTICAL RESERVES

Instead of being set up on the battlefield during Deployment, many units have the ability to be set up on teleportariums, in high orbit, in Reserve, etc., in order to arrive on the battlefield mid-game as reinforcements. When setting up your army during Deployment for a matched play game, at least half the total number of units in your army must be set up on the battlefield, even if every unit in your army has an ability that would allow them to be set up elsewhere. Furthermore, in matched play games, any unit that has not arrived on the battlefield by the end of the third battle round counts as having been destroyed.

STANDARD DEPLOYMENT MAPS

These six standard deployment maps are referenced in the matched play missions in this section. When playing matched play missions, you must randomly select one of these deployment maps. To do so, one of the players simply rolls a D6 – you then use the deployment map that corresponds to the result. The mission will typically say which player makes this roll – if not, it is made by the youngest player.

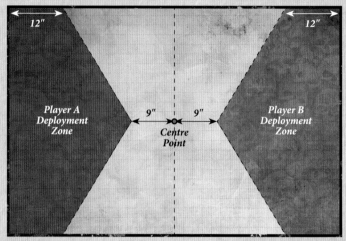

1. SPEARHEAD ASSAULT

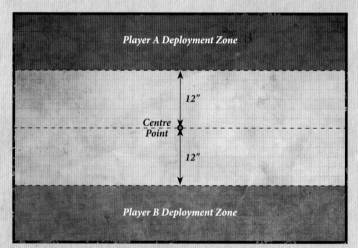

2. DAWN OF WAR

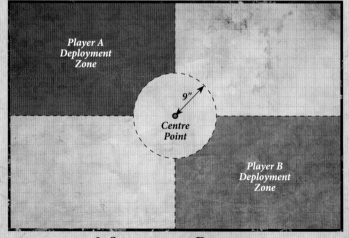

3. SEARCH AND DESTROY

'WE STAND AGAINST THE RISING TIDE OF CHAOS. NONE SHALL MOVE US, OR LAY US LOW. OUR FOES SHALL BATTER THEMSELVES BLOODY AGAINST THE FORTRESS OF OUR CONTEMPT, AND GRIND THEIR BONES TO POWDER UPON THE RAMPARTS OF OUR DISDAIN. AND WHEN THEY ARE NAUGHT BUT DUST UPON THE WIND, WE WILL REMAIN.'

- Captain Lydoro,
Imperial Fists 4th Company

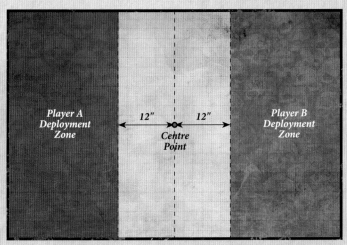

4. Hammer and Anvil

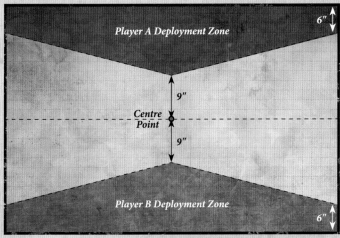

5. Front-line Assault

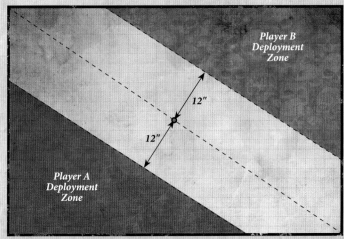

6. Vanguard Strike

'Let the blood flow in a crimson tide. Let it pour through their meager fanes and drown their prating priests. Let it sweep away the Corpse-Emperor's pitiful armies and submerge his rotting worlds in an ocean of gore. So demands mighty Khorne, and so shall it be!'

- Ghadrax the Annihilator, Champion of Khorne

ETERNAL WAR
RETRIEVAL MISSION

The battlefield is strewn with discarded equipment, supplies and other detritus of war that, for various reasons, you wish to recover. You must fight off the enemy while scouring the field to retrieve as many of these vital objectives as you can.

THE ARMIES

Each player selects a Battle-forged army to an agreed points limit.

THE BATTLEFIELD

Create the battlefield and set up terrain. Next, the players set up 4 objective markers; the players should roll off and, starting with whoever rolls highest, the players alternate placing these objective markers until all 4 have been set up. The objective markers can be located anywhere on the battlefield, as long as the centre of each is more than 12" from the centre of any other objective marker and 6" from the edge of the battlefield.

DEPLOYMENT

The player who placed the fourth objective marker determines which of the standard deployment maps is used in the battle (pg 216) and picks one of the deployment zones on the map for their army. Their opponent uses the other deployment zone.

The players then alternate deploying their units, one at a time, starting with the player who did not pick their deployment zone. A player's models must be set up within their own deployment zone. Continue setting up units until both sides have set up their army.

FIRST TURN

The player who finished setting up their army first can choose to take the first or second turn. If they decide to take the first turn, their opponent can roll a dice; on a roll of 6, they manage to seize the initiative, and they get the first turn instead!

BATTLE LENGTH

At the end of battle round 5, the player who had the first turn must roll a D6. On a roll of 3+, the game continues, otherwise the game is over. At the end of battle round 6, the player who had the second turn must roll a D6. This time the game continues on a roll of 4+, otherwise the game is over. The battle automatically ends at the end of battle round 7.

VICTORY CONDITIONS

At the end of the game, the player who has scored the most victory points is the winner. If both players have the same number of victory points, the game is a draw. Victory points are achieved for the following:

Take and Hold: At the end of the game, each objective marker is worth 3 victory points to the player who controls it. A player controls an objective marker if they have more models within 3" of the centre of it than their opponent.

Slay the Warlord: If the enemy Warlord has been slain during the battle, you score 1 victory point.

First Blood: The first unit, of any kind, to be destroyed during the battle is worth 1 victory point to the opposing player at the end of the game. If two or more units from opposing forces are destroyed simultaneously, then both players get 1 victory point.

Linebreaker: If, at the end of the battle, you have at least one model within the enemy's deployment zone, you score 1 victory point.

ETERNAL WAR
NO MERCY

In a harsh and war-torn galaxy, there are many battles where there is only one goal – find your enemy, crush them utterly and take away their means to mount further resistance. Your mission is simple: kill as many enemy units as you can!

THE ARMIES

Each player selects a Battle-forged army to an agreed points limit.

THE BATTLEFIELD

Create the battlefield and set up terrain.

DEPLOYMENT

The players roll off – whoever rolls highest determines which of the standard deployment maps is used in the battle (pg 216) and picks one of the deployment zones on the map for their army. Their opponent uses the other deployment zone.

The players then alternate deploying their units, one at a time, starting with the player who did not pick their deployment zone. A player's models must be set up within their own deployment zone. Continue setting up units until both sides have set up their army.

FIRST TURN

The player who finished setting up their army first can choose to take the first or second turn. If they decide to take the first turn, their opponent can roll a dice; on a roll of 6, they manage to seize the initiative, and they get the first turn instead!

BATTLE LENGTH

At the end of battle round 5, the player who had the first turn must roll a D6. On a roll of 3+, the game continues, otherwise the game is over. At the end of battle round 6, the player who had the second turn must roll a D6. This time the game continues on a roll of 4+, otherwise the game is over. The battle automatically ends at the end of battle round 7.

VICTORY CONDITIONS

At the end of the game, the player who has scored the most victory points is the winner. If both players have the same number of victory points, the game is a draw. Victory points are achieved for the following:

No Quarter Given: Each player scores 1 victory point for each enemy unit that is destroyed.

Slay the Warlord: If the enemy Warlord has been slain during the battle, you score 1 victory point. This is in addition to the 1 victory point you score for each destroyed enemy unit.

First Blood: The first unit, of any kind, to be destroyed during the battle is worth 1 victory point to the opposing player at the end of the game. If two or more units from opposing forces are destroyed simultaneously, then both players get 1 victory point.

Linebreaker: If, at the end of the battle, you have at least one model within the enemy's deployment zone, you score 1 victory point.

+++

ACROSS THE VOID OF SPACE, MEN LIVE AS THEY HAVE LIVED FOR MILLENNIA UPON THE SAND, ROCK AND SOIL OF WORLDS BATHED IN THE LIGHT OF ALIEN SUNS. SO IS HUMANITY'S SEED CAST FAR AND WIDE BEYOND THE KNOWLEDGE OF MAN, TO THRIVE BITTERLY IN THE DARKNESS, TO TAKE ROOT AND CLING WITH ROBUST AND SAVAGE DETERMINATION.

+++

ETERNAL WAR
THE SCOURING

Both sides are sweeping through the area, tasking recon units to identify sites of strategic import. However, not all sites are of equal worth – victory will go to the player who can secure the most valuable sites and cripple the enemy's ability to locate others.

+++

THOUGH WE MAY KNOW
THE BITTER TEARS
OF DEFEAT, WE TRUST
IN THE EMPEROR'S
VICTORY.

+++

THE ARMIES
Each player selects a Battle-forged army to an agreed points limit.

THE BATTLEFIELD
Create the battlefield and set up terrain. Next, the players set up 6 objective markers; the players should roll off and, starting with whoever rolls highest, the players alternate placing these objective markers until all 6 have been set up. The objective markers can be located anywhere on the battlefield, as long as the centre of each is more than 12" from the centre of any other objective marker and 6" from the edge of the battlefield.

DEPLOYMENT
The player who placed the sixth objective marker determines which of the standard deployment maps is used in the battle (pg 216) and picks one of the deployment zones on the map for their army. Their opponent uses the other deployment zone.

The players then alternate deploying their units, one at a time, starting with the player who did not pick their deployment zone. A player's models must be set up within their own deployment zone. Continue setting up units until both sides have set up their army.

After all units have been set up, randomly select one of the objective markers, however you wish, to be the Superior objective marker, and a different objective marker to be the Inferior objective marker (see Take and Hold, right).

FIRST TURN
The player who finished setting up their army first can choose to take the first or second turn. If they decide to take the first turn, their opponent can roll a dice; on a roll of 6, they manage to seize the initiative, and they get the first turn instead!

BATTLE LENGTH
At the end of battle round 5, the player who had the first turn must roll a D6. On a roll of 3+, the game continues, otherwise the game is over. At the end of battle round 6, the player who had the second turn must roll a D6. This time the game continues on a roll of 4+, otherwise the game is over. The battle automatically ends at the end of battle round 7.

VICTORY CONDITIONS
At the end of the game, the player who has scored the most victory points is the winner. If both players have the same number of victory points, the game is a draw. Victory points are achieved for the following:

Take and Hold: At the end of the game, each objective marker is worth a number of victory points to the player who controls it. A player controls an objective marker if they have more models within 3" of the centre of it than their opponent does. The Superior objective marker is worth 4 victory points, whilst the Inferior objective marker is only worth 1 victory point. All other objective markers are worth 2 victory points.

Slay the Warlord: If the enemy Warlord has been slain during the battle, you score 1 victory point.

First Blood: The first unit, of any kind, to be destroyed during the battle is worth 1 victory point to the opposing player at the end of the game. If two or more units from opposing forces are destroyed simultaneously, then both players get 1 victory point.

Linebreaker: If, at the end of the battle, you have at least one model within the enemy's deployment zone, you score 1 victory point.

ETERNAL WAR
BIG GUNS NEVER TIRE

Both sides are attempting to secure a foothold in no man's land, spearheading the attack with overwhelming firepower. For the attack to be successful, your big guns must take up key positions on the battlefield and crush the enemy's heaviest weaponry.

THE ARMIES

Each player selects a Battle-forged army to an agreed points limit.

THE BATTLEFIELD

Create the battlefield and set up terrain. Next, the players set up 4 objective markers; the players should roll off and, starting with whoever rolls highest, the players alternate placing these objective markers until all 4 have been set up. The objective markers can be located anywhere on the battlefield, as long as the centre of each is more than 12" from the centre of any other objective marker and 6" from the edge of the battlefield.

DEPLOYMENT

The player who placed the fourth objective marker determines which of the standard deployment maps is used in the battle (pg 216) and picks one of the deployment zones on the map for their army. Their opponent uses the other deployment zone. The players then alternate deploying their units, one at a time, starting with the player who did not pick their deployment zone. A player's models must be set up within their own deployment zone. Continue setting up units until both sides have set up their army.

FIRST TURN

The player who finished setting up their army first can choose to take the first or second turn. If they decide to take the first turn, their opponent can roll a dice; on a roll of 6, they manage to seize the initiative, and they get the first turn instead!

BATTLE LENGTH

At the end of battle round 5, the player who had the first turn must roll a D6. On a roll of 3+, the game continues, otherwise the game is over. At the end of battle round 6, the player who had the second turn must roll a D6. This time the game continues on a roll of 4+, otherwise the game is over. The battle automatically ends at the end of battle round 7.

VICTORY CONDITIONS

At the end of the game, the player who has scored the most victory points is the winner. If both players have the same number of victory points, the game is a draw. Victory points are achieved for the following:

Key Positions: At the end of the game, each objective marker is worth 3 victory points to the player who controls it. A player controls an objective marker if they have more models within 3" of the centre of it than their opponent. However, if only one player has models from a Heavy Support unit within 3" of the centre of an objective marker, they control it regardless of the number of nearby enemy models.

Destroy the Big Guns: At the end of the game, each player receives 1 victory point for each enemy Heavy Support unit that has been completely destroyed.

Slay the Warlord: If the enemy Warlord has been slain during the battle, you score 1 victory point. Should the Warlord be a Heavy Support unit, this is in addition to the 1 victory point you score from Destroy the Big Guns.

First Blood: The first unit, of any kind, to be destroyed during the battle is worth 1 victory point to the opposing player at the end of the game. If two or more units from opposing forces are destroyed simultaneously, then both players get 1 victory point.

Linebreaker: If, at the end of the battle, you have at least one model within the enemy's deployment zone, you score 1 victory point.

+++

GUNS AND WARRIORS ARE USEFUL BUT IT IS OUR INDOMITABLE WILL THAT PROMISES THE ULTIMATE VICTORY.

+++

ETERNAL WAR
SECURE AND CONTROL

Both sides are attempting to capture the enemy base of operations or other similarly vital objective whilst defending their own. Success on the battlefield will require you to split your army into offensive and defensive forces.

THE ARMIES
Each player selects a Battle-forged army to an agreed points limit.

THE BATTLEFIELD
Create the battlefield and set up terrain.

DEPLOYMENT
The players roll off – whoever rolls highest determines which of the standard deployment maps is used in the battle (pg 216) and picks one of the deployment zones on the map for their army. Their opponent uses the other deployment zone.

Then, starting with the player who chose their deployment zone, each player sets up a single objective marker anywhere in their own deployment zone – the centre of an objective marker cannot be within 6" of any edge of the battlefield.

The players then alternate deploying their units, one at a time, starting with the player who set up their objective marker last. A player's models must be set up within their own deployment zone. Continue setting up units until both sides have set up their army.

FIRST TURN
The player who finished setting up their army first can choose to take the first or second turn. If they decide to take the first turn, their opponent can roll a dice; on a roll of 6, they manage to seize the initiative, and they get the first turn instead!

BATTLE LENGTH
At the end of battle round 5, the player who had the first turn must roll a D6. On a roll of 3+, the game continues, otherwise the game is over. At the end of battle round 6, the player who had the second turn must roll a D6. This time the game continues on a roll of 4+, otherwise the game is over. The battle automatically ends at the end of battle round 7.

VICTORY CONDITIONS
At the end of the game, the player who has scored the most victory points is the winner. If both players have the same number of victory points, the game is a draw. Victory points are achieved for the following:

Take and Hold: At the end of the game, each objective marker is worth 3 victory points to the player who controls it. A player controls an objective marker if they have more models within 3" of the centre of it than their opponent.

Slay the Warlord: If the enemy Warlord has been slain during the battle, you score 1 victory point.

First Blood: The first unit, of any kind, to be destroyed during the battle is worth 1 victory point to the opposing player at the end of the game. If two or more units from opposing forces are destroyed simultaneously, then both players get 1 victory point.

Linebreaker: If, at the end of the battle, you have at least one model within the enemy's deployment zone, you score 1 victory point.

ETERNAL WAR
THE RELIC

Both sides are attempting to recover a valuable relic from the front lines. It might be vital battle plans or maps, an item of spiritual significance or some other irreplaceable artefact that must be recovered – no matter the cost.

THE ARMIES

Each player selects a Battle-forged army to an agreed points limit.

THE BATTLEFIELD

Create the battlefield and set up terrain, then place a single objective marker at the centre of the battlefield to represent the Relic.

DEPLOYMENT

The players roll off – whoever rolls highest determines which of the standard deployment maps is used in the battle (pg 216) and picks one of the deployment zones on the map for their army. Their opponent uses the other deployment zone.

The players then alternate deploying their units, one at a time, starting with the player who did not pick their deployment zone. A player's models must be set up within their own deployment zone. Continue setting up units until both sides have set up their army.

FIRST TURN

The player who finished setting up their army first can choose to take the first or second turn. If they decide to take the first turn, their opponent can roll a dice; on a roll of 6, they manage to seize the initiative, and they get the first turn instead!

BATTLE LENGTH

At the end of battle round 5, the player who had the first turn must roll a D6. On a roll of 3+, the game continues, otherwise the game is over. At the end of battle round 6, the player who had the second turn must roll a D6. This time the game continues on a roll of 4+, otherwise the game is over. The battle automatically ends at the end of battle round 7.

VICTORY CONDITIONS

At the end of the battle, if a model from a player's army is carrying the Relic (see below), then that player wins a major victory. If the Relic is not being carried, then the player with a model closest to the Relic wins a minor victory. If both players have models equally close to the Relic, then the battle ends in a draw.

THE RELIC

An **INFANTRY** model can carry the Relic by moving into contact with it – that model then automatically picks it up. From that point, the Relic remains with the model (move the Relic with the model to show this) until it is dropped, which only happens if the model is slain or flees. A model with the Relic cannot embark in a **TRANSPORT**, leave the battlefield, or move further than 9" in any single phase for any reason.

+++

ALL HAIL THE MARTYRS! ON THEIR BLOOD IS OUR IMPERIUM FOUNDED, IN THEIR REMEMBRANCE DO WE HONOUR OURSELVES.

+++

The mightiest heroes of the Imperium gather upon the steps of a sacred cathedrum, pitting their might against the suppurating traitors of the Death Guard in all their blighted glory.

TACTICAL OBJECTIVES

War is unpredictable and fluid. Strategic objectives and tactical priorities can change at a moment's notice, and targets of military insignificance can transform into ones of vital importance without warning. A good battlefield commander must be dynamic and flexible, prepared to take advantage of an opportunity, and ever able to adapt their battleplan to react to a change of orders from above.

USING TACTICAL OBJECTIVES

A mission will tell you if it uses Tactical Objectives – they are most commonly used by Maelstrom of War missions. If it does, you will need to place 6 objective markers on the battlefield after setting up terrain, but before deploying any units. The objective markers should be individually numbered 1 through 6. These represent potential sites of tactical or strategic import that one or both sides might be called upon to secure. After terrain has been set up, the players should roll off. Starting with whoever rolled highest, the players then alternate placing these objective markers until all 6 have been set up. Each can be placed anywhere on the battlefield, as long as its centre is more than 12" from the centre of any other objective marker and more than 6" from the battlefield edge.

GENERATING TACTICAL OBJECTIVES

The mission will tell you how many Tactical Objectives you should generate at the start of each of your turns.

To generate a Tactical Objective, roll two dice, one after the other: the first dice represents tens, and the second represents digits, giving you a result between 11 and 66. Consult the Tactical Objectives on the following pages and write the corresponding result down. Note that unless the mission states otherwise, the results are not secret; both players should be able to see what Tactical Objectives the other has.

If you own a deck of Tactical Objective cards, you can instead generate your Tactical Objectives by shuffling the deck and drawing the top card. The cards you have drawn should be kept face up, so your opponent can see which Tactical Objectives you have generated, unless the mission you are playing instructs you otherwise.

Note that, whilst there are several Tactical Objectives with the same name, they are all uniquely numbered. When generating Tactical Objectives, keep a note of the numbers you rolled during the game – if you roll the same numbered Tactical Objective during the same game, roll again until a different number is generated.

Tactical Objectives that have been generated are said to be active until they are either achieved or discarded.

ACHIEVING TACTICAL OBJECTIVES

At the end of every turn (yours and the enemy's), you must check to see if you have achieved any of your active Tactical Objectives – the descriptions will tell you how and when they are achieved and how many victory points are scored for achieving them. If you can achieve a Tactical Objective at the end of a turn, you must immediately score the victory points for it – you cannot choose not to do so. Players can achieve any number of their Tactical Objectives in the same turn.

Many Tactical Objectives require a player to control an objective marker. A player controls an objective marker if they have more models within 3" of the centre of it than their opponent does.

DISCARDING TACTICAL OBJECTIVES

Once a Tactical Objective has been achieved, it is discarded. After the achieved Tactical Objectives (if any) have been discarded, the player whose turn it is can select one of their remaining active Tactical Objectives and choose to discard it – this scores no victory points. Discarded Tactical Objectives cease being active and you cannot generate or achieve these objectives for the remainder of the game.

| 11 | SECURE OBJECTIVE 1 | Capture and Control |

A vital objective has been identified in your vicinity. You are ordered to hold it at any cost.

Score 1 victory point if you control objective marker 1 at the end of your turn.

| 21 | SECURE OBJECTIVE 1 | Take and Hold |

A vital objective has been identified in your vicinity. You are ordered to hold it at any cost.

Score 1 victory point if you control objective marker 1 at the end of your turn.

| 12 | SECURE OBJECTIVE 2 | Capture and Control |

A vital objective has been identified in your vicinity. You are ordered to hold it at any cost.

Score 1 victory point if you control objective marker 2 at the end of your turn.

| 22 | SECURE OBJECTIVE 2 | Take and Hold |

A vital objective has been identified in your vicinity. You are ordered to hold it at any cost.

Score 1 victory point if you control objective marker 2 at the end of your turn.

| 13 | SECURE OBJECTIVE 3 | Capture and Control |

A vital objective has been identified in your vicinity. You are ordered to hold it at any cost.

Score 1 victory point if you control objective marker 3 at the end of your turn.

| 23 | SECURE OBJECTIVE 3 | Take and Hold |

A vital objective has been identified in your vicinity. You are ordered to hold it at any cost.

Score 1 victory point if you control objective marker 3 at the end of your turn.

| 14 | SECURE OBJECTIVE 4 | Capture and Control |

A vital objective has been identified in your vicinity. You are ordered to hold it at any cost.

Score 1 victory point if you control objective marker 4 at the end of your turn.

| 24 | SECURE OBJECTIVE 4 | Take and Hold |

A vital objective has been identified in your vicinity. You are ordered to hold it at any cost.

Score 1 victory point if you control objective marker 4 at the end of your turn.

| 15 | SECURE OBJECTIVE 5 | Capture and Control |

A vital objective has been identified in your vicinity. You are ordered to hold it at any cost.

Score 1 victory point if you control objective marker 5 at the end of your turn.

| 25 | SECURE OBJECTIVE 5 | Take and Hold |

A vital objective has been identified in your vicinity. You are ordered to hold it at any cost.

Score 1 victory point if you control objective marker 5 at the end of your turn.

| 16 | SECURE OBJECTIVE 6 | Capture and Control |

A vital objective has been identified in your vicinity. You are ordered to hold it at any cost.

Score 1 victory point if you control objective marker 6 at the end of your turn.

| 26 | SECURE OBJECTIVE 6 | Take and Hold |

A vital objective has been identified in your vicinity. You are ordered to hold it at any cost.

Score 1 victory point if you control objective marker 6 at the end of your turn.

31 — DEFEND OBJECTIVE 1 — *Storm and Defend*

You are charged with the defence of a key objective. It must not be permitted to fall into enemy hands.

Score 2 victory points if you control objective marker 1 at the end of two consecutive turns.

32 — DEFEND OBJECTIVE 2 — *Storm and Defend*

You are charged with the defence of a key objective. It must not be permitted to fall into enemy hands.

Score 2 victory points if you control objective marker 2 at the end of two consecutive turns.

33 — DEFEND OBJECTIVE 3 — *Storm and Defend*

You are charged with the defence of a key objective. It must not be permitted to fall into enemy hands.

Score 2 victory points if you control objective marker 3 at the end of two consecutive turns.

34 — DEFEND OBJECTIVE 4 — *Storm and Defend*

You are charged with the defence of a key objective. It must not be permitted to fall into enemy hands.

Score 2 victory points if you control objective marker 4 at the end of two consecutive turns.

35 — DEFEND OBJECTIVE 5 — *Storm and Defend*

You are charged with the defence of a key objective. It must not be permitted to fall into enemy hands.

Score 2 victory points if you control objective marker 5 at the end of two consecutive turns.

36 — DEFEND OBJECTIVE 6 — *Storm and Defend*

You are charged with the defence of a key objective. It must not be permitted to fall into enemy hands.

Score 2 victory points if you control objective marker 6 at the end of two consecutive turns.

41 — ADVANCE — *Seize Ground*

You must advance swiftly into no man's land to prevent your opponent seizing the battlefield.

Score 1 victory point if no unit from your army is within your deployment zone at the end of your turn.

42 — BEHIND ENEMY LINES — *Seize Ground*

Break through the foe's army and cut off their lines of escape.

Score 1 victory point if you have at least one unit completely within the enemy's deployment zone at the end of your turn. If you have at least three units within your opponent's deployment zone at the end of your turn, score D3 victory points instead.

43 — HOLD THE LINE — *Seize Ground*

It is critical that no foe breaks through your defences. Maintain a strong rearguard to protect your supply lines.

Score 1 victory point if you have at least three units completely within your deployment zone, and your opponent has no models within your deployment zone, at the end of your turn. This objective cannot be achieved on your first turn.

44 — MISSION CRITICAL OBJECTIVE — *Seize Ground*

This area is of extreme importance. You are to lead an immediate all-out assault to capture it.

When this Tactical Objective is generated, roll a D6. Score 1 victory point if you control the corresponding objective marker. If the corresponding objective marker was controlled by your opponent at the start of your turn and you control it at the end of your turn, score D3 victory points instead.

45 — SUPREMACY — *Seize Ground*

The battleground is won one yard at a time. Continue to establish a strong military presence in the area.

Score D3 victory points if you control any three objective markers at the end of your turn.

46 — DOMINATION — *Seize Ground*

Dominate the field of battle. Storm every site of tactical import and leave the foe with no place to hide.

Score D3+3 victory points if you control every objective marker on the battlefield at the end of your turn.

51 — OVERWHELMING FIREPOWER — *Purge*

A show of strength is required. Scour the enemy from the face of the battlefield with the use of extreme firepower.

Score 1 victory point if an enemy unit was destroyed during the Shooting phase of your turn. If 3 or more enemy units were destroyed during the Shooting phase of your turn, score D3 victory points instead.

52 — BLOOD AND GUTS — *Purge*

Close with the foe and engage them in hand-to-hand combat. Show them no quarter, no mercy.

Score 1 victory point if an enemy unit was destroyed during the Fight phase of this turn. If 3 or more enemy units were destroyed during the Fight phase of this turn, score D3 victory points instead.

53 — NO PRISONERS — *Purge*

Exterminate your enemy, show them no mercy.

Score 1 victory point if an enemy unit was destroyed during your turn. If between 3 and 5 enemy units were destroyed during your turn, score D3 victory points instead. If 6 or more enemy units were destroyed during your turn, score D3+3 victory points instead.

54 — AREA DENIAL — *Purge*

It is critical that this area is dominated. No enemy vanguard or guerilla units can be allowed to disrupt our plans.

Score 1 victory point if there are no enemy models within 6" of the centre of the battlefield at the end of your turn. If there are no enemy models within 12" of the centre of the battlefield at the end of your turn, score D3 victory points instead.

55 — PSYCHOLOGICAL WARFARE — *Purge*

Break the enemy's morale, make your foes tremble before you.

Score 1 victory point if your opponent failed a Morale test during this turn. If your opponent failed 3 or more Morale tests, score D3 victory points instead.

56 — MASTER THE WARP — *Purge*

Desperate times call for desperate measures – harness the power of the warp to defeat your foes.

Score 1 victory point if you manifested or denied a psychic power during this turn. If you manifested or denied 3 or more psychic powers, score D3 victory points instead.

61 — KINGSLAYER — *Annihilation*

The enemy commander is a powerful and effective leader and should be slain as quickly as possible.

Score D3 victory points if your opponent's Warlord has been destroyed during this or any previous turn.

62 — WITCH HUNTER — *Annihilation*

The presence of enemy psykers can no longer be tolerated. Eliminate them with extreme prejudice.

Score 1 victory point if at least one enemy PSYKER was destroyed during this turn.

63 — SCOUR THE SKIES — *Annihilation*

It is vital to maintain air superiority.

Score 1 victory point if at least one enemy unit that can FLY was destroyed during this turn.

64 — ASSASSINATE — *Annihilation*

The enemy looks to their champions for courage. Identify and assassinate them.

Score 1 victory point if at least one enemy CHARACTER was destroyed during this turn. If 3 or more enemy CHARACTERS were destroyed during this turn, score D3 victory points instead.

65 — BIG GAME HUNTER — *Annihilation*

The larger the foe, the greater the glory…

Score 1 victory point if at least one enemy unit with a Wounds characteristic of 10 or more was destroyed during this turn. If at least one enemy unit with a Wounds characteristic of 20 or more was destroyed this turn, score D3 victory points instead.

66 — PRIORITY ORDERS RECEIVED — *Priority Order*

This mission is of the utmost importance, and cannot be entrusted to anyone else.

When this Tactical Objective is generated, immediately generate a bonus Tactical Objective – this does not count towards the number of Active Tactical Objectives you currently have in play. Your Warlord is the only unit that can be used to achieve the bonus Tactical Objective – they must be the only unit used to control an objective marker, the unit that destroys the last model in an enemy unit, and so on. If you achieve this, you score both the number of victory points stated on the bonus Tactical Objective and an additional 3 victory points. If this Tactical Objective is discarded, so too is the bonus Tactical Objective.

MAELSTROM OF WAR
CLEANSE AND CAPTURE

The evidence of war can be clearly seen all across the battlefield as the wounded cry for aid and vital resources are at risk of falling into enemy hands. Search for and recover these artefacts at all costs and eliminate any enemy forces that dare oppose you.

THE ARMIES

Each player selects a Battle-forged army to an agreed points limit.

THE BATTLEFIELD

Create the battlefield and set up terrain. Next, the players should place 6 objective markers, as detailed on page 226.

DEPLOYMENT

The player who placed the sixth objective marker determines which of the standard deployment maps is used in the battle (pg 216) and picks one of the deployment zones on the map for their army. Their opponent uses the other deployment zone.

The players then alternate deploying their units, one at a time, starting with the player who did not pick their deployment zone. A player's models must be set up within their own deployment zone. Continue setting up units until both sides have set up their army.

FIRST TURN

The player who finished setting up their army first can choose to take the first or second turn. If they decide to take the first turn, their opponent can roll a dice; on a roll of 6, they manage to seize the initiative, and they get the first turn instead!

TACTICAL OBJECTIVES

This mission uses Tactical Objectives. If, at the start of a player's turn, they have fewer than 3 active Tactical Objectives, they must generate Tactical Objectives until they have 3.

BATTLE LENGTH

At the end of battle round 5, the player who had the first turn must roll a D6. On a roll of 3+, the game continues, otherwise the game is over. At the end of battle round 6, the player who had the second turn must roll a D6. This time the game continues on a roll of 4+, otherwise the game is over. The battle automatically ends at the end of battle round 7.

VICTORY CONDITIONS

At the end of the game, the player who has scored the most victory points is the winner. If both players have the same number of victory points, the game is a draw. In addition to achieving Tactical Objectives, victory points are achieved for the following:

Slay the Warlord: If the enemy Warlord has been slain during the battle, you score 1 victory point.

First Blood: The first unit, of any kind, to be destroyed during the battle is worth 1 victory point to the opposing player at the end of the game. If two or more units from opposing forces are destroyed simultaneously, then both players get 1 victory point.

Linebreaker: If, at the end of the battle, you have at least one model within the enemy's deployment zone, you score 1 victory point.

THE TRULY HEROIC TRUST IN BLIND FAITH.

MAELSTROM OF WAR
CONTACT LOST

All contact with command has been lost and the enemy are doubtless advancing towards your position. Secure sites of tactical import to re-establish communications with all due haste and engage any hostile forces encountered with extreme prejudice.

THE ARMIES
Each player selects a Battle-forged army to an agreed points limit.

THE BATTLEFIELD
Create the battlefield and set up terrain. Next, the players should place 6 objective markers, as detailed on page 226.

DEPLOYMENT
The player who placed the sixth objective marker determines which of the standard deployment maps is used in the battle (pg 216) and picks one of the deployment zones on the map for their army. Their opponent uses the other deployment zone.

The players then alternate deploying their units, one at a time, starting with the player who did not pick their deployment zone. A player's models must be set up within their own deployment zone. Continue setting up units until both sides have set up their army.

FIRST TURN
The player who finished setting up their army first can choose to take the first or second turn. If they decide to take the first turn, their opponent can roll a dice; on a roll of 6, they manage to seize the initiative, and they get the first turn instead!

TACTICAL OBJECTIVES
This mission uses Tactical Objectives. Each player generates 1 Tactical Objective at the start of their first turn. In subsequent turns, if a player has fewer than 6 active Tactical Objectives, they must generate 1 Tactical Objective for each objective marker they control (to a maximum of 6 active Tactical Objectives).

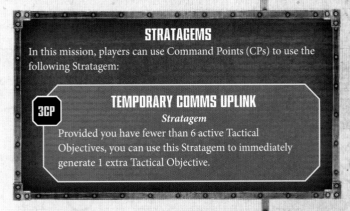

STRATAGEMS
In this mission, players can use Command Points (CPs) to use the following Stratagem:

3CP
TEMPORARY COMMS UPLINK
Stratagem
Provided you have fewer than 6 active Tactical Objectives, you can use this Stratagem to immediately generate 1 extra Tactical Objective.

BATTLE LENGTH
At the end of battle round 5, the player who had the first turn must roll a D6. On a roll of 3+, the game continues, otherwise the game is over. At the end of battle round 6, the player who had the second turn must roll a D6. This time the game continues on a roll of 4+, otherwise the game is over. The battle automatically ends at the end of battle round 7.

VICTORY CONDITIONS
At the end of the game, the player who has scored the most victory points is the winner. If both players have the same number of victory points, the game is a draw. In addition to achieving Tactical Objectives, victory points are achieved for the following:

Slay the Warlord: If the enemy Warlord has been slain during the battle, you score 1 victory point.

First Blood: The first unit, of any kind, to be destroyed during the battle is worth 1 victory point to the opposing player at the end of the game. If two or more units from opposing forces are destroyed simultaneously, then both players get 1 victory point.

Linebreaker: If, at the end of the battle, you have at least one model within the enemy's deployment zone, you score 1 victory point.

IN AN HOUR OF DARKNESS A BLIND MAN IS THE BEST GUIDE. IN AN AGE OF INSANITY LOOK TO THE MADMAN TO SHOW THE WAY

+++

MAELSTROM OF WAR
TACTICAL ESCALATION

What began as a simple raid has long since escalated into full-blown battle, as both sides commit more and more forces to the fray. With every moment that passes, more combatants engage the enemy and another mission-critical target is identified.

THE ARMIES

Each player selects a Battle-forged army to an agreed points limit.

THE BATTLEFIELD

Create the battlefield and set up terrain. Next, the players should place 6 objective markers, as detailed on page 226.

DEPLOYMENT

The player who placed the sixth objective marker determines which of the standard deployment maps is used in the battle (pg 216) and picks one of the deployment zones on the map for their army. Their opponent uses the other deployment zone.

The players then alternate deploying their units, one at a time, starting with the player who did not pick their deployment zone. A player's models must be set up within their own deployment zone. Continue setting up units until both sides have set up their army.

FIRST TURN

The player who finished setting up their army first can choose to take the first or second turn. If they decide to take the first turn, their opponent can roll a dice; on a roll of 6, they manage to seize the initiative, and they get the first turn instead!

TACTICAL OBJECTIVES

This mission uses Tactical Objectives. If, at the start of a player's turn, they have fewer active Tactical Objectives than the current battle round number, they must generate Tactical Objectives until they have a number equal to the current battle round number.

TACTICAL PRIORITY

At the start of the first battle round, but before the first turn begins, each player nominates a single Tactical Objective type (e.g. Take and Hold). You score an additional victory point for each Tactical Objective of that type you achieve. However, you lose a victory point each time you discard a Tactical Objective of that type.

BATTLE LENGTH

At the end of battle round 5, the player who had the first turn must roll a D6. On a roll of 3+, the game continues, otherwise the game is over. At the end of battle round 6, the player who had the second turn must roll a D6. This time the game continues on a roll of 4+, otherwise the game is over. The battle automatically ends at the end of battle round 7.

VICTORY CONDITIONS

At the end of the game, the player who has scored the most victory points is the winner. If both players have the same number of victory points, the game is a draw. In addition to achieving Tactical Objectives, victory points are achieved for the following:

Mission Priorities: If, at the end of the game, one player has achieved more Tactical Objectives of their nominated type (see Tactical Priority, above) than their opponent has of their own nominated type, that player receives 1 additional victory point.

Slay the Warlord: If the enemy Warlord has been slain during the battle, you score 1 victory point.

First Blood: The first unit, of any kind, to be destroyed during the battle is worth 1 victory point to the opposing player at the end of the game. If two or more units from opposing forces are destroyed simultaneously, then both players get 1 victory point.

Linebreaker: If, at the end of the battle, you have at least one model within the enemy's deployment zone, you score 1 victory point.

+++

FACTS ARE CHAINS THAT BIND PERCEPTION AND FETTER TRUTH. FOR A MAN CAN REMAKE THE WORLD IF HE HAS A DREAD AND NO FACTS TO CLOUD HIS MIND.

+++

IT IS BETTER TO DIE FOR THE EMPEROR THAN TO LIVE FOR YOURSELF.

MAELSTROM OF WAR
SPOILS OF WAR

A vital resupply convoy has been intercepted and its cargo lost in the deserted ground of no man's land. You must reclaim these spoils of war before the enemy can reach them, whilst inflicting as much damage upon the foe as possible.

THE ARMIES
Each player selects a Battle-forged army to an agreed points limit.

THE BATTLEFIELD
Create the battlefield and set up terrain. Next, the players should place 6 objective markers, as detailed on page 226.

DEPLOYMENT
The player who placed the sixth objective marker determines which of the standard deployment maps is used in the battle (pg 216) and picks one of the deployment zones on the map for their army. Their opponent uses the other deployment zone.

The players then alternate deploying their units, one at a time, starting with the player who did not pick their deployment zone. A player's models must be set up within their own deployment zone. Continue setting up units until both sides have set up their army.

FIRST TURN
The player who finished setting up their army first can choose to take the first or second turn. If they decide to take the first turn, their opponent can roll a dice; on a roll of 6, they manage to seize the initiative, and they get the first turn instead!

TACTICAL OBJECTIVES
This mission uses Tactical Objectives. If, at the start of a player's turn, they have fewer than 3 active Tactical Objectives, they must generate Tactical Objectives until they have 3.

PRECIOUS CARGO
In this mission, both players can achieve any active Tactical Objective titled 'Secure Objective X', where X is a number between 1 and 6, regardless of which player generated it. In addition, these Tactical Objectives can only be discarded when achieved.

BATTLE LENGTH
At the end of battle round 5, the player who had the first turn must roll a D6. On a roll of 3+, the game continues, otherwise the game is over. At the end of battle round 6, the player who had the second turn must roll a D6. This time the game continues on a roll of 4+, otherwise the game is over. The battle automatically ends at the end of battle round 7.

VICTORY CONDITIONS
At the end of the game, the player who has scored the most victory points is the winner. If both players have the same number of victory points, the game is a draw. In addition to achieving Tactical Objectives, victory points are achieved for the following:

Steal the Loot: If, at the end of the game, one player has achieved more 'Secure Objective X' Tactical Objectives (see Precious Cargo, above) than their opponent has, that player receives 1 additional victory point.

Slay the Warlord: If the enemy Warlord has been slain during the battle, you score 1 victory point.

First Blood: The first unit, of any kind, to be destroyed during the battle is worth 1 victory point to the opposing player at the end of the game. If two or more units from opposing forces are destroyed simultaneously, then both players get 1 victory point.

Linebreaker: If, at the end of the battle, you have at least one model within the enemy's deployment zone, you score 1 victory point.

+++

WE DO NOT HATE THE ALIEN BECAUSE HE IS DIFFERENT, WE HATE THE ALIEN BECAUSE HE HAS NAUGHT BUT HATE IN HIS HEART FOR US.

+++

MAELSTROM OF WAR
CLOAK AND SHADOWS

Enemy patrols are operating in this area, searching the battlefield for some critical objectives. Scout the area under cover of darkness and discover their plans, but be sure not to reveal your own goals. If you can deny the enemy's objectives whilst achieving yours, victory will be assured.

THE ARMIES
Each player selects a Battle-forged army to an agreed points limit.

THE BATTLEFIELD
Create the battlefield and set up terrain. Next, the players should place 6 objective markers, as detailed on page 226.

DEPLOYMENT
The player who placed the sixth objective marker determines which of the standard deployment maps is used in the battle (pg 216) and picks one of the deployment zones on the map for their army. Their opponent uses the other deployment zone.

The players then alternate deploying their units, one at a time, starting with the player who did not pick their deployment zone. A player's models must be set up within their own deployment zone. Continue setting up units until both sides have set up their army.

FIRST TURN
The player who finished setting up their army first can choose to take the first or second turn. If they decide to take the first turn, their opponent can roll a dice; on a roll of 6, they manage to seize the initiative, and they get the first turn instead!

TACTICAL OBJECTIVES
This mission uses Tactical Objectives. If, at the start of a player's turn, they have fewer than 3 active Tactical Objectives, they must generate Tactical Objectives until they have 3.

SECRET ORDERS
In this mission, players keep their Tactical Objectives secret from each other. Only reveal Tactical Objectives when achieving them.

COVER OF DARKNESS
When rolling to hit in the Shooting phase, subtract 1 from the roll if the target is more than 18" away.

STRATAGEMS
In this mission, players can use Command Points (CPs) to use the following additional Stratagem:

1CP	**FLARES**
	Stratagem
	Select an enemy unit. For the duration of your turn, your units can shoot at that unit without penalty from Cover of Darkness.

BATTLE LENGTH
At the end of battle round 5, the player who had the first turn must roll a D6. On a roll of 3+, the game continues, otherwise the game is over. At the end of battle round 6, the player who had the second turn must roll a D6. This time the game continues on a roll of 4+, otherwise the game is over. The battle automatically ends at the end of battle round 7.

VICTORY CONDITIONS
At the end of the game, the player who has scored the most victory points is the winner. If both players have the same number of victory points, the game is a draw. In addition to achieving Tactical Objectives, victory points are achieved for the following:

Slay the Warlord: If the enemy Warlord has been slain during the battle, you score 1 victory point.

First Blood: The first unit, of any kind, to be destroyed during the battle is worth 1 victory point to the opposing player at the end of the game. If two or more units from opposing forces are destroyed simultaneously, then both players get 1 victory point.

Linebreaker: If, at the end of the battle, you have at least one model within the enemy's deployment zone, you score 1 victory point.

MAELSTROM OF WAR
DEADLOCK

Months of bitter fighting have ended in a deadlock, but a fleeting opportunity has arisen for you to strike a devastating blow against the enemy to tip the balance of the war. Strike hard and fast, for with every moment you delay, your tactical options dwindle and the chance for victory slips away.

THE ARMIES

Each player selects a Battle-forged army to an agreed points limit.

THE BATTLEFIELD

Create the battlefield and set up terrain. Next, the players should place 6 objective markers, as detailed on page 226.

DEPLOYMENT

The player who placed the sixth objective marker determines which of the standard deployment maps is used in the battle (pg 216) and picks one of the deployment zones on the map for their army. Their opponent uses the other deployment zone.

The players then alternate deploying their units, one at a time, starting with the player who did not pick their deployment zone. A player's models must be set up within their own deployment zone. Continue setting up units until both sides have set up their army.

FIRST TURN

The player who finished setting up their army first can choose to take the first or second turn. If they decide to take the first turn, their opponent can roll a dice; on a roll of 6, they manage to seize the initiative, and they get the first turn instead!

TACTICAL OBJECTIVES

This mission uses Tactical Objectives. Each player generates 6 Tactical Objectives at the start of their first turn. In the second battle round, players may have 5 active Tactical Objectives, in the third battle round they may have 4, and so on. If a player has too many active Tactical Objectives at the start of their turn, they must discard Tactical Objectives until they have the correct number. If a player has fewer than the correct number of Tactical Objectives at the start of their turn, they must generate Tactical Objectives until they have the correct number.

BATTLE LENGTH

At the end of battle round 5, the player who had the first turn must roll a D6. On a roll of 3+, the game continues, otherwise the game is over. At the end of battle round 6, the player who had the second turn must roll a D6. This time the game continues on a roll of 4+, otherwise the game is over. The battle automatically ends at the end of battle round 7.

STRATEGIC DEADLOCK

From the start of the third battle round, the Command Point cost of all Stratagems used by players is doubled.

VICTORY CONDITIONS

At the end of the game, the player who has scored the most victory points is the winner. If both players have the same number of victory points, the game is a draw. In addition to achieving Tactical Objectives, victory points are achieved for the following:

Slay the Warlord: If the enemy Warlord has been slain during the battle, you score 1 victory point.

First Blood: The first unit, of any kind, to be destroyed during the battle is worth 1 victory point to the opposing player at the end of the game. If two or more units from opposing forces are destroyed simultaneously, then both players get 1 victory point.

Linebreaker: If, at the end of the battle, you have at least one model within the enemy's deployment zone, you score 1 victory point.

+++

TO A SPACE MARINE THE BOLTGUN IS FAR MORE THAN A WEAPON, IT IS AN INSTRUMENT OF MANKIND'S DIVINITY, THE BRINGER OF DEATH TO HIS FOES, WHOSE HOWLING BLAST IS A PRAYER TO THE GODS OF BATTLE.

+++

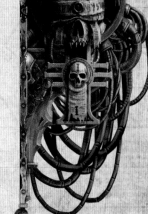

ADVANCED RULES

'Warriors of Ultramar. This is
where we make our stand. If death
is to be our fate, then we shall meet
it with the Emperor's word on our
lips and his light in our eyes. If we
must die, we will die; but we shall
never yield.'

- Marneus Calgar,
Lord of Macragge

ADVANCED RULES

By now, you've scratched the surface of the many ways that you can enjoy the Warhammer 40,000 hobby. The missions that you have already seen are just the beginning – there are always new ways to play and battles to fight!

BATTLE-FORGED ARMIES

Battle-forged armies give you the opportunity to organise your models in a way that reflects the Factions of Warhammer 40,000 as they would be deployed. These battlefield organisations place restrictions on how you form your army, but in exchange provide powerful benefits.

BATTLEFIELD TERRAIN

The battlefield terrain rules describe many of the terrain features found upon your battlefields, from twisted woods and shattered ruins to makeshift barricades and the statues of mighty heroes. These rules help to bring your battlefield to life and introduce a new tactical dimension to your games, as both armies deploy and manoeuvre across the battlefield to take best advantage of the terrain.

THE BATTLEZONES

Battlezones offer an interesting and often dangerous twist to your games by introducing exciting environmental effects – the galaxy, after all, holds billions of alien worlds. Across myriad star systems, on battlefields of ice, lava, jungle and ash, armies engage in mortal conflict. A planet might be beset by radioactive dust storms, shrouded in perpetual darkness or be saturated with warp-stuff. Incorporating these effects into your games with the Battlezone rules is a great way to test the mettle of any commander.

Battlezone rules can be used to enhance any mission. They include additional rules and Stratagems that reflect a specific kind of battlefield, sometimes at a specific time. Battlezone rules usually have an equal chance of affecting both players, and simply choosing to fight your battle in a particular battlezone will present you with new tactical challenges.

EXPANSIONS

Warhammer 40,000 expansions provide new ways to use your collections, and allow you to tailor your tactics for battle across many theatres of war. The Warhammer 40,000 rules are but the tip of the iceberg in a wider hobby where you can fight massive battles with vast armies on each side, tense squad-focussed actions amidst the ruins of an Imperial city, or storm your enemy's lines with an orbital assault spearheaded by Drop Pods and Flyers – anything is possible!

This section will introduce four expansions: Planetstrike, Stronghold Assault, Cities of Death and Death from the Skies. Each of these examines a different exciting aspect of warfare in Warhammer 40,000 and modifies the core rules to better reflect that style of battle. Sometimes these changes are subtle; at other times they dramatically alter the way in which you can use your force on the battlefield. Expansions are great for all styles of play, whether bringing events from the background to life, or pitching your forces into new situations which will test your ability as a commander to the limit.

PLANETSTRIKE

Planetstrike is about planetary invasion – orbital bombardments rain down, hammering defenders as the attackers deploy their troops by dropship and teleport strike. Meanwhile, the defenders blaze away with mighty weapons from their fortifications and ready their elite troops to repel the invaders. The first blows of such a war can decide the fate of a world, and no quarter will be asked or given. The short introduction to Planetstrike later in this section provides rules to represent the conditions of this type of battle, as well as a Planetstrike mission, 'Planetfall', so you can get a taste of planetary invasion straight away.

'When the people forget their duty, they are no longer human and become something less than beasts. They have no place in the bosom of Humanity nor in the heart of the Emperor. Let them die and be forgotten.'

- *Prime Edicts of the Holy Synod of the Adeptus Ministorum*

CITIES OF DEATH

Vicious urban combat is best recreated using the Cities of Death expansion. Fighting a pitched battle across a barren plain is one thing, but a warlord finds a whole new set of challenges when fighting a battle through the war-torn streets of one of the galaxy's innumerable cities. Bitter, short-ranged fighting is the order of the day, with booby traps and snipers making every step into the unknown perilous. Amidst the tangled ruins and rubble, unassuming buildings might prove to hold valuable caches or medical supplies, while high ground is sought by both sides so they might command the battlefield. The overview of Cities of Death later in this section includes the rules you need to fight these claustrophobic battles, and a Cities of Death mission, 'Firesweep', so you can conduct urban warfare yourself.

STRONGHOLD ASSAULT

Stronghold Assault focusses on siege warfare. These gruelling battles are amongst the greatest attacker-versus-defender battles in the galaxy, with armies locked in combat in blood-soaked trenches, or throwing themselves against the walls of monolithic fortresses that bristle with automated weapons systems. The Stronghold Assault introduction includes rules for incorporating fortifications into your battles. It also includes the 'Bunker Assault' mission, which will test both warlords' siege-craft.

DEATH FROM THE SKIES

Aerial combat between squadrons of deadly aircraft lies at the heart of the Death from the Skies expansion. Bombers wreak havoc on undefended forces on the ground, even as agile fighter craft scramble to intercept them. Furious dogfights are fought above the battlefield, where daring pilots engage in duels that could decide the outcome of the war, for whoever can dominate the skies will surely secure victory on the ground. The introduction to Death from the Skies later in this section includes rules for adding a Dogfight phase to your Warhammer 40,000 battles, as well as the 'Tactical Strike' mission which you can use to earn your wings.

MULTIPLAYER BATTLES

The confusion of battle is only compounded when there are more than two warring parties. Each force finds enemies to either side, commanders strike temporary alliances that are broken almost as quickly as they are made, and the centre of the battlefield becomes a killing ground from which few will escape. Awareness of the forces arrayed against you is crucial, and a glory-hungry warlord who seizes the initiative may find the tables turned on them in an instant. This section presents a multiplayer mission, 'Carnage', alongside rules for fighting these chaotic battles.

CAMPAIGNS

Few wars end with a single battle, instead becoming brutal campaigns as warriors and war machines slaughter each other in a relentless and recurring clash of wills. In such contests are heroes born and legends made. Campaigns are an exciting and engaging way to enable players to fight a series of linked battles, adding new dimensions to your hobby. They are great for taking individual battles and giving them a significance that runs into the next game and even beyond, where victory and defeat have consequences for not just the battle, but the war.

You can make a campaign out of any of the missions presented in this book, those in other Warhammer 40,000 publications, or those of your own creation. This section introduces some principles about campaigns, and provides a few suggestions about how to play tree, matrix and map campaigns, alongside a few examples to get you started.

AND MUCH MORE...

As you can see, there's a wealth of missions and extra rules for you to get stuck into in this section, but that's not the end of it. There are always new rules, missions and expansions, so keep an eye on games-workshop.com for the latest releases. You may also find yourself inspired to write and fight your own missions – and we highly recommend it! The more you put into your hobby, the more rewards you will find waiting for you.

'STRIVE, MY BROTHERS, TO CAGE THE BEAST WITHIN, FOR ITS CRIMSON THIRST SHALL MAKE MONSTERS OF US ALL. YET KNOW THAT, SHOULD EVER THE BEAST BREAK FREE, THE SHAME OF THAT MOMENT CAN ONLY BE SALVED THROUGH THE UNMITIGATED SLAUGHTER OF THE FOE.'

- *Veteran Sergeant Gabrian, Blood Angels 6th Company*

BATTLE-FORGED ARMIES

All armies, from the contingents of the T'au to the warbands of the Orks, are – to a greater or lesser extent – structured forces. This section explains how you can organise your units into Detachments; a group of units that fight together and gain a strategic or tactical bonus for doing so.

If a mission you are playing instructs you to select a Battle-forged army, it means that you must organise all the units in your army into Detachments.

An army can include any number of Detachments and you can mix them together however you like. On pages 243-245, you will find several Detachments that can be used with any army, and more will be published in other sources.

To include a particular Detachment in your army, simply organise some or all of your units so that they fit within the restrictions and limitations detailed for that particular Detachment. A unit cannot belong to more than one Detachment, and you will often need to use additional information found on a unit's datasheet, such as Faction and Battlefield Role (see below and right) to determine where it fits in a Detachment.

Each Detachment may contain the following information:

Battlefield Role Slots: These show the number of units of each Battlefield Role (see right) that you must, or may, include in the Detachment.

Dedicated Transports: This details how many Dedicated Transport units the Detachment can include (if any).

Restrictions: This lists any restrictions that apply to the types of units you may include in the Detachment.

Command Benefits: This lists any bonuses that apply if you include this Detachment in your army.

FACTIONS

All units belong to one or more of the many Factions that fight for dominance across the galaxy. A unit's Faction is important when building a Battle-forged army because some Detachments require all units included in it to be from the same Faction. The Factions that a unit belongs to will be listed in the keywords section of its datasheet. For example, a Space Marine Captain has the **IMPERIUM** and **ADEPTUS ASTARTES** keywords, so belongs to both the Imperium and Adeptus Astartes Factions. This means that if a Space Marine Captain was part of a Detachment with the restriction that all units must be from the same Faction, all other units in that Detachment must either be from the Imperium Faction, or they must all be from the Adeptus Astartes Faction.

BATTLEFIELD ROLE

However you choose your army, all units have a Battlefield Role, which is typically shown as a symbol. Apart from providing a useful overview of the types of duties a unit is meant to perform, the role is also of importance when it comes to using Detachments. The most common Battlefield Roles are shown here.

HQ

Troops

Elites

Fast Attack

Heavy Support

Dedicated Transport

Flyer

Fortification

Lord of War

BATTLEFIELD ROLE SLOTS

This section of a Detachment's rules lists the minimum and maximum number of units in each Battlefield Role that you must or may include in the Detachment.

The icons on a Detachment are referred to as slots. Each slot will typically specify a single Battlefield Role. Each slot allows you to take one unit. Red icons are compulsory selections – you must take at least this many units of the appropriate Battlefield Role to include the Detachment in your army. Grey icons are optional selections – you can include up to this number of units with the appropriate Battlefield Role when including the Detachment in your army. Any further units of the same Battlefield Role will need to be taken in a different Detachment. For example, in order to take a Battalion Detachment – which you can see on the facing page – you must select three units with the Troops Battlefield Role, and cannot include more than six Troops units in the Detachment.

Occasionally, a Detachment slot will specify two or more Battlefield Roles, in which case any unit that has one of the specified roles may be taken in that slot. Rarely, a slot will not specify a Battlefield Role, in which case any type of unit can be taken, or it will specify a particular unit or units, in which case only those may be taken.

UNDERSTRENGTH UNITS

Each unit's datasheet will describe how many models make up that unit. Sometimes you may find that you do not have enough models to field a minimum-sized unit; if this is the case, you can still include one unit of that type in your army with as many models as you have available.

If you are using points, you must still pay the points cost as if you had a minimum-sized unit, even though it contains fewer models. An understrength unit still takes up the appropriate slot in a Detachment.

RESTRICTIONS

This section of a Detachment's rules lists any additional restrictions that apply to the units you can include as part of the Detachment. If a datasheet does not adhere to a particular restriction, it cannot be included as part of the Detachment. The most common restriction is that all of the units included in a Detachment must be from the same Faction.

COMMAND BENEFITS

This section of a Detachment's rules lists any bonuses that apply if you include the Detachment in your army. Typically, the inclusion of a Detachment will increase the total number of Command Points your army has available to spend on Stratagems.

COMMAND POINTS

When you build a Battle-forged army, it will have a number of Command Points. These can be spent to utilise Stratagems – each of which represents a strategic or tactical asset available to your army.

All Battle-forged armies start with 3 Command Points. The simplest way to accrue more Command Points is to take more Detachments – many of which increase your total number of Command Points.

You can spend Command Points to use a Stratagem before or during a battle. Each time you use a Stratagem, reduce your Command Points total by the appropriate amount. If you do not have enough Command Points for a specific Stratagem, you cannot use it. Unless otherwise noted, you can use the same Stratagem multiple times during the course of a battle.

The different Stratagems available to players depend on the mission they are playing. Players can always use the three Stratagems presented below, but some missions, battlezones and expansions may introduce additional Stratagems to your battles.

STRATAGEMS

If a player has a Battle-forged army, they may spend Command Points (CPs) to use the following Stratagems in any mission they play.

1CP — COMMAND RE-ROLL
Stratagem
You can re-roll any single dice.

2CP — COUNTER-OFFENSIVE
Stratagem
This Stratagem is used right after an enemy unit that charged has fought. Select one of your own eligible units and fight with it next.

2CP — INSANE BRAVERY
Stratagem
You can automatically pass a single Morale test (this Stratagem must be used before taking the test).

PATROL DETACHMENT

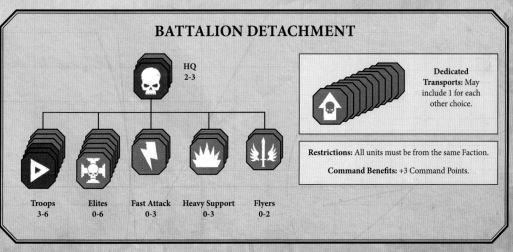

HQ
1-2

Troops
1-3

Elites
0-2

Fast Attack
0-2

Heavy Support
0-2

Flyers
0-2

Dedicated Transports: May include 1 for each other choice.

Restrictions: All units must be from the same Faction.

Command Benefits: None.

BATTALION DETACHMENT

HQ
2-3

Troops
3-6

Elites
0-6

Fast Attack
0-3

Heavy Support
0-3

Flyers
0-2

Dedicated Transports: May include 1 for each other choice.

Restrictions: All units must be from the same Faction.

Command Benefits: +3 Command Points.

BRIGADE DETACHMENT

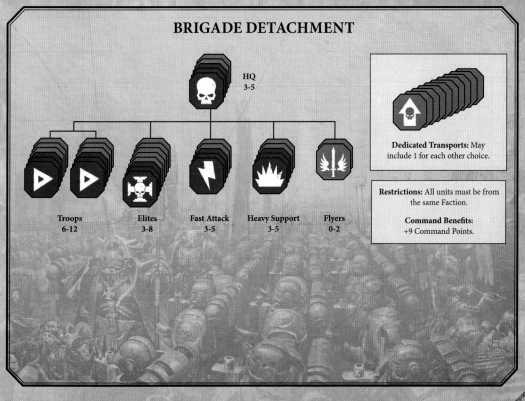

HQ
3-5

Troops
6-12

Elites
3-8

Fast Attack
3-5

Heavy Support
3-5

Flyers
0-2

Dedicated Transports: May include 1 for each other choice.

Restrictions: All units must be from the same Faction.

Command Benefits: +9 Command Points.

VANGUARD DETACHMENT

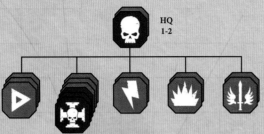

Troops 0-3	Elites 3-6	Fast Attack 0-2	Heavy Support 0-2	Flyers 0-2

Dedicated Transports: May include 1 for each other choice.

Restrictions: All units must be from the same Faction.

Command Benefits: +1 Command Point.

SPEARHEAD DETACHMENT

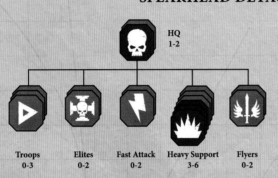

Troops 0-3	Elites 0-2	Fast Attack 0-2	Heavy Support 3-6	Flyers 0-2

Dedicated Transports: May include 1 for each other choice.

Restrictions: All units must be from the same Faction.

Command Benefits: +1 Command Point.

OUTRIDER DETACHMENT

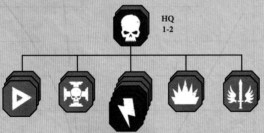

Troops 0-3	Elites 0-2	Fast Attack 3-6	Heavy Support 0-2	Flyers 0-2

Dedicated Transports: May include 1 for each other choice.

Restrictions: All units must be from the same Faction.

Command Benefits: +1 Command Point.

SUPREME COMMAND DETACHMENT

HQ
3-5

Dedicated Transports: May include 1 for each other choice.

Elites
0-1

Lord of War
0-1

Restrictions: All units must be from the same Faction.

Command Benefits: +1 Command Point.

SUPER-HEAVY DETACHMENT

3-5 Lords of War

Restrictions: All units must be from the same Faction.

Command Benefits: +3 Command Points.

AIR WING DETACHMENT

3-5 Flyers

Restrictions: All units must be from the same Faction.

Command Benefits: +1 Command Point.

SUPER-HEAVY AUXILIARY DETACHMENT

1 Lord of War

Restrictions: None.

Command Benefits: None.

FORTIFICATION NETWORK

1-3 Fortifications

Restrictions: None.

Command Benefits: None.

AUXILIARY SUPPORT DETACHMENT

 or   or or   or or or

Restrictions: This Detachment can only include a single unit.

Command Benefits: -1 Command Point. Note that unlike other Detachments, you lose 1 Command Point for each Auxiliary Support Detachment in your army. These are deducted from your total after adding up the bonuses from all other sources.

Hissing and roaring, the living tide of Hive Fleet Leviathan surges across the war-torn battlefields of Praxis II. Against this alien horror stands the Astra Militarum, its mighty battle tanks rising like mobile fortresses from amongst the steely eyed Imperial ranks.

BATTLEFIELD TERRAIN

In this section, you will find expanded terrain rules. You do not need to use these rules to enjoy a battle – the rules for cover detailed in the core rules will suffice to shelter your warriors from incoming fire – but they will add a new dimension to your battlefield and help bring it to life.

WOODS

Twisted woodlands grow on many a corpse-strewn battlefield.

INFANTRY units that are entirely on the base of a wood receive the benefit of cover. If your wood is not on a base, discuss with your opponent what the boundary of the wood is before the battle begins. Other units only receive the benefit of cover if at least 50% of every model is actually obscured from the point of view of the shooting unit.

Models are slowed when charging through woods. If, when a unit charges, one or more of its models have to move across a wood's base, you must subtract 2" from the unit's charge distance.

RUINS

The galaxy is littered with the remains of once-proud cities.

Unless they can **FLY**, **VEHICLES**, **MONSTERS** and **BIKES** can only end their move on the ground floor of ruins.

INFANTRY are assumed to be able to scale walls and traverse through windows, doors and portals readily. These models can therefore move through the floors and walls of a ruin without further impediment.

INFANTRY units that are on a ruin receive the benefit of cover. Other units only receive the benefit of cover if at least 50% of every model is actually obscured from the point of view of the shooting unit.

CRATERS

Many worlds bear the scars of heavy, sustained bombardment.

INFANTRY models that are entirely within a crater receive the benefit of cover.

Models are slowed when charging across craters. If, when a unit charges, one or more of its models have to move across a crater, you must subtract 2" from the unit's charge distance.

BARRICADES

Makeshift barricades make excellent defensive positions.

INFANTRY models within 1" of a barricade, and behind it from the point of view of the firing unit, receive the benefit of cover. In addition, enemy units can Fight across a barricade, even though the physical distance is sometimes more than 1". When resolving Fights between units on opposite sides of a barricade, units can be chosen to Fight and can make their attacks if the enemy is within 2" instead of the normal 1".

OBSTACLES

The advance of many armies has been thwarted by obstacles.

There are two kinds of obstacles: tank traps, which are obstacles to **VEHICLES** and **MONSTERS**, and tanglewire, which is an obstacle to everything else. Units are slowed when they attempt to move over obstacles. If, when a unit Advances or charges, one or more of its models have to move over an obstacle, you must halve the unit's Advance or charge distance, as appropriate (rounding up). **TITANIC** models are not slowed by obstacles.

IMPERIAL STATUARY

The heroes of the Imperium are immortalised in stone effigies.

Models within 3" of Imperial Statuary that are at least 25% obscured by it, from the point of view of the firing unit, receive the benefit of cover.

In addition, **IMPERIUM** units within 3" of Imperial Statuary add 1 to their Leadership.

FUEL PIPES

Promethium and other explosive fuels are pumped across many worlds in armoured pipes.

Fuel pipes follow all the rules for barricades, with the following addition:

Roll a dice each time you make a saving throw of 7+ (usually a roll of 6, plus 1 for being in cover) for a model within 1" of a fuel pipe in the Shooting phase. On a 1, that shot has ruptured the pipe and caused a small explosion; the model's unit suffers a mortal wound.

BATTLESCAPE

The smoking hulls of tanks and the blasted remains of trees speak of the presence of mines or other, more dangerous, traps.

Battlescapes follow all the rules for woods, with the following addition:

Roll a dice each time a model Advances or charges across a battlescape; on a roll of 1, that model has triggered a mine and its unit suffers a mortal wound. Models that can **FLY** can still trigger mines, but only if they charge across battlescape.

THOUGHT FOR THE DAY: A GOOD DEATH EARNS THE EMPEROR'S BLESSING.

HILLS

Hills and elevated positions are often key tactical locations.

Hills, whether free-standing or modelled into the battlefield itself, are raised areas that offer troops on top of them commanding views and fields of fire. Hills are always considered to be part of the battlefield rather than a terrain feature, and so models on top of them do not receive the benefits of cover. Some particularly large hills may block a model's visibility to a target unit, however, so get a model's-eye-view to see if this is ever the case.

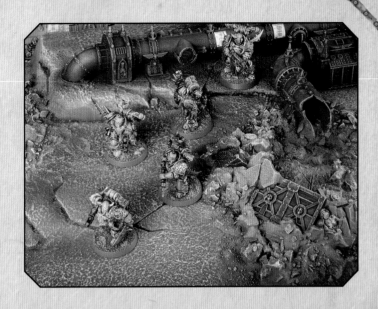

SCRATCH-BUILT TERRAIN

Many hobbyists enjoy making their own terrain features from scratch (thus the term 'scratch-built terrain'). If you wish to incorporate such terrain features into your battlefields, you and your opponent will need to devise your own rules for them. Don't worry – this is very easy to do, especially if you use the rules presented on these pages as examples and inspiration. You could, for example, model your ruins on a scenic base, and agree that the base itself is simply an extension of the ruins and follows all the same rules. Perhaps you will create a river (presumably a fantastical one filled with lava or acid) with entirely new rules, agreeing that the only models that can cross it safely are those that can **FLY**. Some players prefer to say that certain terrain features, such as giant rock formations or imposing sealed buildings, are simply impassable to any models – creating obstacles on the battlefield for armies to manoeuvre around. You could make up some truly exotic rules for your terrain, such as creating a portal to the warp through which Daemons can materialise throughout your battle. Anything goes, so long as all players agree that it sounds like fun!

BATTLEZONES

The galaxy is ablaze with war, and millions of planets shake to the tread of mighty armies. Some are once-verdant paradises reduced to mud-churned ruins, others are hellishly overpopulated industrial hive worlds, while many are utterly inimical to life.

So long as you and your opponent agree, any Warhammer 40,000 battle can use Battlezone rules. They are optional, but Battlezone rules allow you to recreate battles fought in all manner of otherworldly environments, such as in the depths of hive cities, on asteroids hurtling through space, or even amidst the madness of worlds lost to the powers of Chaos. Each battlezone introduces new rules to your missions to represent the battlefield conditions of these varied worlds. They might change the core rules, for example by altering how psychic powers work. They can provide new rules for things like living terrain or tectonic activity, and may grant additional abilities to certain units.

Agree which, if any, Battlezone rules will be used when you are setting up the battlefield, before deployment. Three battlezones are presented here to help make sure that every battle you fight is different. You can find more battlezones in other Warhammer 40,000 publications, and if you feel inspired, you can always make your own!

BATTLEZONE: NIGHT FIGHT

Battles in low to zero visibility are a test for any general at the best of times. When the battlefield is obscured by darkness, howling ash storms, unnatural celestial phenomena or psychic obfuscation, it means enemies can be nearly invisible, reinforcements can be lost, and your objectives can become uncertain.

Low Visibility: When rolling to hit in the Shooting phase, apply the following penalties to your models depending on their distance from the target. If the target unit is exactly 12", 24", or 36" away, use the lesser penalty from the table.

DISTANCE	PENALTY
0-12"	No penalty
12-24"	Hit rolls have a -1 penalty
24-36"	Hit rolls have a -2 penalty
36"+	Hit rolls have a -3 penalty

Fog of War: If a unit arrives on the battlefield after the battle has begun (e.g. as the result of an ability on its datasheet or the Reserves rules), roll a dice the first time it does so. On a 1 or 2, it is delayed and cannot arrive this turn – it arrives in the following turn instead.

STRATAGEMS

In this battlezone, you and your opponent can both use Command Points (CPs) to use the following Stratagem:

1CP

LIGHT 'EM UP
Stratagem

Select an enemy unit. For the duration of your turn, your units can shoot at that unit without penalties from Low Visibility.

Mysterious Objectives: If you are playing a mission with objective markers, any unit that moves within 3" of an objective marker, or is within 3" of an objective marker at the start of the first turn, must identify it. To do so, roll a dice and consult the following table. Each objective marker is only identified once.

D6	RESULT
1	**Sabotaged!:** The unit that identified this objective marker takes D3 mortal wounds.
2	**Nothing of Note:** This has no additional effect.
3	**Grav-wave Generator:** If you control this objective marker, any unit attempting to charge a friendly unit within 3" of this objective subtracts 2 from its charge move.
4	**Targeting Relay:** If you control this objective marker, friendly units within 3" of this objective re-roll hit rolls of 1 when shooting.
5	**Scatterfield:** If you control this objective marker, friendly units within 3" of this objective re-roll saving throw rolls of 1.
6	**Fire Support:** If you control this objective marker, roll a dice at the end of your Shooting phase. On a roll of 5+, choose an enemy unit within 36". That unit suffers D3 mortal wounds.

BATTLEZONE: FIRE AND FURY

The armies clash under a burning sky – far above the conflict, a cataclysmic battle is taking place in orbit, and the casualties of that war descend in burning fragments to bombard the armies on the cracked earth. It is insanity to fight in these conditions, but you will not be found wanting!

Burning Skies: Units that can FLY must roll a dice each time they move in the Movement phase (roll after they have completed their move). On a roll of 1, they suffer D3 mortal wounds.

The Earth Cracks: All Move characteristics are halved for units that begin their turn with any models entirely within a terrain feature, and a unit that charges through such terrain must roll a dice. On a roll of 1, it suffers D3 mortal wounds. Units that can FLY are not affected.

Meteoric Debris: In each of your Shooting phases, place three dice numbered 1, 2 and 3 anywhere on the battlefield, at least 12" apart. You then roll another dice; if the result matches the number of one of the dice, a flaming chunk of debris crashes into the battlefield at the corresponding dice's location and every unit within 6" of it suffers D3 mortal wounds. If the result doesn't match any placed dice, the debris has landed elsewhere on the planet this time.

WARLORD TRAIT

In this mission, your Warlord can choose the following Warlord Trait in place of any other:

Insane Bravado: This Warlord and any friendly units within 8" of them do not have to take Morale tests.

STRATAGEMS

In this battlezone, you and your opponent can both use Command Points (CPs) to use the following Stratagem:

> **2CP**   **ORBITAL BOMBARDMENT**
> *Stratagem*
> In your Shooting phase, you may place six dice for Meteoric Debris, rather than 3. The dice should be numbered 1, 2, 3, 4, 5 and 6.

BATTLEZONE: PSYCHIC MAELSTROM

On countless worlds, psykers unaware of the terrible danger are tapping into powers they cannot control. In extreme cases, a psyker is transformed into a ghastly conduit for the warp, infesting their planet with daemonic corruption while amplifying the psychic potential of all who fight there.

The Warp Overflows: PSYKERS add 2 to their Psychic and Deny the Witch tests.

Psychic Amplification: PSYKERS can attempt to manifest one extra psychic power in their psychic phase, and the range of all psychic powers (where they have a range) is doubled.

Mortal Peril: If you roll any double for a Psychic test, including a double 1 or double 6, the PSYKER suffers Terrors of the Warp (after resolving the psychic power, if it is successfully manifested). This counts as suffering Perils of the Warp, but instead of the usual rules, roll on the following table:

D6	RESULT
1	**A Fate Worse Than Death:** The psyker suffers 6 mortal wounds. If they are slain by this, your opponent may place a Chaos Spawn model, under their control, where the psyker was standing (or as close as possible).
2	**Overload:** The psyker suffers D3 mortal wounds. If they are slain by this, each unit within 6" suffers D3 mortal wounds.
3	**A Door Closes:** The psyker immediately forgets the psychic power that they were manifesting – they cannot manifest this power for the rest of the battle.
4	**Timeslip:** The psyker may immediately attempt to manifest an extra psychic power in this phase (even one they have already manifested).
5	**Possession:** Roll 2D6. If the total is greater than the psyker's Leadership characteristic, they are possessed and controlled by your opponent for the rest of the battle.
6	**Transformation:** Until your next Psychic phase, the psyker has a Strength characteristic of 10 and an invulnerable save of 2+.

PLANETSTRIKE

The Planetstrike expansion allows your armies to battle to the death in a devastating planetary assault. In Planetstrike, players take specific roles – one is the attacker, attempting to wrest control of a planet, and the other is the defender, who will do everything to hold it.

Planetary invasions are swift and terrible affairs, characterised by deafening noise, earth-shattering explosions and the stench of death. Thousands of battle-hungry warriors plunge downwards upon trails of flame and vapour like vengeful angels, pouring from the drop-craft and low-orbiting spaceships that darken the skies above. Megatonnes of ordnance hammer down around these airborne warriors, the detonations so devastating that the skies themselves seem afire. Attack craft roar across the sky through lattices of ruby-red las-fire and rocket contrails, strafing any soldier who dares stray into the open before screaming off through the flak to the next war zone. Pillars of ghostly light probe the skies, their colonnades all but transforming the battlefield into some vast and surreal shrine to the gods of war. The touch of these lights is certain death to any invader caught in their beams, and red-hot debris rains from the skies as batteries of anti-aircraft guns take their toll. Gigantic landers plummet from the heavens, shaking the ground with their impact before disgorging yet more warriors into the merciless meat grinder of a planetary assault.

Below the chaotic skies lies a war-torn landscape chewed up and spat out by the incessant bombardments that precede the invasion. The devastated mudscape is punctuated only by the ruined shells of once-proud buildings and

The defender constructs their garrison – mighty bastions and heavy emplacements bristling with enough firepower to cut down any invaders that dare set foot on the planet.

The attacker launches deadly firestorms from orbit before their forces drop directly into the heart of the fight to wrest the planet from the defender.

A SMALL MIND IS EASILY FILLED WITH FAITH.

by inviolable strongholds that jut like tombstones from the tortured earth. The comparison is apt, for the doomed soldiers who defend these bastions from the storm of violence that threatens to consume them will emerge as corpses or not at all.

It is within this nightmarish and lethal crucible of battle that true heroes are forged into warriors of iron will and exceptional might who march grim-faced through barrages of shrapnel and fire without pause. It is these heroes who determine the fate of the planet, these heroes who defy the enemy to strike them down and tear the prize from their grip. Only the brave or the insane can hope to prosper. Empires have ever been built on the deeds of such dauntless individuals, and by their deeds they may also fall.

PLANETARY ASSAULT

Planetstrike is truly a war on all fronts, in which the enemy can appear at any time, from anywhere – especially from above! Will you play the Defender, setting up formidable fortifications and giving everything you've got to repel the invaders? Or will you play the Attacker, raining hellfire and damnation upon the foe before sending an army of your best troops to claim the smoking remains of their strongholds? Whether you choose to tear the planet from your opponent's grasp or annihilate the invaders raining from the skies, your actions can determine the fate of an entire world.

Planetstrike missions use the following additional rules:

FIRESTORM ATTACK
The planetary invasion is preceded by a fierce firestorm.

The Attacker makes Firestorm Attacks at the start of the first battle round, but before the first turn begins; each mission will specify how many are made. The Attacker first places six dice numbered 1 through 6 on the battlefield, anywhere at least 9" apart. For each Firestorm Attack, roll one dice: every unit within 3" of the corresponding dice's location suffers D6 mortal wounds. **INFANTRY** units hit by a Firestorm Attack can choose to go to ground before the damage is rolled; if they do, they only suffer D3 mortal wounds, but cannot do anything during their first turn.

PLANETARY ASSAULT
The attacker's forces rain from the skies to assault the defenders.

In Planetstrike missions, the Attacker's units are not set up on the battlefield during deployment and instead start the game in Reserve. **INFANTRY** units and units that can **FLY** start the game in orbit, whilst other units start the game in a landing zone, just off one edge of the battlefield.

Roll a dice for each of your units still in Reserve at the end of each of your Movement phases (this is called a Reserve roll) – on a 3+ that unit arrives from Reserve. Note that if a unit placed in Reserve is embarked within a **TRANSPORT**, they will arrive when their transport does, not separately (if rolling, make a single roll for the transport and its embarked units).

If the unit arrived from orbit, place it anywhere on the battlefield more than 6" from any enemy model. If the unit arrived from a landing zone, place it within 6" of the battlefield edge chosen as the Attacker's landing zone.

PLANETSTRIKE DEFENCES
The Defender can use the following rules for defences in Planetstrike:

BASTIONS
These shelter the Defender's forces as they repel invading armies.

Bastions cannot move for any reason, nor can they Fight. Enemy models automatically hit them in a Fight – do not make hit rolls. Each Bastion has a Toughness of 10, a Save of 3+, 20 Wounds, and is removed once it has lost all its wounds. Each has a Ballistic Skill of 5+ and is equipped with four heavy bolters (see right).

The Defender's **INFANTRY** units can garrison a Bastion, moving in and out of it in the same manner as a unit embarking or disembarking from a **TRANSPORT**. Up to 20 models can garrison a Bastion at any one time. Garrisoning units cannot normally do anything or be affected in any way, with the exception that they can still shoot in your Shooting phase. If the Bastion is destroyed, each unit garrisoning it must disembark, but the Defender must then roll a dice for each model just set up on the battlefield; for each roll of 1, 2 or 3, a model that disembarked (Defender's choice) is crushed by falling rubble and slain.

DEFENCE EMPLACEMENTS
Defence Emplacements are used to shoot down invading forces.

Defence Emplacements cannot move for any reason, nor can they Fight. Enemy models automatically hit them in a Fight – do not make hit rolls. Each Defence Emplacement has a Toughness of 7, a Save of 4+, 3 Wounds and is removed once it loses all of its wounds. Each Defence Emplacement has a Ballistic Skill of 5+ and is armed with either an Icarus lascannon or a quad-gun (see below). Add 1 to the hit rolls when shooting one of these weapons at a unit that can **FLY**, or at a unit that arrived from orbit during the Attacker's previous turn. Subtract 1 when shooting at any other target.

WEAPON PROFILES					
	R	TYPE	S	AP	D
Heavy bolter	36"	Heavy 3	5	-1	1
Quad-gun	48"	Heavy 8	7	-1	1
Icarus lascannon	96"	Heavy 1	9	-3	D6

PLANETSTRIKE STRATAGEMS
In Planetstrike games, players can use the following additional Stratagems, depending on whether they are the Attacker or the Defender:

2CP — SCORCHED SKIES
Attacker Stratagem
This Stratagem is used just before you resolve your Firestorm Attacks. You make D3 additional Firestorm Attacks.

1CP — RAPID DROP ASSAULT
Attacker Stratagem
This Stratagem is used before making any Reserve rolls at the start of your first turn. D3 units of your choice automatically arrive from Reserve.

1CP — TARGETING JAMMERS
Defender Stratagem
This Stratagem is used just before the Attacker resolves their Firestorm Attacks. You can move one of the Firestorm location dice up to 2D6" in any direction.

2CP — FORTIFIED STRONGHOLD
Defender Stratagem
This Stratagem is used before the Attacker resolves his Firestorm Attacks. Select a single Bastion. That Bastion has 25 Wounds instead of 20.

PLANETSTRIKE
PLANETFALL

Invading forces orbit above, raining fire upon the foe, their landing parties inbound to take for themselves any fortresses still standing. The defender must weather the storm and repel the enemy, no matter the cost. The attacker must not rest until the world is theirs.

THE ARMIES

The players should first choose who is the Attacker and who is the Defender, then each selects a Battle-forged army. The Power Level of the Attacker's army should be greater than that of the Defender's.

THE BATTLEFIELD

The Defender creates the battlefield; they start by setting up any number of Fortifications (Bastions, Defence Emplacements, etc.). They then set up all other terrain on the battlefield however they choose. Once the Defender has created the battlefield, the Attacker chooses one battlefield edge to be their landing zone – this is where their non-orbital Reserves will arrive from.

Next, the Defender places 6 objective markers. One objective marker may be placed inside each Bastion. Any objective marker not placed in a Bastion must be placed anywhere on the battlefield so long as the centre of each is more than 6" from the centre of any other objective marker, any Bastion or any battlefield edge. If a Bastion containing an objective marker is destroyed during the game, the Defender must place the objective marker where the building used to be.

DEPLOYMENT

The Defender now sets up all of their units, anywhere on the battlefield. The Attacker's units do not start the game on the battlefield, but use the Planetary Assault rules (pg 256).

FIRESTORM ATTACK

The Attacker rolls a D3 and adds 1 to the result for each Bastion that is on the battlefield. The total is the number of Firestorm Attacks that the Attacker makes.

FIRST TURN

The Attacker has the first turn.

BATTLE LENGTH

The game lasts for 6 battle rounds.

VICTORY CONDITIONS

At the end of the game, the player who has scored the most victory points is the winner. If both players have the same number of victory points, the game is a draw. Victory points are achieved for the following:

Storm and Defend: At the end of the game, each objective marker is worth 3 victory points to the player who controls it. A player controls an objective marker if they have more models within 3" of the centre of it than their opponent does. If an objective marker is within a Bastion, count all the models within 3" of the building and all the models garrisoning it when determining who controls the objective marker.

Slay the Warlord: If the enemy Warlord has been slain during the battle, you score 1 victory point.

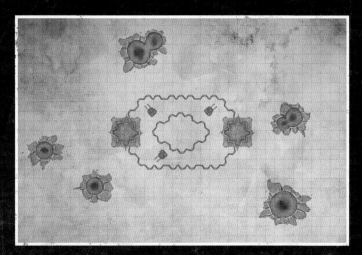

The battlefield shown here is an example of a classic set-up for a game of Planetstrike. The Defender has chosen to place his Fortifications in the centre of the battlefield so that, whichever direction the Attacker chooses to come from, they will be ready.

CITIES OF DEATH

In the nightmare of the far future, armies battle one another to annihilation amid the shattered ruins of vast corpse-strewn cities. The Cities of Death expansion allows both players to recreate the brutal, close-confines nature of urban warfare.

In a galaxy of war, cities make for the bloodiest of battlefields. Bombed from orbit, the blasted city ruins are overrun by hordes of slavering aliens or crushed to rubble beneath the footfalls of titanic war machines. Warriors engage in bitter close-quarters battles whilst mighty battle tanks smash through crumbling buildings, grinding bricks and bodies both beneath their treads. Victory will only be won by an army ruthless and determined enough to drive its enemy from every collapsed building, root out and eradicate every firebase, and level every stronghold to deny even a single sniper a vantage point. Every building, staircase and hallway becomes a battleground fought over by dozens of warriors, no quarter given until the floor is carpeted with the bodies of the dead and the walls are blasted rubble.

Battle lines are drawn from one street corner to another and soldiers dart across shell-pocked roads. No man's land is watched over by merciless snipers waiting for the next fool to stray into their sights.

In these cramped confines, warriors fight on long after their ammunition is spent. With the butts of rifles and scavenged weapons, they bludgeon their foes to death, stabbing and hacking in a frenzy to survive. In such battles, combatants are at their most base and low, and no tactic is too desperate, no rule unbreakable to achieve victory. City fighting takes all the horrors of war and magnifies them. Territory is more important, lives are cheaper, and survival is all but impossible.

Ruined buildings conceal warriors who use their elevated position to gain an advantage over their foes, granting them a superior field of fire and making it harder for the enemy to find effective cover. Assault forces are sent forwards to flush out all such pockets of resistance. Darting from cover to cover, they launch desperate attacks with grenades and flamers to reduce the foe to blasted and charred corpses.

In Cities of Death, key locations are seized and pressed into service as makeshift bunkers, emergency field hospitals or command posts by generals desperate for any advantage. Any buildings that cannot be held are instead rigged with all manner of deadly traps.

Sometimes, a few loyal or well-trained soldiers must be counted on to turn the tide of a city battle. Few in number, such warriors cannot hope to hold ground for long periods against large numbers of enemies and must therefore engage in daring hit-and-run tactics, pinpoint strikes under cover of darkness, and even daring raids launched from labyrinthine sewer networks.

Even the most fast-moving armies can be forced to abandon their usual tactics as they become bogged down in blood-soaked building-to-building warfare.

EVEN A MAN WHO HAS NOTHING CAN STILL OFFER HIS LIFE.

Cities of Death missions use the following additional rules:

CITY RUINS

Unless they can **FLY**, **VEHICLES**, **MONSTERS** and **BIKES** can only end their move on the ground floor of ruins.

INFANTRY are assumed to be able to scale walls and traverse through windows, doors and portals readily. These models can therefore move through the floors and walls of a ruin without further impediment.

INFANTRY units that are on or behind a ruin receive the benefit of cover. **INFANTRY** units that do not move in their Movement phase are better able to make use of available cover in Cities of Death. Until they next move, you add 2 to their saving throws instead of only 1 against all shooting attacks. Other units only receive the benefit of cover if at least 50% of every model is actually obscured from the point of view of the shooting unit.

HEIGHT ADVANTAGE

In urban warfare, every soldier in a tall building is a sniper, raking fire onto those below. Combating foes with such a height advantage is nigh impossible.

A model gains a Height Advantage whilst occupying the upper levels of a city ruin and shooting at a unit that is either at street level or within a lower level of city ruins. To gain a Height Advantage, every model in the target unit must be on levels that are 3" or more below that of the firing model. If a model shoots with a Height Advantage, the target does not receive any of the benefits for being in cover.

STREETS AND ROADS

Forces can move quickly across streets and roads, but doing so often leaves them exposed to enemy fire.

You can move a model an extra 2" if it spends its entire Movement phase on a street or road (move a model an extra 4" instead if the unit Advances). This has no effect on units that can **FLY**.

FIRE IN THE HOLE

In the close confines or building-to-building warfare, grenades are especially effective.

In Cities of Death battles, re-roll all failed wound rolls made when a model throws a Grenade at a unit on or in ruins. Furthermore, if a Grenade makes a random number of attacks, that Grenade always makes the maximum number of attacks instead (e.g. a Grenade D6 profile would instead be treated as a Grenade 6 profile when thrown at a unit occupying ruins).

CITIES OF DEATH STRATAGEMS

In Cities of Death games, players can use the following additional Stratagems:

2CP — SEWER RATS
Stratagem

This Stratagem is used just before you set up an **INFANTRY** unit during deployment. Instead of setting up that unit on the battlefield, they are infiltrating the city's sewer network. At the end of any of your Movement phases, you can set the unit up anywhere on the battlefield at street level that is more than 9" from any enemy model and not in a city ruin.

1CP — MEDICAE FACILITY
Stratagem

This Stratagem is used after both sides have deployed, but before the first battle round begins. Nominate a single city ruin to house the Medicae Facility. Roll a dice each time a model loses a wound whilst occupying that city ruin; on a 6, the model has been healed by the medicae equipment and does not lose that wound.

1CP — BOOBY TRAPS
Stratagem

This Stratagem is used after both sides have deployed, but before the first battle round begins. Secretly nominate a single city ruin to house the Booby Traps and write this down – this cannot be a city ruin that is currently occupied by any models. The first time any model, moves into the city ruin, they trigger the Booby Traps and suffer D3 mortal wounds (D6 if they were Advancing).

1CP — DEATH IN THE STREETS
Stratagem

This Stratagem can be used when a unit with a Height Advantage shoots an enemy unit that is entirely at street level and not in cover. You can re-roll all failed hit and wound rolls when resolving shots at that enemy unit.

CITIES OF DEATH
FIRESWEEP

Both sides are moving forwards to occupy as much of the city as possible, conducting a room-to-room, building-to-building and street-to-street advance. Each force must attempt to claim as many buildings as they can, clearing the enemy as they move.

THE ARMIES

Both players select a Battle-forged army. Neither army can include any Fortifications.

THE BATTLEFIELD

Create the battlefield. Players must set up at least six city ruins, but should place more if they can. The streets and areas between the city ruins should be liberally littered with obstacles, barricades, wreckage and other detritus so that troops have some shelter as they dash from one building to another.

After terrain has been set up, the players must place 6 objective markers to denote the Critical city ruins they are attempting to claim (see Victory Conditions, opposite). The players should roll off and, starting with whoever rolled highest, alternate placing these objective markers until all 6 have been set up. The objective markers must each be located in a different city ruin.

DEPLOYMENT

The player who placed the sixth objective marker now picks one quarter of the battlefield, as shown on the map below, for their deployment zone, and their opponent uses the diagonally opposite quarter of the battlefield as their deployment zone. Next, players alternate deploying their units, one at a time, starting with the player who did not pick their deployment zone. A player's models must be set up within their own deployment zone. Continue setting up units until both sides have set up their army.

POWER LEVEL

After both sides have deployed, determine each army's Power Level by adding the Power Ratings of all its units; whichever player has the lowest is the Underdog. If both have the same Power Level, the player who assigned the deployment zones is the Underdog. If the difference between the Power Levels of the two armies is 10 to 19, the Underdog receives 1 bonus CP; if the difference is 20 to 29, they receive 2 CPs and so on.

FIRST TURN

The player who completed setting up their army first can choose to take the first or second turn.

BATTLE LENGTH

The game lasts for 6 battle rounds.

VICTORY CONDITIONS

At the end of the game, the player controlling the most Critical city ruins earns a major victory. If both players control the same number, the Underdog scores a minor victory. A player controls a Critical city ruin if they have more models on or in that ruin than their opponent.

Player A's Battlefield Edge

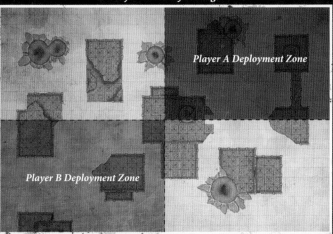

Player A Deployment Zone

Player B Deployment Zone

Player B's Battlefield Edge

The battlefield shown here is an example of a classic set-up for a game of Cities of Death. The battlefield contains several city ruins through which infantry can fight and take cover, and exposed roads, across which the brave can attempt to cover ground.

STRONGHOLD ASSAULT

Across the galaxy, siege warfare is a way of life. In Stronghold Assault one player is the Attacker, throwing themselves against the walls of monolithic fortresses, and the other is the Defender, who will garrison every fortification, gun emplacement and blood-soaked trench to the last.

The galaxy's battlefields are punctuated with monolithic strongholds that reach towards the heavens, studded with enough weapon emplacements and firing ports to hold back entire armies. These fortifications are monuments to the unyielding nature of siege warfare. Many have endured centuries of unrelenting battle, and in their shadows, warriors beyond counting have been slain. Some have even withstood more than ten millennia of grinding war, sheltering troops as they unleash their own fury against the foe.

Nested within the grandest bastions are weapons of such terrible magnitude that they can annihilate the mightiest machines of war, or even cripple a battleship in low

orbit. These jutting fortresses do not stand alone in their endless vigil over the galaxy's battlefields – defence lines and trench networks protect and connect the bunkers and weapon towers at their heart.

However, even the most formidable series of fortifications are naught but walls and barricades without a garrison to defend them. Only when soldiers man battlements and operate weapon systems is a fortification's true defensive potential realised. Even a single squad of warriors can be

transformed into an unyielding foe when occupying a bunker, pouring down firepower upon their enemies with impunity, safe from all but the heaviest retaliation. It is no surprise, therefore, that commanders seek to control these unyielding bulwarks. Control of such assets can be the difference between victory and defeat. As such, they are never defended lightly, nor taken from the enemy without considerable losses.

Strongpoints are inevitably the strategic lynchpins of any occupying army's war effort, and thus become the prime objectives of any enemy attack. The aggressor will launch endless charges across no man's land, attempting to tear down these edifices and slay those sheltering within.

The armour and armaments of fortifications make them invaluable defensive assets. A fully garrisoned fortress can withstand both heavy bombardment and determined assault from a numerically superior foe, but should the walls fall, the defenders' hopes of victory often fall with it.

Many of the Imperium's countless fortresses have succumbed to war over the millennia, torn down in grinding sieges to piles of rubble or blasted by artillery bombardments into shattered ruins. However, for every mighty fortification that has been razed to the ground, a dozen have endured to stand proud – armoured monuments that are testament to the stubborn power and brutal majesty of Mankind.

Stronghold Assault missions use the following additional rules:

BIG GUNS NEVER TIRE

The attacker has brought along their heaviest ordnance to level the defences of the foe.

The Attacker's models can move and shoot Heavy weapons without incurring the -1 penalty to their hit rolls, but only when targeting a Bunker or a Fortress (see right).

DEMOLITIONS

The attacking troops are equipped with demolition tools and explosive charges to breach the enemy's defences.

Each time the Attacker makes a wound roll of 6+ for a model Fighting a Bunker or a Fortress, the structure suffers a mortal wound in addition to any other damage.

STRONGHOLD DEFENCES

The defenders await the onslaught of their enemy, secure in the protection offered by their fortifications and trenches.

The Defender can use the following rules for their defences in games of Stronghold Assault:

DEFENCE LINES

Defence Lines are trenches or armoured shield sections that provide troops with shelter.

INFANTRY models that are within 1" of a Defence Line and behind it, from the point of view of the firing unit, receive the benefit of cover. In addition, these models can take cover at any point during the enemy turn – as soon as they do so, improve their Save by 2 until the start of the enemy's next turn, but they can do nothing until then.

In addition, enemy units can fight across a Defence Line, even though the physical distance is sometimes more than 1". When resolving Fights against units on opposite sides of a Defence Line, units can be chosen to Fight if the enemy is within 2", instead of the normal 1". In order to attack an enemy unit on the opposite side of a Defence Line, an attacking model must either be within 2" of that unit, or within 1" of another model from its own unit that is itself within 2" of that enemy unit. This represents the unit fighting in two ranks.

BUNKERS AND FORTRESSES

These fortifications are used to shelter the Defender's forces as they repel invading armies.

When the Defender creates their army, they can include as many Bunkers and Fortresses as they wish. Each is a single model that takes up a single Fortifications Battlefield Role slot in a Detachment. Bunkers have a Power Rating of 5, whilst Fortresses have a Power Rating of 15.

Bunkers and Fortresses cannot move for any reason, nor can they Fight. Enemy models automatically hit them in a Fight – do not make hit rolls. Each Bunker and Fortress has a Toughness of 10 and a Save of 3+. A Bunker has 15 Wounds and a Fortress has 30 – either is removed once destroyed. A Fortress has a Ballistic Skill of 5+ and is equipped with two Icarus lascannons, a missile silo and up to four heavy bolters (see right).

INFANTRY units can garrison a Bunker or a Fortress, moving in and out of it in the same manner as a unit embarking or disembarking from a TRANSPORT. Up to 20 models can garrison a Bunker at any one time, and up to 40 can garrison a Fortress. Garrisoned units cannot normally do anything or be affected in any way with the exception that they can still shoot in your Shooting phase. If the Bunker or Fortress is destroyed, each unit garrisoning it must disembark, but the controlling player must then roll a dice for each model just set up on the battlefield; for each roll of 1, 2 or 3, a model that disembarked (controlling player's choice) is slain.

CAPTURED FORTRESS

An undefended stronghold is an asset for the attacker to capture and turn upon the foe.

At the start of most Stronghold Assault missions, Bunkers and Fortresses are under the control of the Defender. However, the Attacker can garrison any unoccupied building using the same rules. If they do so, the building immediately comes under their control. Buildings can potentially exchange hands several times over the course of the battle.

WEAPON PROFILES					
	R	TYPE	S	AP	D
Heavy bolter	36"	Heavy 3	5	-1	1
Icarus lascannon	96"	Heavy 1	9	-3	D6
Missile silo*	96"	Heavy 3D6	4	0	1

*The missile silo cannot shoot enemy units that are within 18".

STRONGHOLD ASSAULT
BUNKER ASSAULT

One side has withdrawn behind the shelter of unyielding bunkers, holding the advancing foe at arm's reach whilst calling down withering salvoes of artillery strikes. The attacker must destroy or overwhelm the bunkers as quickly as possible, before the barrages pound them into oblivion.

THE ARMIES

The players should first choose who is the Attacker and who is the Defender, then each selects a Battle-forged army. The Power Level of the Attacker's army should be greater than that of the Defender's. The Defender must include at least one Fortification Network Detachment containing between 1 and 3 Bunkers and/or Fortresses, in any combination.

THE BATTLEFIELD

The Defender creates a battlefield. They start by first setting up their Bunkers and Fortresses within their deployment zone. They then set up as many Defence Lines as they like. Then set up other terrain on the battlefield – we suggest a few ruins or craters.

DEPLOYMENT

After the battlefield has been created, the Defender sets up their army within their deployment zone. The Attacker then sets up their army within their own deployment zone.

TARGETING AUGER

After both sides have deployed, the Defender selects one of their Bunkers or Fortresses to house the Targeting Auger. Whilst this Fortification is garrisoned by one of the Defender's units, they can direct an artillery strike at the start of each of their Shooting phases. To do so, place a marker (such as a dice or a coin) anywhere on the battlefield. Your opponent can then move the

marker D6" in any direction. After this is done, roll a dice for each unit (friend or foe) within 3" of the marker – on a 3+, that unit suffers D3 mortal wounds.

FIRST TURN

The Attacker has the first turn.

BATTLE LENGTH

The game lasts for 6 battle rounds.

VICTORY CONDITIONS

At the end of the game, the player who has scored the most victory points is the winner. If both players have the same number of victory points, the game is a draw. Victory points are achieved for the following:

No Quarter Given: Each player scores 1 victory point for each enemy unit that is destroyed.

Rubble and Ruin: The Attacker scores 3 victory points for each Bunker they destroy, and for each Bunker they have captured and still hold at the end of the game. The Defender scores 3 victory points for every other Bunker still on the battlefield at the end of the game. Each Fortress is instead worth 6 victory points.

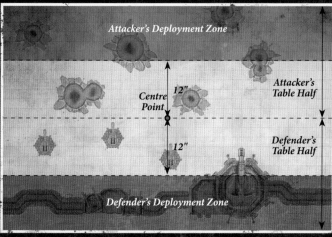

Attacker's Battlefield Edge

Attacker's Deployment Zone

Centre Point

12"

Attacker's Table Half

12"

Defender's Table Half

Defender's Deployment Zone

Defender's Battlefield Edge

The battlefield shown here is an example of a classic set-up for a game of Stronghold Assault.

When setting up the table, any Fortifications that are purchased as part of an army list must be placed wholly within their controlling player's table half.

DEATH FROM THE SKIES

Fire fills the skies as squadron after squadron of aircraft scream into battle. The Death from the Skies expansion allows players to recreate battles where squadrons of aircraft are critical to success and where skilled aces engage in fast-paced dogfights for dominance of the skies.

The clouds burn as squadrons of aircraft tear across the skies and engage in deadly combat. Even as mighty armies clash upon war-torn battlefields, so the skies above play host to battles of their own. Swift fighter wings dogfight furiously with one another, and ace pilots prey upon their victims with sublime skill. Squadrons of bombers thunder in through skies alive with flak, dropping ordnance into the swirling battle below. Meanwhile, attack craft punch through enemy fighter screens to strafe the foe and deliver warriors to the heart of battle. Everywhere, wise commanders seek to dominate the air, knowing that this will secure victory on the ground.

Wings of lightning-fast jet fighters hurtle through acid squalls or weave between the towers of megalithic cityscapes to blow enemy aircraft out of the skies. As their land-bound comrades fight and die down below, these courageous pilots engage in adrenaline-charged aerial duels where a split second's hesitation means death.

All the while, flights of bombers thunder into cauldrons of fire to hammer shield generators, dark idols and super-heavy war engines with lethal ordnance. The destruction wrought by squadrons of heavy bombers obliterates such ground targets wholesale.

Even as this carnage is unleashed, aerial transports and gunships swoop from on high. Strafing runs shred infantry formations, gunning down bestial monsters and turning enemy tanks into fireballs, before disgorging hordes of battle-ready killers from their armoured holds.

Whether forging through sentient rust-cyclones or engaging winged Daemons in the starlit void of space, squadrons of aircraft rule the war-torn heavens.

Hurtling into battle with guns spitting death, wings of combat aircraft fight their own war high above the blood-soaked battlefield.

The first moments of a dogfight are crucial; pilots jockey for position, attempting to tail their quarry and line up for the kill shot. It is an aerial dance in which the slightest mistake can be fatal.

An aircraft may be forced to bug out, temporally leaving combat airspace, usually to shake off enemy fighters. Though it will avoid its own imminent destruction, its absence will be sorely felt on the battlefield, leaving its allies on the ground unprotected and at the mercy of deadly strafing fire and bombing runs until it can return, guns blazing, to wreak vengeance.

Death from the Skies missions use the following additional rules:

FLYERS

All Flyers – that is, units specifically with the Flyer Battlefield Role – can make use of the expanded Flyer rules below. For many of these rules, the Flyers' arcs will be important. Flyers have four 90° arcs: one front, one rear and two side arcs.

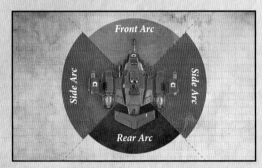

DOGFIGHT PHASE

Aircraft duel to the death in the burning skies above.

In Death from the Skies missions, Flyers can only target enemy Flyers with shooting attacks during the Dogfight phase. This is an extra phase introduced in each player's turn between their Movement and Psychic phases.

In the Dogfight phase, starting with the player whose turn it is, players alternate selecting one of their Flyers and then selecting an enemy Flyer as the target of their Dogfight. Your Flyer can immediately shoot with any of its weapons as if it were the Shooting phase. It can only shoot at the targeted Flyer, however, and cannot use Bombs and similar ordnance during the Dogfight phase. Furthermore, only those weapons that are in arc can shoot at the Flyer, such is the twisting and turning nature of Dogfights. Draw an imaginary line between the centre of your Flyer to the centre of the target Flyer to determine which of your weapons can be fired at that target; turret weapons can shoot in any direction, tail-mounted weapons can only shoot targets in the Flyer's rear arc and all other weapons can only shoot targets in the Flyer's front arc.

You will receive an additional modifier to your hit rolls depending on which of the target Flyer's arcs is facing the shooter, as follows:

• Rear (Tailing): +2 to all hit rolls.
• Front (Head-on Pass): +1 to all hit rolls.
• Side (Deflection Shot): No modifier.

Once your Flyer has resolved its shots, your opponent then chooses one of their Flyers to Dogfight, until all the Flyers that the players wish to Dogfight have done so.

Then move onto the Psychic phase as normal.

Flyers that shoot in the Dogfight phase can still shoot in their Shooting phase as normal, but remember that they can only target enemy Flyers in the Dogfight phase, so will need to shoot at ground-based targets instead.

LEAVING COMBAT AIRSPACE

Sometimes pilots are forced to overshoot their primary target and come around for another pass.

In an exception to the Minimum Move section of the core rules, Flyers can move off the edge of the battlefield – indeed, because of minimum moves, some may be forced to do so. These Flyers are said to have Left Combat Airspace. They can attempt to return to combat airspace at the end of their next Movement phase. To do so, roll a dice; on a 1 or 2, it has been delayed and does not arrive this turn, but you can roll again in your next turn. On a 3+, that Flyer arrives and is set up on the board as follows. Place the Flyer touching any battlefield edge facing any direction and move it directly forwards up to 6" (it cannot turn again). Flyers are always assumed to have moved their maximum distance when arriving on the battlefield in this manner.

Any Flyer that has Left Combat Airspace and has not re-entered it by the end of the game counts as destroyed for the purposes of any victory conditions.

DEATH FROM THE SKIES
TACTICAL STRIKE

A window of opportunity has arisen for your bombers and ground-attack craft to strike at strategically vital ground targets. The attacker must strike fast, for the defender is even now scrambling fighters to intercept the attacking aircraft.

THE ARMIES

The players should first choose who is the Attacker and who is the Defender, then each selects a Battle-forged army. Both armies must include at least one Air Wing Detachment. We recommend that the Defender's army include a few Fortifications as well. The Power Level of the Attacker's army should be greater than that of the Defender's.

THE BATTLEFIELD

Create a battlefield using the deployment map below that is large enough to accommodate both armies. Next, set up terrain. The Defender's deployment zone should contain several defensible pieces of terrain, such as ruins, in which they can take shelter from the air raids.

The Defender then sets up 5 objective markers to denote the Attacker's Ground Objectives. These can be placed anywhere that is not in terrain, or anywhere on a Fortification with Wounds, but each must be at least 6" away from any other (measure to the centre of the objective marker).

DEPLOYMENT

The Defender deploys their army within their deployment zone. The Attacker then sets up their army within their own deployment zone.

GROUND OBJECTIVE

The Attacker must target and destroy the Ground Objectives. If a marker is placed on a Fortification, that Ground Objective is destroyed when the Fortification is. Markers that are not on terrain represent underground targets; these have a Toughness of 6, a Save of 4+ and 10 Wounds (in a Fight, Ground Objectives are hit automatically – no hit dice is rolled).

BUNKER BUSTERS

The Attacker adds 1 to all hit and wound rolls made for their Flyers when targeting Ground Objectives.

FIRST TURN

The Attacker has the first turn.

BATTLE LENGTH

The game lasts for 6 battle rounds.

VICTORY CONDITIONS

If, at the end of the game, 4 or more Ground Objectives have been destroyed, the Attacker wins a major victory. If 2 or fewer have been destroyed, the Defender wins a major victory. If 3 have been destroyed, and the Power Level of the Attacker's army is at least 10 greater than that of the Defender's, the Defender wins a minor victory, otherwise the battle is a draw.

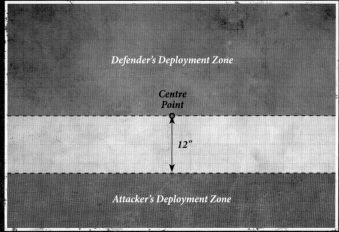

Defender's Battlefield Edge

Defender's Deployment Zone

Centre
Point

12"

Attacker's Deployment Zone

Attacker's Battlefield Edge

MULTIPLAYER BATTLES

The rules for Warhammer 40,000 are written for battles fought between two players, each commanding an army. However, it is equally enjoyable to play multiplayer games between three or more players, each striving separately to defeat their opponents!

In a multiplayer battle there can be as many sides as there are players! Each player must attempt to defeat all of their opponents, using any means at their disposal in order to achieve victory. It is very simple to play a multiplayer battle, and only requires a handful of minor modifications to the core rules, which are detailed below.

MISSIONS

Multiplayer battles are best fought using missions that are designed specifically for them, such as the multiplayer mission presented on the next page, called 'Carnage'. However, it is easy to modify many two-player missions for use in multiplayer games by following these guidelines:

THE ARMIES

To play a multiplayer battle, you must have three or more players. Each player then chooses an army; the models belonging to all of the other players are treated as enemy models.

BATTLE ROUNDS

Each battle round is split into three or more turns – one for each player. Unless otherwise stated, at the start of each battle round, players roll off. The player who rolls highest decides who takes the first turn in that battle round.

After the first player has finished their turn, the players who have not yet had a turn yet roll off. The player who rolls highest decides who will take the next turn in that battle round.

After that player has finished their turn, the remaining players roll again to see who takes the next turn, and so on, until all of the players have had a turn. Then, the battle round is over and a new one begins.

PSYCHIC PHASE

Only one player is allowed to attempt to resist a successfully manifested psychic power – if several players wish to do so, then the player whose turn is taking place can choose which one gets to make the attempt.

CHARGE PHASE

After a player has moved all their charging models, the other players can attempt to perform Heroic Interventions in an order decided by the player whose turn it is. An enemy **CHARACTER** can only perform a Heroic Intervention if it is within 3" of a model controlled by the player whose turn it is.

FIGHT PHASE

Any unit that has models within 1" of an enemy unit can Fight in this phase. Models can be used to attack any enemy models, not just those belonging to the player whose turn is taking place.

Units that charged this turn Fight first as normal. Then, the player whose turn it is chooses an order for all the players (including themselves) to select a unit to Fight with, before the next player chooses a unit. Continue going around in the same order until all eligible units that you want to Fight have done so. If one player completes all of their units' Fights first, or they don't have any units that can Fight, then the other players complete all of their remaining Fights, one unit after another, in the same order. No unit can Fight more than once in each Fight phase.

MORALE PHASE

In the Morale phase, all players must take Morale tests for units from their army that have had models slain during the turn. The player whose turn it is tests first, and they then decide the order in which the other players will take their Morale tests.

MULTIPLAYER STRATAGEM

In multiplayer missions, each player can use Command Points (CPs) to use the following Stratagem:

1+CP

BRIBE
Stratagem

You can use this Stratagem at any time to give any number of your remaining CPs to another player to bargain for a temporary ceasefire, alliance, betrayal, etc.

HINTS & TIPS

In a battle fought between three or more opponents, each general taking part must learn to be cunning! You must be able to set your foes against each other, form temporary alliances, and know when to stab someone in the back before they do the same thing to you. In other words, a successful general needs to be willing to use underhand ploys and tactics in order to win a battle!

A WEAPON CANNOT SUBSTITUTE FOR ZEAL.

MULTIPLAYER BATTLE
CARNAGE

Several armies converge on the same battlefield, each determined to capture it for themselves. Make whatever truces you must and betray whomever you wish, but be careful – when the battle is over, there can be only one victor.

THE ARMIES

In order to play this mission, you will need three or four players. Each must select a Battle-forged army.

THE BATTLEFIELD

Create a battlefield and set up terrain; as it will need to accommodate up to four armies, you might need to use a slightly larger battlefield than normal. Then, place a single objective marker in the centre of the battlefield.

DEPLOYMENT

The battlefield is divided into quarters. The players roll off; the winner chooses one of the quarters to be their deployment zone. Then, the remaining players roll off. The winner selects one of the other quarters to be their deployment zone, and so on, until all the players have a deployment zone.

The players then alternate deploying their units, one at a time, starting with the player who selected their deployment zone first, then the player who selected their deployment zone second, and so on. Models must be set up in their own deployment zone, more than 9" from the centre of the battlefield. Continue setting up units until all sides have set up their armies.

POWER LEVEL AND RANKING

After all sides have deployed, determine each army's Power Level by adding together the Power Ratings of all the units set up in that army. Then rank the armies from highest Power Level to lowest. If two have the same Power Level, the players should roll off. Whoever wins has the higher rank.

FIRST TURN

The player with the lowest rank chooses who has the first turn during the first battle round. The player with the second lowest rank chooses who has the second turn during the first battle round, and so on.

BATTLE LENGTH

The game lasts for 5 battle rounds.

VICTORY CONDITIONS

If one player's army has slain all of its foes, they win a major victory. Otherwise, the player who has the most victory points wins a major victory. If two or more players are tied for the highest number of victory points, the one with the lowest rank wins a minor victory. Victory points are achieved for the following:

Dominate the Field: At the end of each battle round, the objective marker is worth 1 victory point to the player who controls it – keep a running score from battle round to battle round. A player controls the objective marker if there are more models from their army within 3" of the centre of the marker than there are enemy models.

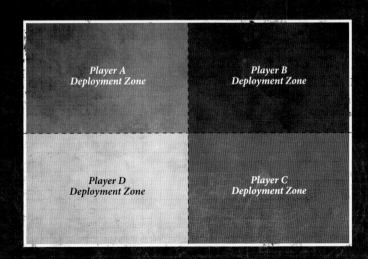

CAMPAIGNS

Taking you beyond one-off battles, campaigns can add a new dimension to your gaming, giving each victory and defeat greater meaning. Essentially, they tell a story that unfolds with every new engagement, where the result of each battle will be affected by the one before and influence the one after.

Once you fight a number of battles with your army, you're likely to find that a narrative develops out of the action on the battlefield. Perhaps one unit gains a reputation for surviving against the odds, or one of your Characters begins a bitter rivalry with one from an army they face regularly.

Campaigns are a great way of developing this natural narrative, providing it with a clearly defined structure and giving each battle you fight greater meaning. In essence, a campaign is simply a series of battles that are linked by a mechanism such as a map, flowchart or overarching story. Campaigns offer a style of gaming where armies gain battle honours and commanders hone their skills as the action progresses.

As you play and progress through the campaign, you will get to know and anticipate the strengths, weaknesses and strategies of your fellow players. Friendly rivalries abound, and are all part of the fun – as well as giving you the opportunity to capitalise on your victories, campaigns also allow you to seek retribution for your defeats!

A campaign can be as small or as extensive as you like. For instance, you could pitch your army against that of a friend and spend a day playing a short campaign that encompasses a skirmish, an epic main battle and a desperate last stand. Several friends could use a campaign as motivation for building their armies, where each week the players add a new unit to their forces and play again. There are many different types of campaign, but here are some examples of the most common kinds.

TREE CAMPAIGNS

Tree campaigns are a series of linked games, with the outcome of each one affecting the conditions of the next. For example, a simple tree campaign could consist of three battles (see below). In the first, one army is patrolling its territory (the defender), while the other must silence the patrols to gain the advantage (the attacker). If the attacking player wins the battle, the next mission sees them use this advantage to ambush the defender's forces. If the defender wins the first battle, the next mission is a rescue, as the attacker has to make a daring strike to retrieve the lone survivor of that

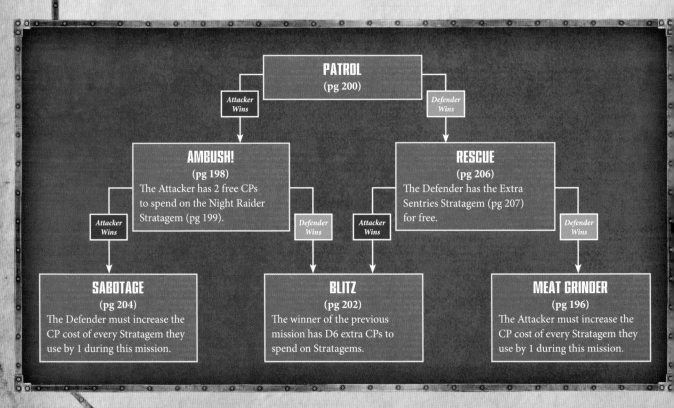

PATROL
(pg 200)

Attacker Wins

Defender Wins

AMBUSH!
(pg 198)
The Attacker has 2 free CPs to spend on the Night Raider Stratagem (pg 199).

RESCUE
(pg 206)
The Defender has the Extra Sentries Stratagem (pg 207) for free.

Attacker Wins

Defender Wins

Attacker Wins

Defender Wins

SABOTAGE
(pg 204)
The Defender must increase the CP cost of every Stratagem they use by 1 during this mission.

BLITZ
(pg 202)
The winner of the previous mission has D6 extra CPs to spend on Stratagems.

MEAT GRINDER
(pg 196)
The Attacker must increase the CP cost of every Stratagem they use by 1 during this mission.

Timidity begets indecision; indecision begets treachery.

failed first mission. The result of the second basttle will determine which mission is played next, and the winner of that mission wins the campaign!

MATRIX CAMPAIGNS

Matrix campaigns require forward planning, with each battle affected by the choices you make at the start. They give you the opportunity to outmanoeuvre your foe in a series of linked games, using guile to win the day, but the mechanics are quite simple. Each player secretly picks an option from a list before each battle – the different choices will come together on the matrix to determine which mission to use. Below is an example that you could use to decide not only the mission you play, but which player has managed to gain an advantage over their opponent. You could use this matrix multiple times in the same campaign, or design your own with your opponent for the engagements that you fight later in the campaign, with additional bonuses or penalties.

MAP CAMPAIGNS

Map campaigns provide a dynamic geographical setting for your battles which you can explore as the campaign progresses. Each player might start with their own territory, marked out on a grid or even a Realm of Battle board modelled to represent the contested world. As battles are won and lost, territory might be taken over, key assets might be seized, and empires carved out that will be forever remembered. The action might not be restricted to battles – you can always write rules for supply lines, reinforcements, natural disasters and so on!

THE NEXT STEP

Once you have developed a taste for campaigning, you can make use of increasingly complex systems – some of these methods can be combined for an even more engaging experience. For example, you can incorporate a matrix into a map campaign and use your knowledge of the terrain to make the best strategical choices.

If you're new to campaigning, however, it's best to start small. While it's tempting to set your sights on conquering an entire star system, a set of linked battles with a manageable objective such as a capturing an outpost is perfect. On the other hand, if you've already enjoyed battling your way through a few games, then dive straight into an epic narrative campaign. This is the perfect forum for unleashing your creative talents, and provides great motivation to finish painting those final units or even build a whole new tabletop battlefield replete with sturdy fortifications, outlandish flora and all the scars of a protracted and hard-fought war.

Campaigns can become great multiplayer battles where pacts are formed and armies expand as the sagas unfold. In fact, stories are at the heart of every successful campaign, and when combined with a sound framework and organisation, they provide the excitement and interest that keeps everyone motivated to win.

		WARLORD A				
WARLORD'S CHOICE		Advance	Hold	Reconnoitre	Flank	Reinforce
WARLORD B	**Advance**	Retrieval Mission (pg 218)	Blitz (pg 202) (Warlord B is the Attacker)	Patrol (pg 200) (Warlord B is the Attacker)	Ambush! (pg 198) (Warlord A is the Attacker)	No Mercy (pg 219)
	Hold	Blitz (pg 202) (Warlord A is the Attacker)	Deadlock (pg 235)	Cleanse and Capture (pg 230)	Meat Grinder (pg 196) (Warlord B is the Attacker)	Meat Grinder (pg 196) (Warlord A is the Attacker)
	Reconnoitre	Patrol (pg 200) (Warlord A is the Attacker)	Cleanse and Capture (pg 230)	Patrol (pg 200) (choose Attacker randomly)	The Scouring (pg 220)	Sabotage (pg 204) (Warlord B is the Attacker)
	Flank	Ambush! (pg 198) (Warlord B is the Attacker)	Meat Grinder (pg 196) (Warlord A is the Attacker)	The Scouring (pg 220)	Cloak and Shadows (pg 234)	Ambush! (pg 198) (Warlord B is the Attacker)
	Reinforce	No Mercy (pg 219)	Meat Grinder (pg 196) (Warlord B is the Attacker)	Sabotage (pg 204) (Warlord A is the Attacker)	Ambush! (pg 198) (Warlord A is the Attacker)	Tactical Escalation (pg 232)

For matrix campaigns, each warlord chooses their strategy in secret before revealing them simultaneously, and then cross-references their choices to determine which mission they will play. In this example, if Warlord A chose 'Hold' and Warlord B chose 'Flank', the two would play the Meat Grinder mission, with Warlord A as the Attacker.

So does the cycle of eternal strife continue. The grinding wheels of conflict crush the bodies of men and the souls of gods until all that is left is dust. Even those who fall do not know peace, for as one battle ends, another begins, and then another. To hope for a better world is to embrace futility and despair. In this world, in this cosmos, in this reality and the next, a single stark truth abides. There is only war.

APPENDIX

DAEMONS

That there are Daemons abroad in the universe, and the link that these entities have with the warp, is not a commonly known or understood phenomenon within the broader community of the Imperium. There are various reasons for this. Quite apart from the rarity of encounters with the denizens of the warp, the hierarchy of the Imperium has always sought to suppress such knowledge. What little awareness exists amongst the peoples of the Imperium is never openly or officially acknowledged. Tales of the warp, and its unpleasant inhabitants, are dismissed as scaremongering or mere superstition.

The Imperium, or at least its more senior agents, is quite determined to prevent the spread of daemonic infestation. It is known amongst the cognoscenti that the ways of the Daemon are deceitful and devious and that they have subtle ways to infiltrate human societies and influence the human mind. Many are the strange, twisted cults and secretive covens of Daemon worshippers that have inveigled themselves into the worlds of the Imperium throughout the course of its long history. Wherever possible, these cults are unearthed and eradicated, but not without great cost of lives, property and sanity.

There is also the very real threat of possession, which, although very rare, is nonetheless feared above all other outcomes. A Daemon with such a foothold in realspace is both difficult to identify, at least in the early stages of possession, and a deadly and dangerous foe. Furthermore, the Daemon is always intent on spreading its taint by establishing cult worship and encouraging yet more possessions. Unchecked, such a creature can wreak untold damage in both the physical and metaphysical spheres.

However, the primary motivation for keeping knowledge of Daemons secret is to ensure that the greater population is not catastrophically disturbed by such revelations and driven to madness, despair and mass civil unrest through the knowing of them. There is a world of difference between understanding that there are vile, antipathetic alien species at large in the universe and knowing that one's immortal soul is at risk from predation by unholy daemonic entities from a hellish dimension a mere thought away from our own. Also, as dangerous as warp travel may be perceived to be, if the general populace were to realise that it was, in fact, through a realm inhabited by Daemons, it is unlikely that anyone would willingly submit themselves to such a means of transport or trust any of the astropathic messages sent through it. The resultant anarchy would be threat enough to completely destabilise an already strained Imperium.

Thus, only the most stout-hearted and iron-willed are permitted to know and retain knowledge of the Daemons and their masters, the Dark Gods. The bearers of this knowledge are few, and they share this information reluctantly. The Inquisition, their erstwhile allies, the Grey Knights, and a few others are among the tiny number of humans who are allowed to know of the Daemons' existence. Most others who come into contact with them are culled to prevent both the promulgation of knowledge and the possible spread of daemonic taint. If they are of sufficient value to the Imperium, they are instead mind-wiped to erase all memories of the encounter.

ASTROPATHIC COMMUNICATION

A brief treatise on the basics of Astropathic transmission (Imp. Ref. 0253870007/SA).

There are many methods of communication within a single planetary orbit and even within compact star systems, ranging from the mundane to the esoteric. However, the majority of the Imperium's colonised worlds are so far apart from other star systems that other means are required to stay in contact with the wider Imperium – to pass messages over such great interstellar distances requires the skills and powers of an Astropath.

Astropaths are the most common sanctioned psykers in the Imperium, having escaped the cruel fate that awaits those without the strength of mind to control their powers, or the will and determination to survive the Imperium's strict training regimes. All major organisations of the Adeptus Terra, from the bureaucratic branches of the Administratum to the furtive offices of the Inquisition, use Astropaths to communicate with each other across the vast distances of the galaxy. These psykers can be found working alongside starship captains, rogue traders, planetary governors and officers from all branches of the military. The Adeptus Ministorum makes extensive use of Astropaths, and has built vast amphidomes and psi-comm spires that rise high over every shrine world, aiding their spiritual broadcasts and creating an interlocking transmission web that at least partially connects many dioceses and parishes, though the most powerful can even reach some of the far missionaries on the edges of the Imperium.

It is said that the Emperor, the greatest of all psychic minds, once held full telepathic conversations with Malcador the Hero, himself a mighty telepath. Though they were at opposite ends of the known galaxy, there was no time delay to speak of, and they may as well have been in the same room. Although human psykers of such extreme potency no longer stride among the stars, so long as the warp is relatively calm, the most powerful Astropaths can single-handedly send messages across several star systems with some accuracy. If all goes well, telepathic communications travel quickly through the warp, crossing many thousands of light years, becoming fainter and fainter, before eventually fading out altogether. Still, such communications vary widely based on the mental strength of the sender, the ability of the receiver to absorb such incoming messages and, perhaps most of all, the unpredictable nature of the warp itself. When the galactic distance required of a transmission is so great that a single Astropath proves insufficient, it is common for them to work in relays, sending messages to various beacons, hubs and Imperial sub-stations to pass along. It is also possible to boost a message by using an Astropath Choir – a group working in synchronicity to broadcast or receive complex messages over unimaginable distances.

It is too complicated and variable to list all of the methods and processes involved in Astropath communications, but the following generalisations should help even a novice understand some of the difficulties of the medium. There are, after all, dozens of types of Trance Broadcasts alone, to mention nothing of Station Reception, Astral Projection or the nearly infinite styles of Divination practised by Astropaths within (and beyond) the purview of Imperial Sanction. Using mesmeric chants to enter a deep trance, a typical Astropath forms the message within his mind and sends it through the warp. The progress of the message is rather like a stone dropped into a pool, as it creates a series of ripples that extend outwards through the immaterium. Some psychics are able to project the message so that it travels only in a desired direction, but even then, some echoes are likely to lap outwards.

Once projected, a message hurtles through the warp until its energy is lost and it fades away, typically a gradual process, but the immaterium is anything but predictable. Communications of this kind have many restrictions; they are brief in length, perhaps comprising only a few images or sentences depending on how the Astropath works, (psychics are as likely to work in abstract pictures and emotions as they are words). As with all things, the very chaos of the warp can alter the form of a message, if only rarely its intent. Unless powered by a mighty source, longer or more complex messages risk getting unravelled in the ripples of the warp, arriving in a jumbled order and risking further, if not complete, distortion. Warp interference is common, as messages can be delayed, muddled or contaminated by any number of fluctuations, such as shifts in warp tides or the intermingling of multiple telepathic signals. Raging warp storms can redirect or simply swallow and destroy messages, blocking communiqués for centuries.

Any Astropath can pick up Trance Broadcasts, although in general it can be said that more discipline is needed to receive messages than to send them. With outgoing messages, an Astropath can concentrate on the clarity of thought, on the message itself, pushing such deliberations deep into the warp. Astropaths in such a trance and actively receiving incoming messages are particularly vulnerable – their minds must open to the eternal noise of that erratic and highly dangerous realm. Not only must an Astropath attempt to sift out the senseless static of passing currents, they must also contend with the residue of ancient messages that sometimes (for no logical reason) drift endlessly, not losing power but continuing to call from some distant past, faint waves of energy lapping across the void. The repercussive warp-waves of major events or cataclysms can also be picked up, sometimes unintentionally, sending more sensitive Astropaths into fits or burning out their minds altogether with the onslaught.

Ominously, some telepathic impulses attract unwanted attention – mischievous warp entities that attempt to alter messages, making them misleading or obscene, redirecting them to the wrong recipient, or perhaps even attaching themselves to the mental transmissions, piggybacking on the message to its final destination. Although rare, it is possible for Daemons themselves to become aware of and attracted to the psychic signals hurtling through their realm. On occasion, they will even trace them back to their source, searching for a way to establish a claw-hold in realspace.

An Astropath who wishes to send a singular message to a specific location – whether it is a particular spacecraft, planet, hive or even an individual – must be able to concentrate his mind to a degree that is unimaginable to a normal human. These messages are launched into the warp not as ripples extending outwards in all directions, but as a single bolt of pure thought. The recipient must be prepared to receive such a powerful transmission, though it is still possible for those in Sweeping Trance Reception to pick up snippets of such messages if they happen to pass through their area of their psychic awareness on the way to their destination.

Success of this kind is linked more to random chance than any degree of skill or accuracy on the part of the recipient.

The need for interstellar communication is enormous, and the Scholastica Psykana is constantly bombarded with requests for sanctioned Astropaths. They are a common sight in the more civilised sectors of the Imperium, easily distinguished by their green robes and sightless, sunken eye sockets. Although only released for duty once they have cleared all sanctioning tests and the holy ritual known as the Soul Binding, in which they face the psychic might of the Emperor himself, the nature of their occupation puts them in nearly constant danger and there have been documented cases of Astropaths becoming corrupted (see crossfile, datascroll Ref. 0062132005).

HIGH LORDS OF TERRA

The High Lords of Terra are the governing body of the Imperium, tasked with interpreting the Emperor's will and enacting his rule across the largest empire in the galaxy. On their command, the armies of the Imperium move; only their edict can approve a Space Marine Founding, and on their orders the Black Fleet sails and their grim tithes are collected. Yet how, beneath the Benevolent Emperor, has such an organisation come to be?

The Senatorum Imperialis has, at its roots, many echoes from ruling bodies formed before the birth of the Imperium. In the beginning of the age, the Emperor himself ruled, although he formed about him a council of advisors comprised of key individuals. This top circle contained the Fabricator General of Mars, the Paternova of the Navigator Houses and Malcador the Sigillite, perhaps the Emperor's greatest ally during the Unification Wars of Terra. As the Emperor left the home world of Mankind to lead the Great Crusade, he left the legendary Malcador to more or less act as regent in his stead.

Over the course of that vast military campaign, which reclaimed the galaxy and freed Humanity from enslavement, the Emperor discovered the lost Primarchs and brought them into the fold. As the Great Crusade began to branch off in many new directions, the Emperor grew to rely on his new battle council. After the decisive victory at the Battle of Ullanor, when Mankind's reascension was no longer in doubt, the Emperor left military matters in the hands of Horus, his newly appointed Warmaster, and returned to Terra.

Whilst Horus directed the rest of the Primarchs in the expansion and security of this new realm, the Emperor formed the Council of Terra. This formalised the role of the Emperor's previous advisors

and the group started off with a half-dozen men. This council, under the leadership of the Emperor, was to become the body of government that would administrate the myriad bureaucratic tasks needed by the newly formed empire. Already, under the far-seeing eyes of Malcador, the Adeptus Administratum was born, new branches immediately forming beneath its auspices. It was a bright start for the new Dawn of Mankind envisioned by the Emperor.

In addition to the Council of Terra, the Primarchs – under the Warmaster – were to head the military branches, now in the latter days of the Great Crusade and spread far across the galaxy. As it turns out, this was a contentious decision. Some of the Primarchs took great exception to being administrated by those deemed less worthy of such honours than themselves. It cannot be proven, but doubtless this turned out to be one of many growing resentments that allowed the Ruinous Powers to infect and corrupt several of the Primarchs.

Following the calamities of the Horus Heresy, the Emperor was interred upon the Golden Throne and could no longer rule his realm directly. Several legends tell of the Emperor's last words, spoken as he was attached to the vast machinery that would allow his mind to live on. Full of foresight beyond mortal men, the Emperor's final instructions were for the rule of the Imperium. In that time of great change, Malcador too was gone, and it had been he who had proven best able to enact the Emperor's vision. His role, and the leadership for the coming reformation, fell to Roboute Guilliman, the great Primarch of the Ultramarines. It was he who set up the new ruling body, the Senatorum Imperialis, or as it is now more commonly known, the High Lords of Terra. It was their duty to interpret the will of the Emperor and, in his stead, to command the Imperium. The number of this ruling council was set at twelve, with Roboute Guilliman himself taking a seat under the title of Lord Commander of the Imperium, the old term Warmaster having fallen out of favour for obvious reasons.

Since those days, the number of seats on the High Lords of Terra has largely remained the same, fluctuating during various points of crisis before eventually returning to its original number. Each seat is filled by a leader from one of the most powerful organisations of the Imperium. A complex web of tradition, skulduggery, promises of support, threats of retaliation and considerations of mutual interest binds them together and determines who holds office and who does not. In practice, some of the Imperium's organisations and institutions are so powerful and vital that it would be unthinkable for their leader to not be granted a seat upon the High Lords of Terra. Naturally, however, over the long millennia, the unthinkable has happened many times over, though the existing High Lords often put in place measures to ensure that their seat is a permanent one – that upon their deaths their position is automatically filled by the new head of their organisation. The following offices are almost invariably represented as High Lords because they form the cornerstones of the Imperium, the most important of its ancient institutions:

- Lord Commander of the Imperium, Roboute Guilliman
- Master of the Administratum
- Fabricator General of the Adeptus Mechanicus
- Paternoval Envoy of the Navigators
- Inquisitorial Representative
- Master of the Adeptus Astra Telepathica
- Ecclesiarch of the Adeptus Ministorum
- Grand Master of the Officio Assassinorum
- Master of the Astronomican

Those nine posts are virtually sacrosanct and, with the notable exception of Roboute Guilliman's long absence, there are very few times in the history of the Imperium when these seats upon the High Lords of Terra became empty and were not filled with a successor from the same organisation.

It is worth noting that a specific Inquisitor does not typically hold the position of Inquisitorial Representative on his own, but instead, the seat is retained for whichever individual is sent on behalf of the Inquisition for a particular session. Similarly, the place of the Paternoval Envoy is open to whoever is the Envoy of the Paternova of the current ruling family of Navigators. The Paternova himself never leaves the Palace of Navigators, for it is forbidden for him to do so.

The remaining three posts are usually filled from amongst the following mighty officials:

- Lord Commander of Segmentum Solar
- Lord Commander Militant of the Astra Militarum
- Lord High Admiral of the Imperial Navy
- Cardinal(s) of the Holy Synod of Terra
- Abbess Sanctorum of the Adepta Sororitas
- Captain-General of the Adeptus Custodes
- Grand Provost Marshal of the Adeptus Arbites
- Chancellor of the Estate Imperium
- Speaker for the Chartist Captains

It is an oddity that, throughout its history, very few members of the Adeptus Astartes have served as High Lords of Terra – given the importance of Humanity's most elite fighting force and the fact that the first council was initiated by Roboute Guilliman, the Primarch of the Ultramarines. This seems to have been set up intentionally by Guilliman, who knew that at times of great need, Space Marine leaders would have no choice but to step in, but should otherwise remain outside the ruling structure. Some

say the Primarch's discouragement of Space Marines serving in the Senatorum Imperialis was based upon the Emperor's original Council of Terra – which was separate from his Military Council, and a ruling body that did not include any members of the Adeptus Astartes. Guilliman clearly believed – as his great work, the Codex Astartes, points out – that it is the Space Marines' duty to serve Mankind, not to rule it.

In its long existence, the High Lords of Terra have gone through many changes. They have been forced to give one of its seats over to a religious leader (the Ecclesiarch, who joined shortly after the Imperial Cult was named the sole religion of the Imperium in early M32), wiped out to a man by assassination (on the orders of a slighted Grand Master of the Officio Assassinorum, an event known as 'the Beheading') and dissolved altogether by the ruling Ecclesiarch (during the civil war known as the Age of Apostasy). Many members have disappeared under suspicious circumstances and the Inquisition has been asked to investigate a number of times (although many have suggested that at least some missing Lords of Terra have disappeared because of the Inquisition). Yet always, despite the many power struggles and strife, the High Lords of Terra have continued to interpret the Will of the Emperor and thereby rule the greatest empire in the galaxy.

EXCERPTS ON WARP TRAVEL

Notes of Sharim Calypso, Adjutant advisor to the Imperial Navy. Ref. MCS17-82h.57c

The Questio Logisticus branch of the Adeptus Administratum has a division devoted to tracking median travel via common warp routes. Although only two millennia worth of data has been compiled, it has thus far proven little, save what is already known – to enter warp space is a deadly and unpredictable risk.

By way of an example, note the logbook of the Proxxian traders that operate in the Nephilim Sector. They primarily transport forced labour, from the hive world of Proxx to the isolated mining colonies of Hephastian, approximately three times each Terran year. The distance is dozens of light years and requires a fleet to traverse the immaterium. The route is anything but predictable, despite being classed as a semi-fluctuating passage (the most stable rating). Typical voyages range between one and six weeks, but the more extreme journeys have taken as much as 1,200 years and as little as two minutes. Some 22% of expeditions have, as of yet, not arrived at their destination – although given the time disparity, one can only estimate what percentage have been lost and which are still en route. In distance, this is a relatively

short voyage; the numbers only grow worse with longer journeys.

It is my observation that little more can be learned from further computations and that the old Navigator maxim, 'Trust in the Emperor's Light', remains the one truism of value concerning warp travel.

STC SYSTEMS

Created at the developmental apex of the Age of Technology, the Standard Template Construct (STC) system was a way to ensure that all the recently far-flung human colonies across the galaxy could build anything they needed, from air-purifiers to military-grade weaponry, hab-buildings to plasma reactors. The user simply asked the machine how to build what was needed and it would calculate everything – from locally available materials to the means of manufacture and assembly – and present the most efficient way to achieve what the settler asked. The STCs were designed so that the least-accomplished user could still fabricate the vehicle, building, or weapon they needed. For all intents and purposes, the STCs were the sum total of Man's technical know-how at its zenith of power.

Every human colony had at least one STC system, although most colonists never tapped into anything like the more advanced constructs, finding the more rudimentary machines and weapons far more useful. It is highly probable that few of the theoretical or most highly advanced works were ever attempted. Over the passage of time, a majority of the STC machines were lost, destroyed in battle or by natural disaster, or began to fail, overcome at last by corrupted databanks, too much jury-rigging in place of knowledgeable maintenance, or simply the fatigue of thousands of years of use. Those lucky planets that still maintained even a partially working STC system grew to guard it jealously as the Age of Technology slipped into the anarchic madness of the Age of Strife. Soon, the galaxy-wide realm of Man was fractured, each world cut off from all but its closest neighbours. The madness, warfare and warp-spawned invasions, along with a great backlash against technology, ensured that few of the great works of the previous era survived.

Today, there are no surviving STC systems. It was common practice, however, beginning in the Age of Technology, for colonies to produce hard copies of many of the more standard designs. Over the years, these have been copied repeatedly, with varying levels of accuracy. Yet, as commonplace as many of these designs once were, now any copy is a rarefied item, even more so for any that carry precious first-generation printout information. During the Great Crusade and later, during the period known as the Forging, thousands upon thousands of previously colonised planets were reclaimed for Humanity. Many STC reproductions were found amongst these worlds and, it is rumoured, even some partially working systems were unearthed. These long-lost troves of forgotten technology were mostly discovered buried amidst the ruins of greatly regressed worlds, but occasionally they were found enshrined within locked vaults, guarded by those to whom the name STC, or even its purpose, had long passed out of understanding. Any such findings are greedily collected by the Adeptus Mechanicus; the Tech-Priests rush such treasures back to their secretive forge worlds, where they can be thoroughly studied, hoarded, worshipped and copied.

One result of the STC system, and its pivotal place in human development, is that many worlds utilise designs and machinery of a similar type. Of course, the millennia have wrought changes in the basic utilitarian devices prescribed by the STC, but many humans adhere religiously to the old designs. STC designs were intended to be able to cope with anything, given the unpredictable nature of colonies in previously unexplored space. Therefore, designs were often big and brutish, hard to damage and easy to repair. Examples of recovered STC technology are still being built and remain in use, including such military hardware as the Rhino Armoured Personnel Carrier and the Land Raider, as well as the atmospheric pumps that still keep the air (almost) breathable in even the largest hive-blocks. The Adeptus Mechanicus still searches for copies of undiscovered templates, or perhaps a fully functioning STC system. Until then, gone are the secrets for the trident-shaped Proteus Cannon of Mars or the force field generators that guard the Palace of Xerxes, and countless other marvels whose workings even the most adept of the Tech-Priests can't begin to fathom.

ABHUMANS

Abhumans are evolved from human stock, but changed or mutated to a greater or lesser degree. They differ from true mutants in that they conform to a recognisable physical standard, breed true, and are no more prone than normal humans to further mutation. There are billions of abhumans living within the Imperium and they are tolerated and exploited by the authorities very much as the rest of the population. It is rare for them to reach positions of authority or power within the Imperial hierarchy and many are subject to popular derision, fear or prejudice. Many abhumans are recruited into the service of the Administratum and its various sub-divisions, including the Imperial Guard and the Imperial Fleet. In the Imperial Guard, they are organised and fight in dedicated squads or companies, segregated from their human comrades.

The Adeptus Terra officially recognises seventy-three stable abhuman strains within the Imperium. Of these, forty-six types are now listed as extinct, and no records have been received of a further twelve strains for over a generation, suggesting that they too have died out or been assimilated back into the general population. The status of the remaining fifteen abhuman races is quite varied and there is permanent disagreement about their specific classification amongst the adepts of the overseeing sub-division of the Adeptus Administratum: the Tithes Chamber Notaries, sub. Planetary Census (Abhumans). The most noteworthy and contentious matter concerning the adepts is the Ogryn (Homo sapiens gigantus) matrix of abhuman strains. This complex group is currently officially listed as seven distinct types (Alpha, Theta, Type IV, Type VIIa, H.S. gigantus gigantus, H.S. gigantus cranopus and the mysterious Grey Ogryns), but many in the Chamber doubt that these are all separate types, and revision of the classification is therefore pending.

Ratlings (Homo sapiens minimus), Squats (Homo sapiens rotundus), Beastmen (Homo sapiens variatus), Troths (Homo sapiens verdantus), Longshanks (Homo sapiens elongatus), Pelagers (Homo sapiens oceanus), Felinids (Homo sapiens hirsutus) and Neandors (Homo sapiens hyannothus) comprise the remaining classified, and officially recognised, abhuman races. Of these, Beastmen are subject to severe persecution and have been placed on the Register of Proscribed Citizens (Class A-G worlds) by the Adeptus Arbites. This effectively precludes them from settlement on, or transportation to or from, more than three hundred thousand worlds of the Imperium and forbids their conscription as an Imperial Tithe obligation. All of this is a sure sign that they will soon lose abhuman status completely and be reclassified as true mutants. Troths, Felinids and Neandors are endemic, and restricted to the worlds of Verdant, Carlos McConnell and Hyannoth IV respectively. The remaining abhuman races are variously present across the entire Imperium. In some regions they are plentiful and common, living in large colonies or even populating entire worlds, while in others they are scarce and virtually unknown.

BLACK SHIPS

The great fleet of Black Ships belongs to the Adeptus Astra Telepathica. Independent of the Imperial Navy, they are the second-largest fleet in the galaxy. There are many thousands of Black Ships, but only the highest-ranking adepts in the Adeptus Astra Telepathica know the true scale of the fleet and the vast scope of its operations. New vessels are constantly commissioned to replace inevitable losses and to further increase the fleet's size. Thus it is that each year, more and more planets of the Imperium are visited and stripped of their psykers for transportation to Terra.

The captains and other senior officers of the Black Ships are senior adepts of the Adeptus Astra Telepathica. The ships' crews are indentured workers drafted from a number of Imperial worlds situated relatively close to Terra. The Astra Telepathica have ancient contracts with these worlds, ensuring a steady flow of suitable recruits in return for exemption from Imperial Tithes. All crew are rigorously tested and scrutinised for any latent psychic abilities or sensitivities and are regularly mind-scrubbed to purge any taint or infection.

Navigators for the fleet of Black Ships are all members of the Granicus, Ptolemy and MacPherson Navigator Houses who work exclusively for the Astra Telepathica. Inquisitors, alone amongst Imperium officials, have secured Rights of Passage aboard the Black Ships and have leave to travel freely throughout the entire fleet. They are also wont to oversee the identification, capture and incarceration of particularly recalcitrant or rebellious psykers in whom they have a personal interest. Generally, few other Imperial agents are permitted aboard these dread vessels but occasionally Space Marines, Sisters of Battle or higher-ranking members of the Adeptus Terra may be accommodated at the captain's discretion.

A Black Ship is a dreadful environment for psykers. Psychically sensitive crew spend most of their time in the shielded upper decks of the main bridge, as far removed from the containment holds as possible so as to avoid the unpleasant effects of the security measures in place. There are numerous devices and routines directed at the great holds to confuse and confound psychic abilities. Each ship has a troop of specially trained adepts whose sole function is to focus their own psychic energies into an Occluding Sphere – this strange metaphysical device broadcasts an invasive signal into the mind of any nearby psyker, severely disrupting their ability to concentrate or reason and therefore largely curtailing their ability to utilise their talents. In addition to this, oppressively loud and discordant noise is pumped into the holds, which are dimly illuminated for the most part but frequently lit with bursts of strobing light to shatter the twilight. Food and drink for the captives is laced with sedatives. The captive population is regularly moved from one hold to another. All of this serves to keep the psykers in a helpless, confused and compliant state. The most dangerous psykers (as identified by Inquisitorial scrutiny) are kept in separate isolation cells deep within the bowels of the containment holds.

Every day, dozens of Black Ships complete their epic journey and arrive at Terra, whereupon they disgorge their cargoes of human psykers. Each ship can hold thousands of psykers within their vast holds, so each and every day, tens of thousands of psykers are sent to the processing halls, graded and passed on through the myriad departments and institutions responsible for ensuring that the Tithe is put to its allotted uses.

COMBAT LIFE SAVER

Lesson 243.77fIVs.
HOW TO FIELD DRESS A LAS WOUND

Laser weapons are easy to produce and maintain, assuring they are amongst the most common weapons in the galaxy. Las weapons do not fire a projectile or slug, but instead project a high-energy pulse. This beam can range greatly in strength, depending on the size of the las weapon and the rating of its power source. The largest of the las weapons – such as the lancestrike batteries employed upon spacecraft of the Imperial Navy – produce beams that can sear away entire hab-blocks, leaving only smoking craters hundreds of feet deep. On average, however, las weapons are much smaller. Even the humble laspistol, within close range and with no atmospheric diffusion of shot, has the power to blast away a foe's face on contact, with the beam penetrating the skull and burning a hole through the brain, causing immediate death.

A las-pulse will shear through flesh to produce a cauterised hole surrounded by blister-burns. When first striking flesh, a las-pulse will cause a flash-burn effect on impact, as the heat of the discharge causes the immediate surface area of the target to be vaporised. This can, to the untrained eye, take on the same wound aspects as those left by high-density explosives, but there are major differences when it comes to field dressing las wounds. While the brief exploding flash of initial contact is highly visible, it is rarely the major concern. It is typically the continuing projection of the las-beam boring into the body that causes the most extensive damage – the beam will punch through any internal organs and is capable of severing limbs.

The following steps should be employed when confronted with a las wound:

I) Approach. Do not treat until you have ensured the victim is removed from the source. Las weapons produce a narrow amplified beam of light. Most often this is a short burst, however, should the shaft be ongoing and still present, it is dangerous to approach – entering the beam will cause you to become a casualty as well.

II) Expose. Identify the impact site and determine the extent of the flash burn. Lift away any clothing covering the burnt area, without pulling material over the burns. Leave in place any material that has been seared into the burn area. If the victim is wearing armour, be aware that some materials absorb heat, leaving the area dangerous to touch. In a hazardous environment (such as chem-zones, rad-sites, or other such dangerous areas) do not cut away any protective covering – apply the dressing directly over it.

III) Evaluate. Find the penetration level of the beam. Has the beam passed through the victim causing an exit wound? It is best to check as soon as possible. The extreme heat cauterises the wound, leaving minimal bleeding, however, rapid swelling will begin around the area almost immediately, making later diagnosis more difficult. If the las wound is only a glancing hit, in a limb, or shows no signs of striking a vital organ, proceed with Field Dressing Type I. If you suspect the las wound has penetrated a vital organ, go straight to Type II.

IV) Field Dressing (Type I). Using the cleanest material available, place the cloth lightly over the burn, covering the entirety of the wound. If the victim is able, he may hold the dressing in place. Use strips to bind in place (wrapping around limbs or torso) and tie tightly enough to avoid slipping. Do not break blisters or apply ointments to flash burns.

V) Field Dressing (Type II). Cover the wound as quickly and completely as possible. This is cosmetic, to hide the lethal wound from comrades, and may also allow the victim some false comfort. The swelling that follows is bound to cause catastrophic bodily failures. Death is effectively inevitable, and redistribution of resources can commence immediately.

SERVITORS AND SERVO-SKULLS

Duty to the Emperor need not end with death, and this is abundantly clear in the forms of some of his lowliest servants: servitors and servo-skulls.

Servitors are the basest form of biomechanical life – task-adapted slaves whose mechanical components are designed so the whole can perform a single laborious function. They are mindless machines of living flesh and metal that obey their programming without question. A servitor's mind is essentially blank, and only the most rudimentary instincts remain.

Servitors make up the bulk of the Martian population but can be seen toiling away tirelessly throughout the Imperium. Many work in hostile environments where an unmodified human body would quickly perish. Because they are specifically adapted, they vary tremendously; some have mechanical legs or arms for lifting, others have computer terminals sprouting from their bodies where they interface with more complex machines. There are weapon-toting gun servitors, heavy mining cyborgs, holomats and living holographic recorders with bulging vid-lens optic receptors where eyes would be, to name just a few. Servitors are also seen on the battlefield, accompanying senior Tech-Priests as servants and guardians, using their limited skills to operate dangerous machinery or weaponry.

While many servitors are adapted from artificially cultured drone bodies, others are the remains of humans who have committed some terrible crime. The most severe punishment for a criminal in the Imperium is not death – that would be wasteful and hardly serve as a useful deterrent. Instead, the convicted are turned into servitors. The malefactor is first mind-wiped and then augmented and reprogrammed to perform some rudimentary function too tedious even for the menials of the Adeptus Administratum. Ex-convicts who become servitors wear a brass plate upon their body proclaiming their crime, as a warning to all who would transgress against the laws of the Emperor or the Omnissiah.

Unlike the ignominious fate of criminals, the fate of those who die in honoured service to the Emperor is sometimes to be allowed to continue their labours in the form of a servo-skull. Made from polished human craniums, servo-skulls are most closely associated with the Adeptus Mechanicus, but can be seen providing assistance to high-ranking officers and officials throughout the Imperium's many institutions. Usually modified to facilitate communications or archiving of some kind, many of these macabre devices have pict-recorders, loud-hailers and scrivening devices built into them. They might also have weapons, simple manipulator pincers, illumination emitters, any number of sensors, or even surgical tools, depending on the needs of those who keep them. The most immediately obvious feature of a servo-skull, however, is the tiny gravity repulsor array that allow them to float through the air.

Servo-skulls also frequently sport opulent, protective metal coatings which, along with their small size, make them extremely durable. More than one battlefield has been found long after the last shot was fired, with a single servo-skull floating over the ash and debris – the only remaining witness to attest to the valour or cowardice of those who died there.

INDEX